Printed by Rich Books Los Angeles., in the United States of America.

First printing, June 2019.

Rich Books
Shelly Rich and Kristen Campbell

therichmess@hotmail.com
kristencampbell1904@yahoo.com

Chasing Sober™

Kristen Leigh Campbell
with Shelly Rich

A Memoir of Hope and the Infinite Chase of Sobriety

I love it when people that have been through hell walk out of the flames carrying buckets of water for those still consumed by the fire.

Stephanie Sparkles

Table of Contents

·Prologue·

I turn on the light and tiptoe softly into my closet, closing the door gently behind me. I'm home alone, so my attempts to be quiet or secretive can only be subconscious, in my head somewhere is me, knowing that I'm up to no good. I have a single, solitary "desperation" needle hidden in here, a "just in case" needle. I know exactly where.

I look at my arms, stretched out rummaging under my loosely folded sweaters, my hands are shaking. My fingers sent like detectives march forward reluctantly on orders to find my old worn-out makeup bag. They succeed.

My arms, except for the artwork, don't look like mine anymore, scarred but healed; they're clean, normal arms. They're upstanding citizen arms, good girl arms. My fingers too, now delicate and beautiful, all of the spaces in between perfect, there's not a scab or dried spot of blood to be found. I pull the makeup bag down, briefly flashing back to all of the contents it used to hold, makeup never being one of them. I tug on the small broken zipper and look inside to find my past.

One lonely little needle, lifeless, but welcoming, sits at the bottom of the tiny bag. "Hello old friend," it seems to say. It's my last needle. "Last" sounds strange as it drifts through my thoughts. "So does sober," I think. The warring words in my head go back and forth fighting for validation. I take a deep breath, trying to get control, "They both sound uncomfortable," I whisper. "But you're sober," I remind myself. "Don't worry," I remind myself back, "I know."

•

·Chapter One·

I locked the bathroom door and put my backpack on the sink. It's dirty, dimly lit, wadded up paper towels and toilet paper litter the floor. The smell makes me gag. The mirror is icky. I stare at myself through the rust, water spots, and graffiti etchings, my strung out reflection just as disgusting as my surroundings. Hollow eyes, dark circles, pick marks, the fact that I was rail thin for the first time in my life without trying scares me, although that part is not as disturbing as the rest. I try not to think about it and pull out my stash and my kit.

Yes, kit, thanks to the needle exchange program. If there were experiences that cemented the fact that I was a major junkie, it would be visiting the needle exchange truck. I guess that, using in a filthy gas station bathroom and having to look at myself in the mirror to shoot up, check, check and check. I was certifiably a drug addict. My veins were shot; tiny dots of dried blood all over both arms only confirmed the mirrors assessment of me. I melt my small lump of heroin on a spoon and then soak it up with the cotton.

Plunging the syringe into the fluffy white ball I fill it up. I start puffing my cheeks in and out, then hold my breath, keeping my neck straight and stretched out I'm on the hunt for a place to shoot. I'm scared. I relax my face, my heart is racing. I run the needle under the cold tap. It's too hot. The fact that I know how to do this, that I know it's too hot gives my stomach a flutter. I am now a bona fide heroin addict. This was the end of the road for most. Would it be for me too? I knew I had crossed the line; shooting heroin was on a whole other level. I was ashamed, to resort to putting a needle in my neck, why? It was definitely not a good sign.

I puffed my cheeks again several times looking for the veins in my neck. I tried not to think, but the thoughts keep coming. "What happened to me that I'm doing this? Something had to happen that makes me want to check out, avoid my life, but what?" I jab the needle into my neck, pulling slightly to see if there's blood, any good drug addict knows that if there's a spot of blood you've registered. Check, I've registered. I continue, pushing the syringe all the way down. Even though it's in a vein in my neck I can taste it on my tongue, another fun fact from a user. In a few minutes I won't be thinking about me anymore. I won't care again, that's what this is about, right?

I rinse the needle and shove it back in my bag with the rest of my kit. I keep hearing a baby crying, but can't figure it out. It's crying and crying. It needs help. I throw my backpack over my shoulder and unlock the door. I step out, but I'm at a gas station and I'm all alone. Still, I hear the crying. It's getting worse. I'm looking around, but there's no one there. In fact, there are no people at all, no cars, no traffic, no one, it's desolate. The crying is getting worse. The baby sounds mad now. It needs help. I start crying too. "Where's the baby?" I want to help it, but I can't find it.

"Kristen! Kristen, wake up!" My husband Chase shakes me awake holding our newborn daughter, shrieking to be fed. My heart skips, my stomach sinks, and I'm sweaty. I start to panic. I feel anxious like I might be sick. Did I just use and I have a baby? What's happening to me? I try to wake up. Was it real? It felt so real. I look around the room trying to breathe.

"I think she needs to nurse," he says nervously. "What's going on with you? Are you okay?" Chase, not used to babies or crying, hands her over hopeful she'll calm down. I take her and gently kiss her perfect little head. "Shhh...It's okay, everything's okay, Mama's got you" I coo softly, examining my arms as I pull her close. They were both clean. It was a dream, I'm so relieved. Thank God it was just a dream.

"Didn't you hear her crying?" Chase asks. Sounding more like an accusation than a question, I look down at our tiny baby doubting myself. Am I already awful at this? Does he think I'm not going to be a good mother? I've had the thoughts too; mostly while I was pregnant. Will he be a good father? Will we be good parents? Are we capable? We weren't perfect, but we had made our marriage work and anyone who's ever been married knows that isn't easy, especially at first and especially for us.

"It's fine; I just had one of those dreams again." Me, consistently obsessive-compulsive, my self-doubt is on high as I speak. "In the dream, I kept hearing a baby crying, but I couldn't find it. I didn't know if it was real or not." I look up at him, not sure what to expect, "It's not a big deal right? She only cried for a minute and look, she's perfect now."

Chase stands in front of me, now the picture of fitness, his current addiction has become exercise. Shirtless, in his bike shorts, he runs his hand through his short blond hair, "I know, but you got to get it together Babe. I don't want her getting so upset or having an anxiety disorder because of us. I mean, I don't want to mess her up." He's sexy even when he's being an asshole. Trying to soften it, his playful grin melting the hurt, he adds in a goofy voice, "Right Babe? You know what I'm saying?" I look down again so in love with our little being, "I know." I answer quietly, "I don't want to mess her up either."

Now, it was as simple as a bad dream. It used to be my reality. I was the girl in the gas station, the strung-out junkie in the mirror. My husband too was trapped in a lifestyle of drugs and alcohol. We're both sober now, *Chasing Sober* really. Once you've been an addict, it never leaves. Believe me, it is always a chase, every day, every hour, sometimes down to the minute. Working hard to distance ourselves from years spent in the chaos and confusion of addiction, we will both be *Chasing Sober* for the rest of our lives. But for now, today, in this moment, everything is good.

I'm mesmerized by our perfect baby. I keep staring at her, still in disbelief that she's ours. Beautiful with so much promise, I gently caress her sweet, soft head, a blank slate yet to be influenced by us or the world we live in. Full of possibility and potential, my greatest hope is for her to have a better life than mine, a life free from addiction, self-loathing and issues, a simple, normal, everyday life. Was it possible? I knew both my husband and I would play the biggest role in how she would turn out and, even if we did our very best, you never know what might happen.

I'm sure my mom had the same aspirations for me when I was born, a hope that I would be a good person, have a measure of success, a happy life. Sadly though, from a young age, I had issues. Problems, internal and external, together, too much for me to handle I turned to alcohol and drugs to rescue me. My journey of abuse and self-destruction started innocently enough, with a beer.

I had my first at thirteen and immediately loved the way it made me feel. Or not feel. Drinking mostly with friends, I'd have only one or two and feel pretty looped. Eventually, I started drinking more and drinking alone. Stealing beer from my dad or my friends' parents, it easily became three or more. I liked it too much. I was able to check out, my environment and circumstances disappearing with the buzz, life no longer seemed so real or unbearable. I never knew for sure what made my life feel so bad or why I wanted to escape? Perceived things, or real things? Maybe it was everything? Growing up it was a question I'd ask myself all the time.

My closest friends all drank, each of us escaping something or someone. Unhappy or lonesome homes, parents who didn't care, cared too much, siblings, stepparents, stepchildren, too many rules, or no rules. Of course, those were only confounded by school and social issues, homework and grades, the inadequacies and fears, real and imagined that almost all teenagers face. Getting obliterated erased it all, at least temporarily.

Within a matter of time, we graduated to hard liquor. My personal favorite was Jack Daniels. I started stealing bottles of it anytime I was at a place that sold alcohol. Daring and unafraid, I started drinking every day. I easily blacked out, drinking too much too quickly. I didn't mind, it was the cheapest and easiest way to keep avoiding all of the things going on in my life that I either hated or couldn't figure out, or both.

No one sets out to be an alcoholic or drug addict and everyone's reasons are different. Some factors from my childhood could have influenced it or it could have been that I had an addictive gene, even ending up an alcoholic and drug addict under perfect circumstances.

I will say that my life was uncomfortable for me for as long as I can remember. I just never fit in well. My parents divorced by the time I was two. The fix-it baby that wasn't, I arrived and only made things worse. My mom told me I came hard wired with anxiety; I never slept, cried a lot, hated the car and had major separation issues. In general, I was an extremely stressed out baby. Adding that to a faltering marriage killed it.

I split time between my parent's separate homes from two on. My dad, I'm sure in an attempt to avoid any financial obligation to my mom, chose fifty-fifty custody. This was a living arrangement with the only consistency being constant change. Every week, three days at one house, then four days at the other, then swap. These two completely different people and their homes with opposite rules, philosophies and parenting styles made my life complicated, ever-changing and unstable. Many children could have managed and come out unscathed, I wasn't one.

As I got older, I tried to tell myself that I loved it, that I had the best of both worlds but it was never that easy. My mom with her A-type personality was driven. From the start, she was hardworking, dedicated and disciplined, one of those that made things happen instead of just talking. Not to fault her, but after she and my dad split she was pretty much married to her work. My dad was the polar opposite; even though he had a great job he lacked ambition and was ambivalent at best about working. He loved going to the beach, riding his bike, smoking weed and in general was a perpetual teenager.

My dad, most likely looking for someone to take care of him, started dating pretty quickly and eventually remarried. While my mom's time was devoted to me when I was with her, my dad's time became divided. His new girlfriend and her two children moved in and it affected everything. Our time together, our relationship and our growing household all now competed for his attention. As a kid, navigating this situation on my days there, was confusing, the relationships between all of us through the years would end up having a profound effect on my childhood, my choices and my life.

I think in the beginning I was excited to have a brother and a sister, at my Dad's Wedding I was happy. I was open to the idea of an extra mother, initially, I even liked Marianne but, the instant family at my dad's house wasn't without challenges. The boy, Sam was a few years older and bullied me, the girl, Taylor was my exact age and the perfect child that I could never be. The "extra" mother, never a mother to me, hated me. Mean to me from day one I never knew why. I was a three-year-old when they started dating and only five when they got married. Showing her obvious preference for her own kids, she showered them with attention and affection, ignoring me and rarely if ever even touching me.

Through the years there were hundreds of scarring and slightly abusive behaviors, things I couldn't understand at the time, but remember well. Insidious too, no one else seemed to notice. They were insignificant things, but things that mattered to kids, things that teach a sense of fairness, how they fit in and how to relate in the world. Loving her own kids and just tolerating me all of those years made me think something was wrong with me. Everything else on top of that, only added to my insecurities, laying a foundation, from a young age, that I wasn't worthy or good enough.

I remember her always serving her kids first, every meal, sometimes treating me like I wasn't going to get anything. As simple as giving us cereal in the morning came with a message that I didn't matter as much. I'd sit patiently as Sam and Taylor chatted happily and began eating while my stepmother would take several bites out of mine, setting the bowl down in front of me, half eaten. Maybe she did it to all of us, but I only noticed my own. Born obsessive-compulsive, germs and shared food, among other things, would disturb me and ruin my meal every time, sometimes to the point that I wouldn't be able to eat. Disgusted, one of my hard and fast rules to this day is never sharing dairy.

The thought of her spoon in my cereal every morning was torture. There were a million other things too, maybe just as unimportant, devaluing me emotionally little by little. Did she do it purposely? Could always having to sit in the back seat while her kids took turns up front really do any harm? Getting dropped off at school and watching her hand her own kid's lunch money, then telling me she didn't have enough for me? Did that damage me? Using my room as a laundry room on a regular basis, did it really have an impact on me?

I mean, literally, every time I went to my dad's there were piles of clean clothes folded all over my bed. His household never felt welcoming to me in the first place, the laundry situation only made it worse. That, combined with my stepmother's reaction about having to put it all away because I was there made me sad. I heard it, I saw it, but, worst of all I felt it, I was an inconvenience. My room, from a child's perspective, was never really mine. It was the laundry room at my dad's. My dad, oblivious, would never say or do a thing about it.

Did any individual thing really diminish me or affect how I felt about myself? Probably not, but over the years, all of it combined? It seems probable, all of it, everything she did, going into my head from the time I was little, telling me I was worthless. For a long time, it stayed with me. At my dad's I was the outsider, between the way I was treated and the constant moving from his house to my mom's meant I was always a visitor. I never felt like I belonged, anywhere.

Even though my mom's house was different, in my mind, I was still a guest, only staying for a few days at a time. It was her house or my dad's house, "my" house never really existed, like me it was always somewhere in between. At least going to my mom's felt warm and welcoming, most of the time. I had my own room that waited for me with all the things I loved and, as it should be, everything remained untouched from the time I left until I returned. Even though she was affectionate, loving and completely attentive to me when I was there, I would still feel uneasy. It was just me, I didn't know why.

My mom was great, the best really, fun and adventurous we would always be on the go, bike rides, the beach, camping. She had a tribe of friends and her sister, my Aunt Cindy with her two kids were usually around, we were constantly out having fun and enjoying life. My mom was my best friend from the time I can remember, I loved her more than anyone and with her was where I always wanted to be. I knew it wouldn't last though, I'd start to get comfortable and relax, I'd almost let my guard down but then it would be time for me to leave again and I'd be without her.

I hated thinking about it all, it was the past and that's where it should stay, or should it? Coming to terms with the past and acknowledging it was over and didn't have to affect me now could help me move forward. I deserved a better future and so did my family. I laid my sleeping baby in her bassinet, covered her and turned on the baby monitor. I checked on her several times before getting into the shower. I could hear Chase in the other room talking on the phone, most likely his work. Even though he was on Paternity Leave they called him all the time. Hearing the shower would make him nervous, he'd wonder why I didn't tell him, he'd worry about the baby, obsess about her being alone.

Apart from being ex-addicts, we were both current obsessive compulsives and, as I mentioned mine was from childhood so it was a force. As if one wasn't enough, the two of us were off the charts. How were we not going to mess her up? I tried to change the thoughts swirling around in my head, "She will be fine, she will be fine, she will be..." Like clockwork, Chase pops his head in the bathroom door, "Where's the baby monitor? I should have it with me? Can you even hear it in the shower?" Answering his own questions and shaking his head, he takes it and leaves. We were going to mess her up.

·Chapter Two·

Within a few weeks, we were more comfortable and relaxed with being parents. Although sleep deprived, we were in love with the baby and fell into a pretty easy routine. Our out of control eating habits were going to have to change though. We had promised each other to do Weight Watchers after Jordan was born, so in addition to being all things baby, we started dieting. I had gained over seventy pounds during my pregnancy. Chase gained too, blaming sympathy eating; he ballooned right along with me. Starting a few weeks ahead of me, like most men he had already shed a million pounds and was looking like a high-performance athlete within the first few days. Feeling a bit competitive, I was ready to catch up.

One benefit of our combined OCD and addictive tendencies was that everything we did, we were all in, completely consumed. For us, whether we were all about eating, or all about dieting and exercise, doing it together was intense. We were both overly preoccupied with food, I still am. An emotional eater, I grew up chubby, using food to pass the time, comfort me and distract me from a life that was extremely uncomfortable. Over time it became ingrained in me to eat, hate myself for eating, and then turn to an insane diet in an effort to obtain an unrealistic "ideal weight" and body type. Eventually, there was never a time that I wasn't thinking about my weight.

Chase was similar; he obsessed about eating then beat himself up about his weight. Being a guy, I never thought much about his reasons, only why it always seemed easier for him to get a handle on it. Our shared sobriety only intensified our food issues. It wasn't uncommon for people in recovery to change their focus from drugs or alcohol to other "allowable" addictions. For us, we both chose food, our relationship had started with a shared love for food and now, our "addiction" to food and eating was like a part of us. It was what we did. I know we were obnoxious to some, especially those trying to have a meal with us, but we couldn't help it.

The funniest part is we were equally obsessed. Like a scene from "What about Bob," we were both Bill Murray, making every bite an event, our meals always a highlight or celebration. Even though it was love, hate, gain, lose, we both were addicted to everything about eating. My pregnancy had only given us an excuse.

Determined to lose the weight and get back in shape, we started weighing, counting calories and working out. Fanatics, we talked about it, thought about it, fought about it, planned meals and workouts, competed, and literally spent most of our free time immersed in eating healthy, losing weight, and fitness. Beyond crazed, we measured every bite on a scale, read the fine print on packages and computed even our tiniest indulgence on our phones.

Our lives revolved around taking care of the baby and food, we were ridiculous and we knew it. Anyone who was around thought we were nuts. We'd even take our little scale to restaurants, constantly asking the poor servers how many ounces or calories they thought was in our meal and customizing everything we ordered. The best part was we were so much alike, we understood each other and for the most part, we had fun. Chase was my best friend and we loved being together, and to me, that meant the odds of us staying together were good. That alone would give our baby a better start than us.

It would be nice to say that I wasn't affected by my parents' divorce, especially since I was so little when it happened. I never had a memory of them being a couple and very rarely did I even see them together. When I did there wasn't much communication and it was even less after my dad remarried. Their relationship was strained and encounters with the two of them together were always awkward, at least for me. Today would be awkward.

"Hey Bub, what's taking you so long? We're supposed to be there in twenty minutes." In our tiny, shared bathroom, I'm finishing my makeup and respond to him in the mirror "I know." Chase checks himself out, then looks at me, "Come on your fine, I don't want to be late, you're the guest of honor, this day is all about you. Besides, I don't want people to think we're not on top of things like we can't swing being on time to a function because we have a kid."

He's right; it had become important to us to make a good impression. This was our first family event with a baby, it was my College Graduation. For me it was more than a proud moment, it was another representation of how far I had come. Having a lifelong hatred of all things related to school, I had been a high school dropout, never receiving much of the education that had been offered. Today though I would be graduating from College with a Bachelor's Degree, it was hard to believe. "I'll be ready in a minute, don't rush me." I finish with my makeup and put my hair up in a ponytail. I pull it out and brush it again. Chase stays watching me fuss with my hair, "I'm really proud of you, you know that right?"

Tenderhearted, Chase looks and acts tougher than he is. He's tall, with a thicker build, short blond hair and soft blue eyes that are mischievous but sweet. He's partially covered with tattoos, his armor, they convey a lot about him. In a glance you can sum up parts of his life, the past, the present, his likes, and dislikes. The Raider Tattoo, one of his favorites, combined with his personal style only adds to his overall appearance of being more "hood" than mainstream.

Mine too, I'm 5'6, with long highlighted blonde hair, brown eyes and average to medium build. I also have a number of tattoos, a varied collection that represents different times and people in my life, both good and bad. As popular as tattoos are and as much as I love them, I know there's still somewhat of a stigma attached to people who have them. I don't care though, for me they're constant reminders of a life I never want to go back to and a time period I never want to relive. Moving forward, there are beautiful ones, dedicated to my new life, my family and children, treasures that keep me *Chasing Sober* and grateful, humble to the fact that I made it out when so many others don't.

Chase was right; we needed to be on time. I had to get my cap and gown and figure out the lineup. For others, maybe it was okay to be late or not care as much about what people thought. For us, two convicted felons, in recovery with a mess of tattoos, and a different look, we had to win people over on other merits. Being on time could go a long way in someone's initial assessment of us and we both made it a habit to make little things like that count. I was excited to get there, proud of myself even. In a matter of hours I would be a College Graduate. I felt and looked great and, I was becoming more confident in myself and the idea that Chase and I were going to be good parents. We had this and I wanted the world to know that today, in this moment, we had both kicked addictions ass.

It was a surreal moment for sure, the truth was I never thought I would have an education. My aversion to school started when I was small and continued throughout my life. The first school I went to was perfect, even though the woman that watched me was a train wreck. She was loud and aggressive, rough even, pushing us around and enforcing a militant schedule. Mechanical in a way, there was no love or lightheartedness; I don't remember playing or having fun. To me, she met the basic needs and that was it. Being with an obnoxious daycare worker all day only intensified my anxiety. I guess from the beginning, it wouldn't matter where I was, I would be anxious and insecure. Everything made me nervous. Uncomfortable in my own skin most people in my life only exaggerated those feelings.

My mom, when I was with her, was the only one that I felt a sense of security from. The daycare was the one constant in my life and it was even more unsettling than going back and forth between my parents' homes. Most days I cried all the way to school and from drop off couldn't wait for someone to come and get me. Being so small I wouldn't know which days were whose, so every evening I'd stand at the gate, never sure which parent I was waiting for.

As I got older and changed classrooms, my experiences with school improved. The school I went to, Baldwin Academy, and many of the people there would end up playing huge roles in and throughout my life. It became a comforting and secure place for me with caring people that always welcomed me, never judged me and only extended kindness and love. I was never turned away, even at my absolute worst. I met several of my best friends there, lifelong and to this day, still a big part of my life.

Erica was one of them; she was my age and attended the same program as me. Erica's Mom, also one of my closest friends and still a huge part of my life today, was one of my teachers. There were others there too who would become mainstays for me, sticking by me even as my life eventually imploded. I stayed there through first grade and although I continued to hate school in general, Baldwin Academy and its prestigious little campus furnished a safe environment for me. I loved it and I loved the people there. In the end, it had provided and would continue to provide, a sense of stability, the one thing that would be missing throughout most of my life.

Unfortunately, my mom moved me to a public school after first grade; a school that was free, and closer to her house. I hated it. Pulled from the safety of my small Private School, my best friends and, all of the people I knew and loved, I was forced out of my comfort zone into a world of mass children. It was devastating for me. I went from knowing everyone and feeling safe, to not having a single friend. No one seemed to notice how much I was suffering. I felt alone and at six years old I became depressed. I was most likely certifiable, but my mom wouldn't hear of it. She had to go to work and I had to go to school, that was the bottom line; my dad, of course, didn't get involved. I was alone all day, refusing to participate or even try to make friends; it was only a matter of time before my mom gave in and at least allowed me to go to the same school as my step-sister.

Maybe in an attempt to get my Dad's wife to treat me better or to improve the rapport between the two homes, my mom for a time even tried to befriend my evil stepmother, Marianne. It never went over well, there was no depth to my stepmother, she was overly preoccupied with appearances and things and; my mom just wasn't like that. They had very little in common other than me, and of course, since Marianne hated me that left nothing.

The two women responsible for raising me, making decisions for me and, my overall well-being, had absolutely nothing in common and could barely tolerate each other. I suffered the consequences. Marianne, spiteful and vindictive treated me even worse as the adult relationships deteriorated. The friendship and the schooling, both short-lived, ended up generating even more problems for me.

My new school environment wasn't entirely better anyway, at least in the beginning. My only friend was my step-sister, Taylor, who just happened to be the most popular child there. She excelled at everything while I continued to flounder. On top of that, she was the teacher's pet, an ideal student and, idolized by everyone. Everything she said and did, in my skewed perception, was perfect.

Of course, the problem wasn't with her being amazing and loved at school, it was with me and the feelings I had about myself. In my mind, I was the exact opposite; real or imagined I saw myself as unlikable, ugly even, odd. I was the beautiful girl's weird step-sister. As much as I grew up loving and admiring her, our relationship would be complex. As a child, I didn't understand why, but I didn't feel good about myself. Constantly eclipsed by what I saw as my perfect step-sister, regardless if it was real or imagined, it would play heavily into my already faltering self-esteem and growing insecurities.

This no-win situation was made even worse when we'd be forced to dress alike. This may have worked for Taylor but definitely not for me. She was petite and thin with shiny blond hair and big blue eyes. Like a living doll, she looked adorable in anything. I was average, shorter, and did I mention I was chubby? I had mousy brown hair with basic brown eyes and a shaggy haircut. Sometimes I'd even be mistaken for a boy. I never felt cute. More unflattering than my appearance though was my awkwardness. I can't even explain it, I was just so uneasy being me.

Regardless, for a time I loved Taylor and she loved me, one of my only friends at a time when I felt so alone. I tried really hard not to compare myself to her, even after she started calling my dad "Dad" and talking about how she spent more time with him than me. I tried to make it into a good thing, another commonality, but I was a kid, there wasn't much I could do about it anyway. At the time, I didn't think any of it bothered me. It must have though because all of the memories are so painful.

To me, it seemed like my dad never really got involved. In fact, I always assumed he was uninterested in us, or maybe it was just me. In all the years that I struggled, my dad never once sat me down and explained that he was my dad and that I would always be special and important to him. He never really told me how much he loved me, or that he would always be there for me, nothing like that ever happened. Really it was the exact opposite, he never was there for me, half the time I wondered if he even knew what was going on in my life.

Other than fighting with Sam and hearing him argue with Marianne about how awful "her son" was, he didn't say much. If he did, it was usually after one of their arguments, short-fused and annoyed with all the noise and chaos of having three kids and a wife that micro-managed him, he'd tell everyone to "shut up," or "to leave him alone." For the most part, my dad didn't put any effort into the family or into being a good dad. From my viewpoint, he was an observer. I guess I thought that since he didn't notice anything else, he most likely didn't notice our appearances, even when we were being dressed alike and I was being made fun of.

Of all the things I believe Marianne did to torture me, one of the worst and, most blatant, was when she gave me a nightmare perm. Interestingly, my beautiful sister remained perm free; it was only me that had to endure the frizzy strands of short fried hair. I don't think my dad even noticed. He never said a word, nothing good or bad. For me, it meant Marianne could do whatever she wanted to me and my dad would just allow or overlook it. Not my mom, she was pissed. Fuming mad, she called my dad, telling him in no uncertain terms that Marianne was forbidden to touch me or my hair and she was forbidden to make any decisions like that for me in the future.

My mother's reaction was another telling sign that it wasn't a good look for me; I knew without a doubt that I was hideous. My mom, although she always looked nice and made sure we were clean and well put together, was never about looks or brands and labels. Again, it wasn't who she was, so naturally, she didn't have much input. Even if she did, for the most part, keeping the peace would have been more important to her. Marianne, on the other hand, was so worried about appearances, that she made everything about how you looked. She was always pushing for both Sam and Taylor to be popular, the best dressed, and most attractive. I didn't merit her consideration, just easier for her to buy two of everything, mine two sizes larger than to bother choosing something I might like.

She was the type to put on a show, wanting everyone to think she was the master of the blended family. In public, she played the role of the perfect stepmother, but behind the scenes, just like her treatment of my mother, I was barely tolerated. She treated me like garbage and that was the way it was. It was so bad that even Taylor would cry, apologizing for how awful her mom was towards me.

My mom thought I exaggerated and my dad, trying to avoid any conflict with his bitch of a wife would laugh it off, sputtering the same line all the time, "Oh come on Kris, it's not that bad." My dad, true to character, never took a stand; for anything, especially me. My mom's house was better, but not perfect. I feel like she tried to make up for us not being able to be together all of the time by being fun. The busier we were the less we had to think about any of the issues I was having.

In the earlier years sometimes Taylor would be allowed to come with me on my mom's days. Taylor, for lack of other options, became my new best friend, convenient and almost always available; we became inseparable for a while. I loved her like crazy, most likely co-dependent on my part, I thought I needed her.

Outside of my mom's house I still didn't seem to fit in anywhere. I didn't want to be different, but I was. Frustrated with my own life and circumstances, I started bullying kids at my school. One little girl, I targeted started crying when she would see me. At first, I did it to be funny, but when I started getting attention and gaining friends for it; I really got out of hand. I started scaring her, picking on her relentlessly, calling her names and telling her that I hated her. Eventually, I even told her I knew where she lived and that I was going to come to her house in the middle of the night and kill her. I was seven.

I must have been pretty bad, unfazed by being sent to the office, at the time, I didn't really care, and wasn't sorry. When my mom showed up, maybe unsure of what to do; I don't remember her doing anything. No one really seemed to care, almost as if that was what was expected from someone like me.

The following year Sam, my stepbrother, was shipped off to live with his dad in Colorado. He and my dad were constantly at odds and fighting. I guess they couldn't really have him or the tension he caused around anymore because Marianne was pregnant; there was a new baby on the way. I wasn't crazy about Sam, he constantly teased me and fat-shamed me, taking out all of the frustration and anger he had for my dad, on me. Still, he was a part of our family; to me, I didn't understand it. The broody and rebellious stepbrother, he'd wrestle me to the ground or punch me, constantly trying to start fistfights and arguments. Most of my complaints about him fell on deaf ears and on rare occasions when I was acknowledged, my dad just laughed and would say, "That's what brothers do."

Marianne never bothered to stop him, let alone correct him. Instead, looking for reasons to blame me for his bad behavior, she'd tell me, "That's what you get, I'm sure you did something to deserve it." Regardless, his leaving was strange for me. "Too much to handle," was what I heard and then he was gone. In my mind, no one really mattered. We were disposable, at least at my dad's. The fact that he was Marianne's own child and she could just discard him like that was troubling to me. I had this looming feeling that I could be next. Would my mom want me? I didn't think she would, at least not all of the time. Where would I be sent? My living situation, precarious for as long as I could remember, to me, was always in question.

My stepsister Katie was born several months later. I loved babies and couldn't have been more excited, everyone loved her. Baby Katie was a welcome addition to my dad's house, good-natured and happy; she brightened the tense environment for me, at least for a while. I remember throwing all of my dolls on the floor and stomping on them, shouting, "I don't need you anymore!" I may not have needed dolls, but at eight years old going on nine, I still slept with my mom at her house and I slept with Taylor at my dad's.

As happy as I was about the baby, I remained confused about Sam and how easy it was to just get rid of him. Not my dad. My dad, no longer competing with Sam for Marianne's attention, appeared happier. Although her focus was always on the baby, he seemed okay with that, maybe content to be the only male in a household of females, he wasn't as angry. With everything in my life changing, I tried to adjust, but emotionally I couldn't. Inside I was in constant turmoil, wondering if I really would be next, the thought of being away from my mom started to consume me with anxiety.

By the time I was nine, I was overweight, obsessed with calorie counting and wore giant boy shirts with tight sports bras to try to hide myself and my developing body. Adding to my angst, a trip to the Orthodontist revealed that I needed my mouth spaced and braces. Already self-loathing, the changing anatomy and the braces only made me feel more self-conscious and insecure. Although school was more bearable and I was doing better socially, (who doesn't pretend to like the school bully) academically I continued to struggle.

Forced into making my own friends after the school separated me from Taylor, I started to have a wild streak. Citing that I had become too much of a bad influence, I was angry and became even more of a bully; I cursed all of the time and tried to be the constant cut-up or class clown. Now worried about talking in my sleep and everyone finding out that I swore, I even tried to start sleeping alone. On the outside I was the "Intimidator," as well as the "Entertainer" and "Funny Girl," but inside I was a mess. Never believing I was good enough, I believed everyone's life was normal while mine was different. Continuing to see myself as a big misfit, moving from house to house, I longed to just fit in somewhere, anywhere.

As I entered the double-digits, things continued to spiral out of my control. In a constant state of despair and always wanting to disappear, I never dreamed things could actually get worse. They did, though, starting with my mom moving away from the beach to an area twenty miles east, called Scripps Ranch. She also had a new boyfriend, which is when I found out that my mom was all about me unless she had a man in her life. I immediately hated everything about both. The move, on my mom's days, put me in an area where everything and everyone was unfamiliar. This left me at my dad's on his days, with my mom no longer conveniently around the corner, or accessible.

Constantly having a pit in my stomach and feeling more unsettled than ever, I tried to adjust to my mom's new house and the distance between us while I was at my dad's, but I couldn't take the creepy guy. A crack head with no job or money, he ended up moving in with us. Forced to be around him on my days with my mom it was painful, I couldn't bear it, even wishing that one of us would die, preferably him. My fun mom was gone, our good times together, fleeting. Instead, I watched in disgust, as my now distracted mother handed the disturbing loser money and paid for his existence. No one could understand it. My Dad and Marianne even joked about it, almost taunting me, "You know your mom, she loves a project." I think my dad knew firsthand. Of course, my mom could care less what everyone thought, she went on with her life, working, spending time with the crack head, and fitting me in between the two.

I never felt so alone. In my screwed up perception, now there was nowhere I belonged. I wasn't wanted or welcome anywhere and that eventually pushed me over the edge. Severely depressed, overweight and not able to communicate how bad it was, for the first time I was suicidal. I didn't even know or understand what true depression was, but I knew I wasn't right. It wasn't until my mom was away on a business trip and I wouldn't get out of bed that anyone realized I needed help. At my dad's house, he and Marianne had no idea what to do with me, or more to the point couldn't be bothered. In a panic, my dad called my mom.

My mom, usually able to help and knowing how to handle almost any situation, was at a loss. She flew home and started with the basics, which included taking me to my pediatrician and getting my very first "substance" to "fix me." Diagnosed with severe depression, they prescribed medication and sent me to a Child Psychologist. I also ended up getting tested for Learning Disabilities and Attention Deficit Disorder, which in the end, they also added to my diagnosis.

None of this helped. If anything, all of it only made me feel worse. Now I had a "label" and was "medicated," a troubled child that had to go to therapy. My life hurt and there was no one who could help, nothing that would make it better. To top it off I was sent to a therapist that wasn't kid friendly or even kind. I resented her and having to go. Twice a week sitting with another adult that could really care less about me was a painful replay of everything that was already going on in my life. The last person I wanted to talk to about my personal feelings or issues anyway, she was no help.

Overwhelmed with it all and taking antidepressants and anxiety "meds" that made me feel strange; I just wanted to end it all. I struggled with constant thoughts of killing myself, but I couldn't do it. I think mainly because I wasn't sure how to go about it, but also because of my mom. I loved her too much and felt bad for her. She was doing everything she could to try to help me and she would have blamed herself. It wasn't her fault that I was this way, but she took it on. My mom was determined to do whatever it took to make me feel better, she wouldn't give up. My dad, true to character, did nothing. Not one thing. Just like the day I couldn't get out of bed, he left it to my mom to take care of things and try to get me put back together.

Consumed with an awareness of my dad doing nothing and questioning it all in my head, I'm startled by Chase, "What's taking you so long Babe? We need to leave." I hated remembering my past, it was a total downer for sure, but I was doing it a lot lately and didn't know why. Like everything else, there were no answers, only a continuous why? Why was I depressed as a kid? Why was my dad not involved? What was so bad that I would even consider killing myself? I was ten years old. Ten and I wanted to die, why?

"I'm just thinking about things," I answer, trying to sound normal and not wanting to recap. "What things?" he asks cautiously. He's holding Jordan, who lights up when she sees me; her reaction to me is everything. "The past, I guess, my parents, how much I hated my life." He looks at me confused, "Is this about Marianne and your sisters not coming today?" Kissing the baby as she squeals, I answer truthfully, "No, I don't want them there; they don't deserve to be a part of this." Joking around and in another one of his silly voices he asks, "Are you depressed? Do you have Postpartum Depression?" I laugh lightly, "No, I just don't want Jordan to have to go through anything I had to go through." Chase, not sure what to say silently stands watching me play with the baby. "I just want Jordan's life to be different, I want us to stay together and be good parents, promise me?" Hugging me he promises, "We will Bub, we will."

·Chapter Three·

"I'm just having lunch and then, uh, I'm thinking about, um, going for a bike ride." I sit across the table, from my dad, listening to him stammering through the tail end of his phone call with Marianne. I continue to eat, annoyed, all of a sudden feeling alone. I look at Jordan asleep in her stroller, then to the waves crashing along the beach. I'm overthinking again and I can't stop. At a local boardwalk eatery, my dad and I have been hanging out a lot, maybe too much.

I try to tune out his conversation, but it's impossible. I keep listening, knowing he won't mention me, as much as I try not to let it bother me it always does. Feeling ashamed, it pushes old buttons. I'm back to being the outsider, questioning myself just like I did when I was a kid. It's weird, what am I to him? I'm embarrassed, my heart sinks as I think of it, I feel like a mistress but, it's my dad. I am his daughter, why can't he let my stepmother know we're together? He's not just leaving me out of the discussion, but he is literally hiding the fact that he's with me. He's with me and his grandchild and he can't or won't mention it. Again, I'm back to why?

I'm irritated now. It's been going on for a few years, but I usually ignore it. I feel like I can't anymore. He hangs up and starts filling me in on his relationship issues. Oblivious, he now talks openly, sharing way too much information about my stepmother. I listen hesitantly, torn between wanting to know and not wanting to know. Basically, I still can't stand his wife so it's satisfying to hear that they're not getting along. It's validating when he tells me "She's' a bitch" and complains about how difficult she is. Really though, I don't want to know. It's creepy and it makes me feel like the mistress again, somehow a part of his dirty little secret, but it's his secret, not mine, so why does it make me feel so ashamed of myself?

"Dad, why didn't you tell her we're together? Why don't you ever tell her we're together?" I want to confront him, but it doesn't come out. It stays in my head with all of the other things I'm afraid of, things that might lead to something bigger, scarier, things I won't know how to handle. I watch him talking, my heart is racing, I'm listening, but I don't want to. I'm uncomfortable, but I don't move. I will for my baby to wake up so I have a reason to stop him from talking. In my head are a million "why" questions swirling around, getting more and more intense. He's never even aware of me. He's blabbing away, filling me in on how mad everyone was that they weren't invited to my graduation.

Now he's talking about my stepmother and my two sisters like it's us against them. I follow blindly for a moment, my emotions rising as he keeps talking. I'm confused though, I look at him realizing he's not my ally and it's not us against anyone. It's me alone with my own father and he's intentionally hurting me. I want him to stop, but I can't stop him. I picture it, all of them bashing me, hating that I've succeeded at something instead of failing. I think of them being happy that I was a drug addict, free from having to have anything to do with me, but is that really how they felt? I criticize myself for thinking bad about them but stop. I know that's how they are and in my heart, as sad as it makes me, I know it's true.

I feel upset now. I picture my dad there with them during the discussions, he probably doesn't join in. Or does he? I'm anxious; consumed now by my emotions; my breathing is shallow and my heart races. Does he even stick up for me? I know he doesn't, he never has. I want to scream for him to stop. Instead, my stomach sinks and I keep listening to him, wondering why I'm allowing my dad to do this to me.

The waitress brings our check, which I'm sure we'll split; all the while my dad keeps talking. Confused, I try to focus on what he's saying, but all I can think of is that for as long as I can remember he's pitted my sisters and me against each other. He's always told me things that they've said about me or things they've done behind my back that would hurt me, cause me not to like or trust them. Marianne too, my dad has constantly shared personal and intimate things about him and his wife, literally telling me how much his wife dislikes me and all of the reasons she doesn't want to be around me. Why? Why would my own father do that? My sisters and I no longer have much of a relationship and my stepmother and I are like adversaries, barely able to be in the same room with each other. After all these years, we've never been more distant.

It isn't new or different that he does it, but for some reason, like everything else, I'm just noticing it more. I think as a parent, he could have been, no, he should have been, building our relationships. My dad should have been encouraging us to love each other, to get along and stay in each other's lives, but he never has. Instead, my dad is and always has been the divider.

Sickened, the mistress thing comes to mind again. If he keeps all of us separated and at odds, then his secret relationship with me and the time we spend together stays a secret. With none of us talking or seeing each other, my dad can hide me, hide our relationship. Is he embarrassed about me? My heart sinks again, my new awareness of how dysfunctional we are is making my skin crawl. My relationship with my dad is even more disturbing than when I was a kid only now I'm choosing it. In my mind, again, I ask myself why?

"We're splitting this right?" My dad is predictable, I put my credit card down with his and we wait for the waitress. He continues to talk while I think about my graduation and how special it was to me. My stepmother and my sisters being there would have definitely marred it. I was thirty years old and a recovering Drug Addict, an accomplishment so ordinary for many, for me was extraordinary. Earning a Bachelor's in Psychology, the degree itself was enough; I didn't even need to use it to make it worthwhile. Just to know that I was able to go from recovering Heroin Addict to College Graduate helped in a way, cement my separation from addiction. For the first time in my life, I started to believe in myself and feel good about my own abilities. My dad and his family, for whatever reason still made me feel inadequate, to them, I would never be good enough.

My dad and I part ways after lunch, but I can't stop thinking about everything. It couldn't be normal, we couldn't be normal. Hiding me and keeping our relationship a secret from his wife was only a part of it, my dad constantly causing a division and disconnect between me and my sisters, again was only a part of it, those things had gone on for years. It was the new awareness that he had never really been there for me as a parent; I couldn't really even define his role in my life. We had never had a traditional father, daughter relationship and I was just starting to notice it. What were we?

I try to think of him ever giving me fatherly advice, of him caring enough to offer guidance or direction in my life, but I can't. I can't remember him being supportive or encouraging; I can't even picture him helping me. I don't think he's ever contributed to anything for me financially, I mean once I get started, the list goes on, and there's nothing. There's literally nothing that my dad has done for me that stands out or is significant. Why? What was I to him? Since having a child of my own, I was continuously reliving the past, especially my dad's role in my life, both past and present. I'd try to shake it and for the most part, kept it to myself, but there was something troubling me about my dad and it wasn't going away.

With my graduation behind me, I could technically start on the path to becoming a psychologist or counselor; I could start helping other people. The strangest thing was I didn't want to, not yet. I wasn't ready. I really wanted to be a mom. When Chase and I discussed it, we agreed that for the time being, I didn't need to go to work. I'm sure this concerned my mom. My mom, my biggest fan and greatest supporter outside of my husband, had offered to help me financially while I went back to school. I'm sure her reasons were based more on me having a career and climbing the corporate ladder than what I had in mind. Not much of a corporate sort, I entered the agreement with a more realistic idea of becoming a counselor, helping people like me and my husband, get and stay sober. For me, being a new mom was enough; if I didn't have to work I didn't want to. If it was possible, I wanted to be with Jordan.

For me, being a stay at home mom was the job of a lifetime. I loved it, each and every minute of it. Being in recovery, I had to be scheduled, stay busy and make good decisions. Good decisions, for both Chase and I, meant making the choice to be around people that weren't triggers. With the freedom I now had it was important for me to plan what Jordan and I would do each day and who we would spend our time with. The handful of people included my parents, Chase's family and a few close friends that I had never used with. Since my mom still worked full time, she could spend a few hours here and there or on occasion meet us for lunch, but she wasn't available to just hang out except for the weekends.

I made plans from time to time with Chase's Mom, his sister, a few choice friends and, my dad. Trying to stay planned was actually part of the reason I had been spending so much time with my dad lately, but why was he always available? Why did he want to hang out with me? Was it strange or was it normal? Strange was starting to win out in the battle going on in my head. Like always, I ignored all of the warning signs that I was having in favor of what I thought might be my dad loving me. It wasn't easy though; our being together was for some reason, oddly uncomfortable.

Both of my parents, after moving, eventually ended up back in the beach area. My mom bought a condo overlooking the bay while I was a preteen and, my dad bought a house about two miles away, a few years later. Although in different neighborhoods, they were both close to the ocean and, near enough to my house that it was convenient for us to see them regularly. Again, trying not to overthink it, I ended up spending the most time with my dad. We'd go to lunch, take the baby to the beach or for a bike ride, he'd come to our house or we'd go to his house. Marianne worked full-time so she was gone all week and, on weekends she chose to spend most of her free time with my sisters. My dad's job was freelance so his schedule always seemed wide open.

Strangely, he became my go-to person to do things with. We spent, on average three days a week together and occasional weekends. He and my husband got along well and we'd all spend a Saturday or Sunday together a couple of times each month. Usually, we'd end up at the beach, they'd toss the Frisbee around for hours while Jordan and I watched or she napped and, I'd get to relax. It was easy with no expectations and I thought I was happy until something would pop into my head. It was bizarre, here was the same dad that had never been there for me, taken an interest in me, or even helped me through any of the challenges I faced, now an active part of my life and one of my closest friends. Why? I couldn't explain it.

Estranged on and off through the years, my dad and I only started spending time together after I got clean and sober. We really reconnected when Chase reached out to him to ask if he could marry me. Even then, it was occasional at best. To be honest, I never really thought about how much time we were spending together, it just happened. While I was pregnant I was diagnosed with SPD, or more technically, "Symphysis Pubis Dysfunction." I was assigned bed rest and ended up with more time on my hands than usual. Most of the people I knew had to work, while my dad was always free. Initially, it was just lunch here and there due to the limitations of my condition. Once Jordan was born and I was feeling up to it, we could do more activities and our time together increased. It was so gradual I never even noticed.

It wasn't just spending so much time with my dad that was weighing on me, there were other things too. Strange things had been popping into my head out of the blue. I'd try my best to dismiss them, put them out of my mind, always telling myself how awful I was for thinking like that. Only on occasion would I question whether any of it was actually real. It wasn't until Jordan was about six months old and she and I went back to my dad's house after a few hours at the beach that something finally clicked.

He was going to watch her while I used the guest bathroom to rinse off. Stepping into the shower, I didn't take off my bathing suit. Subconsciously it was a habit, a strange form of protection I invented when I had to stay at my dad's. When I noticed it, it scared me. It was like I was a child again, showering in my sports bra. Soaking wet and with alarms sounding in my head, I scrambled to shut off the water and get out of the shower.

Still in my swimsuit, I toweled myself off and get dressed. With wet hair dripping down my back and soaking my shirt, I rushed to the living room, to find my dad holding Jordan on his lap and watching sports on television. "That was quick," he said, sounding so normal and innocent, I was instantly consumed with guilt. Trying not to panic and berating myself for even thinking it, I looked to his groin area to see if he was excited holding my baby girl. I felt sick and instantly ashamed. There was nothing.

"Pops, we've got to go." I took Jordan and hurried to strap her into her car seat. I wanted to change her diaper, in case she fell asleep on the way home, but I didn't want to do it in front of him. In my head, I was confused and embarrassed. My self-talk telling me how ridiculous I was. Feeling like I was crazy, all I could think was, "my poor dad." He stood up to give me a hug and with goose bumps and hunched over, I hugged him without letting him get close. "Okay, I guess I'll talk to you tomorrow," he said as he walked us to the front door.

I snapped the baby seat in the back and got into the car. My dad, completely unaware, smiled and waved goodbye from his porch. I drove around the corner, pulled over and burst into tears. I could hardly breathe, my thoughts a combination of "What is your problem" and "There is a problem." I didn't know which to believe. Composing myself, I checked on Jordan in the backseat and started to drive home. I couldn't get it out of my mind though.

This wasn't the first time something like this happened. There were other times when I felt like something was wrong, but I'd always talk myself out of it. Or someone else would. The first time I mentioned anything about being uncomfortable around my dad was to my mom. I was thirteen. I was still in therapy and taking medication for depression and anxiety. Even more, messed up than before, I had started drinking and smoking pot. My dad had moved out of the beach to a more rural area called Alpine. He, Marianne, Taylor, and Katie all lived in a huge house that seemed like it was out in the middle of nowhere.

Having to go all the way out there literally made me nauseous. I couldn't stand it. The drive was at least forty plus minutes each way on a desolate highway. I felt so far away and separated from my mom, it made me sick. Single again, my mom and the few friends I had would be so far away that I would literally have panic attacks the entire time.

Having spent years feeling isolated and alone when I was at my dad's house, being at his new house was a million times worse. As if it wasn't already bad enough, my dad and Marianne had managed to turn my sisters against me, I'm sure telling them that I was a screw-up; I was crazy or not right. Whatever was said, both of my sisters over time were unsure of me and my mental stability. I hated it out there and I hated all of them. I tried to tell myself it didn't matter, that none of them mattered, but all of it broke my heart. Regardless of how much I hated it and all of the reasons I didn't want to be there, I still had to spend fifty percent of my life with my dad.

My being uncomfortable at my dad's house wasn't new; it had been building up for a long time. Now though, it went beyond me feeling like I didn't belong, now there was a bigger problem. I just wasn't sure how much I could trust myself to know whether it was real or imagined. I wanted it not to be real, but my self-talk was constant. There was a chattering in my head begging me to say something, only day after day, I could never get up enough nerve to actually let it go beyond my thoughts. Finally, at my mom's for the first time in days, I felt like I would go crazy if I didn't speak up or tell someone about it. Sad and confused, I sat in my mom's kitchen trying to work up to how I was going to tell her. I was scared. Once it was out, it was out. I wouldn't be able to take it back, ever.

I watched her turn off the oven and look around for the oven mitts, wondering how she was going to react. As rare as it could be we're making dinner together, I'm at the island cutting and putting cucumbers in the salad, it's just us and it's too quiet, eerily perfect. "Mom, I feel like my dad's staring at my boobs!" There it was out. Out in the universe for someone to hear and either validate me or tell me I was crazy. Believe me, I wanted to be crazy, but it was so real and I was getting more self-conscious and uncomfortable by the minute. Without hesitating, my mom replies "Don't be ridiculous Kristen; your dad would never do that!" Okay perfect, I was crazy. It was confirmed by my own mother.

My mom continues, seeming annoyed with me, "What would even make you think such a thing? Really Kristen!?" I know her, not usually a reactive type; I can tell she's trying to stay calm. I'm actually done talking about it, but I'm pissed about her attitude, so I force myself to continue, "Because he seriously stares at my boobs all the time and my evil stepmother is constantly complaining about them, so I think there's a problem with my boobs over there!"

My mom keeps busy and doesn't look at me, I can't tell if it's an act, or if she's really still making dinner. I mean the rice cooker's done, the enchiladas are out cooling on the stove top and I finished the salad before I even brought up the "boob topic." I start feeling guilty. I shouldn't have said anything. My mom is right, my dad wouldn't do that. Or would he? Feeling sad, mad and now crazy, I go to my room. What's wrong with me? Why would I even think that? My poor dad, I try to get it out of my head only there's a voice in there telling me, "It's the truth."

There were a million other signs that something wasn't right. Whether it was real or imagined, even with medication, I was consumed with anxiety about it. I didn't even want boobs. I wore thick sports bras all the time, trying to keep them flat and inconspicuous. They were tight too, so tight I'd have the lines etched deep into my body when I'd take them off, not that they'd be off for long. Scared, at my dad's house, I would even shower with them on, trying to towel them as dry as I could before getting dressed. Obsessed, I wore them all day every day and slept in them at night. I also wore giant boy's shirts and had even started wearing boy's clothes and shoes. I wanted to be invisible and unnoticed, especially at my dad's. So was I crazy? I guess if my mom said so.

I felt bad about myself for weeks after that. I couldn't believe I even said it out loud. Now I wasn't alone in thinking I was disgusting, my Mom must have thought I was pretty sick and disgusting too. I continued to numb myself with alcohol, drinking more and more frequently. After I shared my feelings with my mom, I struggled with whether or not she was right. If my dad would never do such a thing though, why did I think that he would? Confused about it all and not knowing what else to do, I became preoccupied with getting and staying completely hammered, it became a preoccupation.

I started ditching school with friends and would experiment with Cocaine, Crystal Meth, Ecstasy, Mushrooms, and Acid. I loved it all. The more drugs I used, the more friends I had and the more removed I was from my painful existence. From the time I told my mom about the problem with my dad, there was never a time afterward, at least for the most part, that I wasn't under the influence of something. My dad, as always, never noticed anything and if my mom started to suspect, I'd blame my depression medication.

While at my dad's, I'd hide out in my room, consistently drugged, keeping myself numb. If I could get away with it, I'd get drunk too. At my mom's, the workaholics, it wasn't as lonesome, I had the freedom to do what I wanted, spending time with friends using drugs, drinking and having fun. The partier on the outside, inside I was scared. Lonesome and still in turmoil, I felt worthless and unlovable. I connected and maintained friendships with others that seemed to be social outcasts too, others like me who were substance abusers seeking relief. While my mom worked, I got lit. Rarely at school, I partied all the time and started becoming interested in the opposite sex.

My interest in boys was normal, but my feelings about myself weren't. Thinking I was worthless, it was easy to talk me into doing things I may not have been comfortable with or didn't want to do. I had little experience but was beginning to figure out that using my body was a way that I could get things I wanted or needed, including drugs, alcohol, and money. By the time I was fourteen, school was the least important thing to me, the wonderful feeling of not feeling was all I cared about. I was a teenage catastrophe and there wasn't much that anyone could do about it.

I pulled into the driveway in a fog, the afternoon with my dad disturbing on so many levels, now seemed like it was ages ago. Flooded with memories and feeling heavy about our lunch, I think of my dad and his "top secret" relationship with me and now my innocent child. I'm not sure what to do. Based on years of sharing things that were in the "gray" area, or bringing up topics that were "uncomfortable" and made people think I was crazy, I did what I always did, I tucked it away. I'd tell myself that everyone was right; I was crazy. I'd repeatedly ask myself what was wrong with me and why did I think this way? The only difference is now, I was a wife and a mother, I had a husband and a child that deserved my best. Was I my best if I kept pretending that everything was fine when it wasn't?

I take my sleeping baby from the car and go into the house. The problems facing me with my dad are overwhelming. I could choose to do nothing. Years ago choosing nothing meant I could block it all out by getting drunk or high, completely free myself from any thoughts or even feelings about the things bothering me. What were those things, though? I put my sleeping baby in her crib and turn on her lullabies. My heart is so full of love for her; I know I can never take that path again. I was sober now, almost five years sober. I wanted to stay sober. Why was I even thinking like this? Wait, was it my dad? Was my dad a trigger? With Twinkle, Twinkle, Little Star playing in the background, I go to the other room and call my sponsor.

·Chapter Four·

Within a few weeks of lunching with my Dad, I had started back with a famous support group. As much as I loved it, I hadn't been very regular about it in the past. Feeling a bit invincible with all of the good things going on in my life, my sponsor kindly reminded me that continuing to work the program and going through all of the steps would be key to my staying sober. I had been sober for several years now and had never completely read the "Big Book" or completed all of the twelve steps, recently I hadn't been attending meetings regularly and having a sponsor was even new to me. I decided to start fresh, determined I dedicated myself to finishing the book, working the program, going to meetings and maybe making an appointment with a therapist.

Not being much of a reader, the "Big Book" wasn't the easiest, but I started. The therapist's phone number, shared with me by my sponsor, was scrawled on a random scrap of paper and stuck under a magnet on the refrigerator. Only occasionally reminding me to make an appointment, within a few days, it went unnoticed. The Meetings though were no problem. Being very social and actually knowing quite a few people from my past that were attending, I easily added it to my schedule and became a regular. I chose a woman's group and went twice a week, leaving Chase in charge of Jordan.

Feeling enthusiastic about my new commitment I encouraged Chase to get on the bandwagon too, but for whatever reason, he wasn't interested. Working full-time, trying to carve out opportunities to keep fit and helping with the baby was about all he had to give at the time. As much as I wanted both of us to be on the same page with our sobriety and being actively engaged in the steps to stay sober, I knew I couldn't force him to do anything. I was on my own, at least for now.

The meetings definitely helped and I was inspired by so many that were in the process of sobriety, some having years and years of being successful and mastering addiction, while others were in attendance without so much as a day free of using to account for. Chasing Sober was real to me and I loved it. Immediately, I felt compelled to be there and be regular. I wanted to be the best that I could be. Maybe eventually I would even be in a space where I was able to help others.

With my OCD in full swing, I happily took care of my house, my husband and Jordan. I exercised regularly, weighed every bite of food, counted calories and fully immersed myself in all of the aspects of working the program. Being so busy it was easy to avoid my dad. I knew that my problem wasn't time with my dad, but not confronting the nagging feeling inside of me that he had done something to me. The something, still undefined, wasn't good. So, as much as I was making progress in all other areas of my life, avoiding my dad and the issues bothering me couldn't stay unresolved forever.

A few weeks later I made an appointment with the therapist and threw the scrap of paper away. What was I going to say to her? How would it go? Should I just start by telling her I think my dad might have done something to me? Right away it started my inner critic, trying to convince me that nothing happened, that I was crazy, that my dad would never do a thing like that. Only this time the more I tried to convince myself that nothing happened the more thoughts I had that something did. I didn't want this to be true. I missed my dad, not the dad from my past, but the dad I had now. The funny dad, my friend that I had lunch with and went on bike rides with, the person Chase and I went to the beach with, Jordan's grandpa. My poor dad, why would I think such a thing? What was wrong with me? I couldn't take it anymore; I called the therapist and canceled my appointment.

I drove with Jordan down to the beach, put her into the jogger and started on a run. I was mad at myself, I knew I had to do something; I either had to make up my mind and confront the issue or let it go. I ran faster as my mind raced with things from my past darting around wildly. Winding through all of the normal people on the boardwalk, I kept questioning myself, "What is my problem, why am I such a mess?" My child was six months old now and "it," whatever "it" was that happened with my dad, was always on my mind. The truth was I didn't know what "it" was. I wasn't really sure what happened, what was done to me.

What I did know is that even now, if we were with my dad, I was always on edge, worried about him staring at my breasts or looking at my body. I knew too that he was constantly lying to his wife and dishonest about being with me, his own daughter and, the worst was I knew that if he held my baby I was obsessed with checking to make sure he didn't get excited. It was sick and I was disgusted with myself for even thinking it, but it wasn't going away, it was only getting worse.

I honestly didn't know what to do about it. Parts of me felt like it was all in my head, but there were too many other things. Things that made me believe there was a reason for me to be reluctant around him and not trust him. The saddest part was that no one had protected me; I couldn't take the chance of letting that happen to Jordan. If my dad was going to be in my life I had to confront the issue, right?

The following week I was sitting at the therapists. Alone in the waiting room, I'm ten minutes early. I'm seated near the door, it's quiet and as expected, I'm feeling anxious and alone. Like when I was a child, I am worried about being judged. My past is uncomfortable, even left darting around in my head, to let it out and actually talk about it scares me. Most of what's bothering me is vague. Talking about it and looking for answers will make it real. Am I ready for real? My past is already rugged and rough, painful really. Will me dredging up the details about it do any good? I think about leaving, but I know the thoughts will never go away unless I address them.

Did he just look at me? Or did he touch me? I start to wonder if he ever had sex with me and I quickly dismiss it. "Kristen really!" The voice in my head starts in on me, "What's wrong with you, that's too much," I quietly think that "too heartbreaking" is more like it. Wouldn't I have known, though? I think back to the first time I had sex, it was an older man I met at Discount Tires. I was thirteen, almost fourteen and his name was Alan.

Why am I thinking about this? I stop myself and then start again. Feeling relieved that I can remember and that it wasn't my dad, I relax a little. My inner critic uses the opportunity to remind me of how filthy and disgusting I am and guilt chimes in to share that my poor dad is innocent.

My first time was anything but special. Horrible and dirty, it would be another secret in my life, a secret that confirmed I was less than and worthless. Out of my mind most of the time on ecstasy, pot, and alcohol, it was summertime and my good friend Erica needed to take her car in to fix a bad tire. It was late in the day and the two mechanics working there told us we were cute. Older than us, we thought it was cool when they let us stay in the car and get high while they put it up on a lift and repaired the tire, free of charge.

We hung around visiting until they got off work and then went to one of their houses where we continued to smoke pot, drop acid and drink. After both of our friends went home, Alan and I were left alone. Within a few minutes, he started to get close to me and kiss me. By then I was so drunk and so high I was barely conscious. I easily gave in. I had nothing to lose. I was a teenage drug addict, alcoholic with no self-worth or self-respect. Besides, regardless of how I felt about myself, I knew now that I could use my body in exchange for "favors."

Alan was a loser, twice my age, he was a drunk and a stoner, who happened to live in of all places, a house across the street from my mom. He would be classified today as a pedophile or even a predator, but at the time I was naive to those types of things and unaware. I had no feelings for him or about him, to me, it was a place to hang out and get and use drugs. Most likely drawn to the idea that I had somewhere to go and that there was someone outside of my mom to take an interest in me, it wasn't a good situation but at the time it provided an escape for me.

Fueling my preoccupation with not fitting in and being abnormal was the fact that under the circumstances, because of the age difference, we weren't allowed to go anywhere or do anything. We could only be together in secret and the secret was just between us. Outside of his house, "we" didn't exist. He'd tell me all of the time that we couldn't really be in a relationship or he'd get into serious trouble.

Within a short time, I found out I was pregnant. I had constant waves of nausea, couldn't keep anything down and my squished and hidden boobs were all of the sudden unable to fit in my already ample sports bras. Those symptoms combined with the fact that I hadn't had my period very long and it had stopped led me to believe that I had a problem. I rode my bike to CVS to get a Pregnancy Test, but the clerk told me I was too young and wouldn't let me buy it. So, I rode over to Rite Aid and stole one. I rode back to my mom's, read the instructions and peed on it. The plus sign lit up within minutes.

Once it was confirmed that I was pregnant my life, already chaotic, went spinning further out of control. It was worse once I found out that I was pregnant and alone. The creepy neighbor wanted nothing to do with me other than to make sure that I would keep quiet about "us" and get an abortion. He never thought to help with the money it cost or even offered to drive me. He ended up being just another adult in my life to prove that no one could really care about me. I scheduled my own appointment, called my friend Erica to take me and, used my birthday money to pay for getting rid of what would have been my first child. After that, I never stayed sober long enough to think about any of it.

"Kristen?" Startled, I look up at the therapist in the doorway. "Oh, hey." Not what I was anticipating, she's older with short, dark hair and serious glasses. Dressed casually she looks like she's my mom's age, maybe a little bit older. She's thin, with no boobs and an attitude. I'm not sure why I notice the boobs and I feel awkward. Maybe it's the topic I need to talk about. Regardless, I don't think I'm going to like her. She isn't warm. I have a feeling I might need warm. "Come in and have a seat. I'm Dr. Hadley but you can call me Liz, most of my patients call me Liz."

"Okay, Dr. umm, Okay Liz." I don't want to call her Liz. I sit down on the edge of a small armchair and look around her office trying to take it all in without being obvious. I look at all the diplomas and awards hanging up and then to the personal items on her desk. There's a picture of a little dog. I try not to laugh, it's like a kid's school picture, but with a dog. Why a dog? She begins our session with a rundown on pricing, late fees, missed appointments, etc. etc. I try to keep up and have an open mind, but I don't think I can share anything with a woman like this. I'm feeling negative and try to shake it.

"So Kristen, tell me why you're here?" Thinking I shouldn't just blurt out that my dad may have touched me, I give a brief rundown of my life, my parents, my stepfamily, and half-sister, my trouble with addiction, my marriage, and my baby. I begin to tell her that there's something troubling me about my past, but she interrupts me. "Tell me about your marriage, Kristen." She stares at me without blinking. She's very power-driven and it's making me feel even more uneasy. "Okay, but I'm not really here about my marriage," I say politely. Trying to stay calm and in control, I take a deep breath, "I'm here about..." She cuts me off again, "Yes, but a lot about the intimacy in your marriage can help us get to the bottom of what happened to you when you were a child."

I think about my marriage. I mean it isn't like the fairytale romances you see on television but it's good. I guess I could tell her that Chase doesn't really like to take out the trash or do a lot of housework, but he does help me with Jordan. My marriage? I start to get nervous now, is there something wrong with my marriage too? Trying not to tear up, I answer "Well, I sleep in a sports bra most of the time and on occasion, a giant man's shirt."

"Does your husband ever say anything?" she fires back. "Well, he has, in the past." I share this hesitantly, waiting for her to respond, hoping it doesn't mean anything bad. "Has he asked you to take off the sports bra?" she asks bluntly. "Well, not really," I hesitate again, "He just asks about it from time to time, he tells me that most women can't wait to get home and take off their bras, I guess he wonders why I'm in it all the time, why I'm sleeping in it." I fake smile and add, "I guess he thinks it's funny." "Is it? Is it funny Kristen?" she asks me while she's writing something in a notebook. "Well, not funny like, well, no, I'm just more comfortable with it on," I answer sadly.

The questions go on for a while. They're all very uncomfortable and none of them really have much to do with the reason I'm there. My answers are confusing even to me and I try to keep from crying. She starts asking me a lot of things about Chase and how he acts, his family, his upbringing, his work. Then she touches on my Mom and her role in my life, then my Dad and our relationship. I'm not sure whether I even have enough time now to ask her about my dad and what's been happening.

Just as I'm getting up the courage to share, she tells me in a very direct and condescending manner that she believes I may be Bipolar and that for the time being, while I was in therapy, I should separate from my husband. Stunned, I hand over my credit card for the co-pay, wait for her to return it and leave without saying anything else.

Mad, I get in the car and call my Mom. She's watching Jordan and I'm hoping she'll keep her a while longer so I can run some errands. Knowing I went to a therapist, but not specifics, she asks how it went. I tell her how awful it was and that the advice was for me to leave Chase. We both agree she's ridiculous and that I need to find someone else and we hang up. I start the car and head to Target.

It wasn't the first time I'd been to a therapist I didn't like or that was no help. I had been to several throughout my life. The trouble with therapists was that so far none of them had ever really been able to help me. So why did I bother going? Why was it that I needed help? Couldn't I work things out on my own? My thoughts were all over the place as I drove.

I couldn't imagine why someone who barely knew me and had never met my husband would suggest that we separate. I mean really, we were a family, with a small child. I loved my husband. My husband and my daughter were everything to me. They were my family now. I finally had a family that I knew loved me and wanted me, and I loved them and wanted them right back. She was way out of line. Thinking about family, for whatever reason, I'm back to the abortion and how ruined I was, how alone I felt. Randomly, I consider the fact that I could have a sixteen-year-old child. I feel regretful for a moment, thinking I literally could be the mother of a teenager, a young boy or girl that most likely would be learning to drive. Of course, it would never have been possible; I wasn't capable then, not to mention the effects of all the drugs and alcohol. My skin crawls as I think of the father, who most likely would have gone to jail.

Hitting every red light and fighting the onset of rush hour traffic, I continue to dwell on my past. I'm painfully reminded of going through that experience all alone and the aftereffects the abortion had on my psyche. I saw myself as more worthless than ever and deliberately checked out. The neighbor quietly moved away and a young family moved in. I took any drugs I could get my hands on and continually drank myself into oblivion. I was on a total crash course and there was nothing anyone could do to stop me.

Completely dropping out of high school, against my mother's wishes, I spent my time aimless and lost, no longer caring about anyone or anything. I stayed high all of the time, taking psychedelics along with my routine combination of alcohol and pot. Higher than a kite and out of it almost all of the time, when I wasn't I was depressed and despondent, unable to cope.

My dad, as expected, did nothing to help. Instead, he made matters worse by telling me I was no longer allowed at his house. Not like I was ever really welcome or wanted to be there, but now I wasn't "allowed." Marianne decided I would be a bad influence on my half-sister Katie, who had just turned six. My Mom, my last hope, with her stoic composure and all of her best efforts, tried desperately to reach me, but she was at a loss again. She could only tell me how disappointed she was in me and that I needed to stop, begging me to get my life together. Maybe because I had been a suicide risk in the past, there was a fear that if anyone did anything too drastic, I might try to take my own life.

They were such bleak times for me that there were many moments when I thought I would be better off killing myself. There was really nothing anyone could do. My dad with his own life and second family wanted little to do with me or any problems in general. My mom had to work. That meant she had no way of making me go to school, keeping me from my friends or preventing me from using drugs and alcohol. She was the only one who was even trying to help me, but I couldn't be stopped.

On the rarest of occasions when my mom would get a glimpse of the real me, she would plead for me to at least finish school. I don't think my mom was fully aware of where I was mentally or the extent of my drug use. I was regularly consuming huge amounts of Quaaludes and Barbiturates while still smoking pot and drinking until I blacked out. When I was aware of her, which was seldom at best, I would feel sorry for her. I would be sad that things were this way and that she had to live in a constant state of worry and frustration. As bad as I felt, I couldn't stop. Life without being high was not worth living, at least to me.

Ultimately, my mom signed me up for an alternative schooling program called Futures High that started in the fall. I would be turning sixteen in September, which was perfect because in order to go to this school I needed to be able to drive myself there. I would have to get my Driver's License and a car. Thinking it could help change me and the course of my life and again, not knowing the extent of my drug and alcohol abuse, my mom helped me with driving classes and bought me a new car. The consequences of missing school or using drugs or alcohol meant I would lose the privilege of driving.

I tried to sober up, at least enough to make it to the two days a week I had to be at my new school. Futures High couldn't have been better for me. The instruction was one on one with a teacher, they didn't give grades lower than a C and if I didn't do the homework I never got an F, it would just be reassigned until it was completed. The best part of this school was that there were other people there like me who I could get high with between classes and after school. For once in my life I wasn't the biggest loser on campus, I actually fit in and started to feel good about myself.

I was still thinking about Futures High when I pulled into the Target parking lot. I turned off the engine and pulled out a sticky note and started to make a list. My mom, still helping us out financially, had brought to my attention that I was a little too swipe happy, regularly using our shared credit card far too much. Maybe if I stuck to a list I would do better. My mom, who had never given up on me, was a huge support in my life and now in my family's life. Through all of my addiction, in and out of jail, sober living houses, rehab, and relapses, she was always there. Even now, I didn't know what I would do without her. The least I could do was to be more reasonable with my spending.

My dad, the polar opposite, had basically disappeared during that period of time, I think there were years where I never saw him, his wife or even my sisters. Intermittent at best I don't remember him being around much through most of my worst years. Why would he vanish when I would have needed him the most? In between writing down items on my list, I was still obsessing about the past. Why couldn't I just let it go? Where was my dad and why wasn't he there for me back then?

I remind myself that my dad had never really been there, but the alarms are sounding. I try to silence the voice before it starts, but it's no use, it races around in my head, stirring up a million questions, big, scary questions, questions left dormant for years that are now demanding answers. "Why Kristen? Why can't you figure it out?"

I flinch as it surfaces, did my dad know something? Was he afraid of being exposed? Did he think he might have been responsible for the awful turn my life took? I shuddered as I tried to get the thoughts to go away. Even silently begging them to leave me alone, telling them to "Get out, get out." I have to stop thinking about it. I have to stop. It isn't fair to anyone to keep this up. I needed to let it go. I hate myself for thinking such awful things about my own father. He wasn't perfect, but he was my dad.

Maybe I was crazy; maybe all the drug abuse was affecting how I remembered things. Whatever it was I knew I had to stop dwelling on it. Feeling a bit nauseous I try to breathe and relax some. Tensing up instead, it dawns on me that I haven't been myself lately. In a flicker of a moment, I realize my period was late too. Of course, it all made perfect sense, I knew I was pregnant. It was exactly how I felt before with Jordan and... "Stop, Kristen, just stop." I shake the past from my thoughts as I excitedly jot down pregnancy test on the list and try to get a handle on myself.

Pregnant again, I couldn't be happier. I loved being a mom, the thought of another baby was super exciting to me and I was thrilled. If I was pregnant though, my new baby deserved a positive and happy place to be for the next nine months, not a screwed up mental case unable to decide whether she was molested or not. With a new determination to let the past go I take my list and head into the store, beaming about the future and the possibility of another baby.

·Chapter Five·

Not quite into my second trimester, I paced outside of the doctor's office waiting for my Mom to show up. Jordan's on my hip, happy just to be held and have her pacifier, unaware of anything going on. We've just come from having lunch with a good friend of mine where I had finally, after the customary 12 weeks, been able to share my good news. It was a lunch cut short by uncomfortable evidence that my new pregnancy could be in jeopardy. I made an emergency appointment with my doctor and then called my Mom to meet us. Always reliable, she pulls into the parking lot within a few minutes of us and rushes over. She interacts with Jordan and takes her as we walk into the office building and wait for the elevator.

"What's going on Kristen?" looking at me, she pushes her sunglasses onto her head and lets the baby play with her car keys. My call to her was brief, only a request that she comes to help with Jordan while I went in to see my doctor for an emergency issue. She's a mix of concern and frustration as she continues, "Kristen what's wrong?" I try not to take it personally, my Mom is scheduled, a planner, meeting at the last minute without knowing why has her wound up. She looks at the baby, then back to me as we step into the elevator. The small space seems tight. I'm anxious enough about my appointment and it only intensifies as I realize that my Mom might not be that happy about me having another baby, especially so soon. I hadn't really thought much about her reaction, until now.

"I hope you're not pregnant Kristen." Okay then. That was settled, she's not happy. But I am. "That would not be responsible," she continues. Blunt and to the point her neck and chest are getting flushed. Jordan, as if she understands what's going on, looks back and forth from me to her grandmother like she's at a tennis match; she waits for me to respond. Saved by the elevator door opening, I step out trying not to feel deflated by her comments.

"I'm sorry you feel that way," I respond quietly as I walk through the door of the doctor's office and go to check in. Disappointing my Mom now was so much different than when I was younger. I was so used to it then and so out of it most of the time; it really didn't affect me as much. Anything that bothered me, I escaped, dulling all of my thoughts and feelings with drugs and alcohol. Now, as a sober person, and a mother myself, it was distressing. It bothered me that anyone would be disappointed in me, especially my mom.

Called quickly, I'm led to the exam room, stopping on the way at the ominous scale. My heart sinks; I've been eating everything in sight based on the little plastic stick and its bright pink plus sign. I still struggle with weight and body image issues; the scale as long as I can remember has been a lifelong enemy. I hate how much control the three little numbers have over my life and how I feel about myself.

"Do I have to weigh?" I ask the nurse, hopeful. "Yes, its routine, but you can close your eyes and I'll write it down without mentioning it if you like." A kindred spirit, I conclude by her size she must have scale issues too. Doesn't everyone? I kick off my flip flops in the last ditch effort to shave off any amount possible and step reluctantly on my nemesis. I'm still thinking about my Mom and her reaction as the nurse charts my weight.

I can see why she would be upset. Since Chase and I have been married she has been helping us out financially. She lets us live in one of her investment properties for minimal rent, she helps with some of our monthly expenses, we use her credit card as needed and, she takes us on family vacations twice a year. Beginning to feel a little guilty, I understand why she's more concerned than elated.

The nurse guides me to the exam room and asks me a few questions, noting my answers on her chart. She pulls on some gloves and preps me for a blood draw. I know already this is going to be uncomfortable and as always, awkward. The nurse, on the hunt for a good vein to draw from, comments after several minutes, "Your veins are..." "Shot?" I finish her sentence. "Yes, I'm a recovering addict." I stretch out my hand and point to a Swastika Tattoo, between my thumb and forefinger. "They usually have to get it from here." Feeling embarrassed, I wonder how much I weighed and think of asking her just to change the focus. Instead, I confess, "It's not how I feel now." She's black and heavy set so I'm two for two. This time she just ignores me.

It's true, it's not how I feel now, but there was a time period where I was involved with and influenced by people that were hateful, angry and violent. Intrigued by them, I managed to get introduced to the group through a friend of mine Julianne, from Futures. Jul's, like me, was a misfit and a rebel. She was a beautiful girl with a mixed up family and a love for everything they hated. Her focus back then was on a group of Skinheads, one in particular named Andy.

There was something very attractive to me about Skinheads; in my life the more outrageous the better and they were outrageous. They were tough, covered in tattoos, and rebellious. They also liked to do the same things I liked to do, which was going to shows, concerts, drinking, using drugs and fighting. I wasn't raised to hate people and the fighting was fairly new to me, but with this lifestyle and these people, I was able to let out aggression that I wasn't even aware I had. Even though I was never exposed to violence and my family wasn't racist in the least, my draw to people that were seen as social outcasts and being accepted by them, made it easy for me to embrace their beliefs and transfer the hate I had for myself to others.

Once I befriended these people I started to hate by association all Black, Jewish, Mexican and Gay People. I was mean, angry and aggressive. I started getting shocking tattoos, including a Swastika, coloring my hair, dressing wildly and smoking cigarettes. I was transformed into someone I didn't recognize and while most traits were undesirable, there was something to be said for how strong and capable I was becoming. With all of my hate and anger directed out towards others, I felt better about myself. Freer in a sense, I was confident about finishing high school, I was more popular than ever, and as far as I was concerned, I was a new and improved version of myself.

My relationship with my new group of friends was limited by my schedule, apart from my two days of school at Futures; I was able to land a job at Baldwin Academy, my favorite little pre-school from when I was a toddler. All of the same people were there and I felt welcome and loved. I knew from the start it would only be a matter of time before I would ruin it, I was a preschool teacher and a drunk at the same time. I laced my coffee with my drink of choice, Jack Daniels before work and had a hidden flask for sips throughout my shift.

My drinking was definitely out of control, an obsession. Passing out in the evenings and unable to get up most mornings, I'd often show up to work doing the "Walk of Shame," wearing my clothes and make-up from the day before. Most days I was able to manage without anyone noticing, or so I thought.

While I was working at Baldwin and finishing school, I met a boy my age named Justin. We were at a party in a nearby neighborhood called Clairemont, seeing him across the room; I had never been so attracted to anyone. New and different for me, from the moment we met there was a chemistry between us that made me feel invincible, excited and on top of the world. It was a first, experiencing such good feelings, I was almost happy. I loved it, not quite as much as getting high, but close. From that first night, we were inseparable. The best part was that I was beyond drunk and had been snorting Cocaine for hours, but he didn't seem to mind. Justifying myself and my lifestyle, it seemed to prove that if someone so good could like me as I was, I must not have been that bad.

Justin was good looking, on the taller side; he was strong with a nice build, dark hair, and beautiful green eyes. Clean-cut and tame, he was a senior at a normal high school in our area. He partied, but nothing like I did, it wasn't the main focus of his life like it was mine. The first night we met we were intimate, but it was different from all of my other experiences. He was kind, caring, and gentle. We became good friends; enjoying each other's company, he took me on dates, out to dinner, movies, we spent time together just having fun. As much as we cared about each other, and even though I may have been his first true love, my first true love would always be alcohol. Alcohol and drugs were everything to me, they were my life.

Consumed not just with drinking, but getting drunk, I was delusional. I believed I was in control of my life and making good decisions. The truth was that day after day, I was on a constant bender and still taking massive amounts of drugs. Smoking pot to me was as normal as brushing my teeth, a part of my daily routine. My life was anything but in control. In my mind, I believed people thought I was on the right track, working, going to school, young and in love with someone who actually loved me back. All of this and my friends and I had recently started our own clothing line, blatantly called "Red Eyed." I felt unstoppable, on fire, my life was working. Only it was all an illusion and I was the only one not seeing it.

The "Red Eyed" business came to life when my friends and I were looking for some cute Marijuana Shirts to wear to a party on April 20th, aka 4:20. Four-Twenty is a holiday type celebration for Marijuana Enthusiasts, as well as, a time each day to light up. When we couldn't find anything worthwhile, we started brainstorming and came up with our own logo. Deciding to start our own company, we sketched and colored our design, found a silk screener, got our business and resale licenses and started a marketing plan all on our own.

Our "Red Eyed" brand was a huge hit, we couldn't keep the t-shirts, tank tops, or sweatshirts stocked. We plastered the town with our stickers and raked in the cash. My cash went to pay for all of the drugs and alcohol I was consuming, while my friends were more reasonable, spending some of their money on partying, and putting some away. I was so out of control that no one could keep up with me. Proud that I could drink everyone I knew under the table and ingest copious amounts of drugs while still functioning, I would never have guessed that they were all concerned about me. So concerned, that they were planning a big change for me.

I graduated from Futures a few months before my eighteenth birthday and knew without a doubt, that I would never in my life have to go to school again. Complete freedom, I was ready to direct all of my attention to our new business venture, partying and Justin who had been my boyfriend for the past year. My Mom threw a huge Graduation Party and was thrilled that I had a High School Diploma. She definitely felt let down when I told her I had zero interest in college. She had been saving for years, hoping I would grow out of my debased lifestyle and start to take my future more seriously. Wrong.

Being involved in a new relationship herself, she didn't put up much of a fight, just her now routine disappointment lecture, which fell on deaf ears. I still lived at her house, but between her hectic work schedule and staying with her boyfriend, she was gone most of the time. I generally had the place to myself, had people over and did whatever I wanted. This included coming and going as I pleased and not answering to anyone. For me, in my distorted view, things couldn't have been better.

My hustle with the shirts was real. I thrived on being a businesswoman and our clothing line was booming with interest in our company continually growing. We couldn't have been more excited about all of the money rolling in. My girlfriends and I would go into stores and show people the samples, the stores would place their orders and we would deliver all of the items once they were made. It was a great set up with a ton of freedom. I was lit all of the time, high on life and drugs and I loved it. I lost my teaching job at Baldwin just as "Red Eyed" started to take off.

Fired for coming to work drunk and because I threw a little girls pair of shoes into the middle of the street when she wouldn't keep them on, I wasn't too surprised. Instead of being bummed, I looked at it as an opportunity to focus all of my time and energy on building our company into a huge success. Not having a schedule and being totally unaccountable to anyone, within a few weeks I realized I still needed more of a routine and a regular paycheck. I got a job as a nanny for a family that had an Autistic Child. He was only two at the time, so I was still able to drink, get high and take drugs all day, my secret, sadly safe with him.

Driving around and conducting business, under the influence and with a two-year-old in tow was anything but professional. Even though we were more of a casual company, it was causing friction with my business partners. As much as I thought I had it all under control and that no one noticed, I was a nightmare. I was constantly stealing alcohol from local stores, even using the baby and his stroller now to hide several bottles at a time. I had started cheating on my boyfriend and I had been arrested more than once for shoplifting, along with possession and being under the influence. Other people in my life, including my closest friends and my boyfriend, all seemed to be partying too, but I was unaware that they were able to go days without anything. They were capable of being completely sober, comfortable even. I, on the other hand, had to be and was under the influence of something at all times.

I never noticed that they had all been trying to get me to stop or at least slow down. I was completely oblivious even when they were starting to conspire against me. On a day that we had planned to go out and sell our shirts, one of my friends insisted on driving. I always drove; I was the driver, period. Although I was surprised, I wasn't lucid enough to be suspicious of her motives. I got ready, taking pride in my appearance; I showered, did makeup and hair, then psyched myself up to sell our "Red Eyed" merchandise. I laced my coffee with Jack, took a few bong hits and waited for my girls to pick me up.

My friends showed up as planned and we took off, but we weren't heading towards any of the stores. Instead, we were driving through a neighborhood. I didn't think much about it at first, but pulling into a driveway at an unfamiliar house in North Pacific Beach, I started asking questions. I didn't recognize any of the cars and there was no sense that there was something strange about to happen. I couldn't figure it out.

"Whose house is this?" I asked, completely naive to what was about to go down. Looking at it, I remembered that I had been there before, that it was a friend of my mom's house. "Hey, what are we doing here?" Still clueless, I got out of the car and followed blindly along. "We're just picking up some fabrics," answered one of the soon to be traitors. Walking up to the door, my mom opens it and doesn't say anything. I'm confused, but still not thinking too much about it. "Hey Mom, what are you doing here?" Still silent, she ushers me inside, where I see my dad. It's so bizarre, I'm tripping out that my parents are together in this random house. I couldn't even remember the last time I saw my dad. Temporarily weirded out, I continue to look around, spotting my boyfriend sitting across the room. Then I notice a strange man that I've never seen before, getting up and coming towards me.

I still have no idea what's going on as he approaches me and holds out his hand, "Hello Kristen my name is Bob, and I am an alcoholic." Confused, I shake his hand as he explains that he was an interventionist, specializing in alcoholism. Still not computing, I wipe my hand on my jeans while everyone sits down. "Wait, an Interventionist? What?" I look around again as the guy sits down, telling me to take a seat. In my head, I'm wondering "How they know this clown and who does he think he is telling me what to do?" Defiant and still in my head, "I'm not sitting down." Instead, I sit, looking around, wondering why everyone is so quiet. They're all staring at me. "Wait, what the...," once I figure out what's going on, my heart sinks. Are they here for me? No, no way. I must be here for one of them? What is this? I'm annoyed; all I keep thinking is that I can't believe they're wasting my time like this.

I look at my Mom who is stoic and composed, I'm irritated especially if this is for me. She has some papers in her hands and her hands are shaking. She looks at me, through me really, a vacant look that scares me. It's me; it dawns on me that this really is for me. This is an intervention for me! My annoyance turns to anger, I'm so mad that I start shaking too, I want to bail and think about it, but remember that I don't even have a car. Outraged, I just want to go and sell shirts, and now I'm stuck. I wasn't interested in getting sober, screw this intervention. I keep thinking to myself, "Why is this happening? They're all wasting my valuable time when I could be out making some money."

The strange guy from the treatment center starts talking, but I immediately tune him out. I hate him, I don't even know him, but I hate him for being here and screwing me over with this intervention bullshit. I ignore everything he's saying and look around at all the traitors from my life, knowing they must have been devising this stupid plan for weeks. I'm burning up with anger and feel betrayed. How could they do this to me?

They all take turns reading their trumped up, emotional letters then start crying and making it a scene. It's embarrassing; I'm uncomfortable with the things they're sharing. It's all too personal and private; they're laying out all my faults and shortcomings like I'm not even there. It's shocking, isn't this designed to show how much they care about me and love me, how much they want to see me turn my life around? What about them? What about their drug and alcohol use?

What hypocrites! My friends and boyfriend were all getting high with me and we were all drunk together a few days ago. I'm even more incensed as I look around the room, all of them acting so innocent, it's so ridiculous when I think how two-faced they are. I feel no remorse. If anything, I'm getting angrier by the minute, thinking about how much more I'm going to drink and use when I get out of there.

Then everything changes, everyone turns on me, threatening me and harassing me. Unbelievably, it's all mean; the new tactic now is clearly intimidation. I look over to the alcoholic guy waiting for him to settle everyone down, but he does nothing. The dialogue changes from, "You need to get help," to "If you don't get help." Now hostile; various threats are being hurled at me. They've turned into a firing squad, each person taking a turn at shooting me down with their version of what an awful person I am, each repeating in their own words how disappointing I am and basically resorting to scare tactics. They start telling me, "If you don't go to rehab you're going to lose everything and none of us will have anything to do with you." It was so sad. Hurt and alone, just like always, it's me against the world. Now, without my mom, all I can think about is getting loaded and blacking out to all of this.

"Why would they want to do this to me, it's so malicious." The most hurtful to me was my Mom. My own mother was turning on me or at least that's how I felt. In all of the years, she was the one person I could always count on no matter what and now she too was against me. I was devastated by her and what she was saying. I started to cry uncontrollably. She was talking to me with everyone in the room watching as she destroyed me. She's done with me, done with my addiction, my lifestyle, continuing like a steamroller running me into the ground, she was taking my car and, should I choose not to go to rehab I would no longer be welcome in her home.

Not believing it could get any worse, in front of a roomful of people who have now become my enemies, my mom, in one final act of shaming me, shares that she caught me in bed with a boy named Cameron at her house. She follows up with what a disgrace I am. Breaking not only the "Mom Code," but also the "Girl Code," I only stare in disbelief. Why would she do that to me? My boyfriend looks stunned. Most likely broken-hearted, he just glares at me. My Dad sitting there dumbfounded, as usual, doesn't say a word as everyone else in the room seems to keep taking turns ripping me to pieces.

With the fervor growing against me, my friends are now stating that I was going to be kicked out of our business and, they plan to disown me. "What? I started that business, you can't do that!" All I can think is how much I hated them. Then Justin seemed to pull himself together enough to condemn me too, sharing that he could never stay with anyone like me, "a slut, a liar and a useless addict." "You'll lose everyone and everything," is all I kept hearing. I was sad on the inside, but I knew anger was better. Anger wasn't painful; it was powerful, helping me not to care, I let the anger and resentment blaze, hate burning for each and every one of them and their betrayal. The more I thought about it the more rebellious and indignant I got. How could everyone turn on me like this? Especially my mom, I couldn't take it anymore.

I didn't want to hear it anymore. I didn't care. I hated them all for doing this to me, even my dad, why did he bother to come. He didn't even have the balls to say anything. Screw them all is how I felt on the inside, but on the outside, I had to come up with a plan, buy some time. With no other options at this point, I deceitfully agreed to go to rehab.

Once I caved, all of them except for Justin who quietly left tried to hug me and insist that I had made the right choice. Inside I was methodical, putting on the show that they wanted to see. I had absolutely no intention of getting or staying sober. I knew even as I got in the car that there was no way I'm staying in rehab. I seriously have no interest in being sober, ever, regardless of who walks out of my life or what I lose.

My Mom and Dad, in a strange and uncomfortable alliance, take me to The McDonald Center in La Jolla together. I wasn't even able to get any personal belongings, pajamas, a toothbrush, a flask; I went with nothing but the clothes on my back and my purse, which only had my wallet, a lighter and a pack of Camel Lights. My Mom was talking to the air most of the way there, confident that this would be a great chance for me to straighten out my life and that I could still go to college. I could make something of myself instead of being a drunk or an addict, blah, blah, blah, all the way there.

My Dad occasionally agreed, but his agreeing was hypocritical too, considering he had been getting stoned and drinking my entire life. I tune them both out and tried to think of who would be willing to come and get me and how I could get out of there. My newest tattoo, The Swastika, catches my eye. I smile, reminded of exactly who to call.

There's a knock on the door startling me back to my appointment, I'm sitting in a hospital gown, waiting for the results of my blood test and exam. My doctor, Dr. Abrams enters first with the nurse following behind. I look at them wondering briefly what they must think of me, still feeling uncomfortable about my dumb tattoo. I turn my attention to the chart the nurse is holding, hiding my undisclosed weight. I want to know now, but don't have the nerve to ask.

My Doctor is friendly, but always in a hurry, so I know it will be quick. After congratulating me and confirming that I'm pregnant, she estimates a due date at the tail end of May. She briefly explains that I have SPD again and after prescribing bed rest and encouraging me to take it easy; she asks if I have any questions. I look at the nurse hesitantly and courageously ask her what I weighed. She laughs out loud as she tells me and it lightens the mood. They leave the room together and with everyone smiling as they go, I feel relieved.

I look down at my hand and peel the tape, lifting the cotton ball; I stare at the tiny hole and hint of blood that's left underneath. The familiarity of this moment has me captive; taking me back to a life that no longer exists. The tie off she used, the needle, the blood, and the cotton ball, all once a daily part of my existence, for me, this is a weird trigger. My heart beats wildly in my chest, anxiety or excitement; I'm not sure which, my body is reacting to just the thought of using drugs. I catch myself and take a deep breath.

"Stupid," I think as I toss the tape and cotton ball into the garbage can. Will there ever be a time that I won't be drawn to my past? The dialogue in my head continues, "No, of course not, you're a drug addict." I look at the dot of blood again, "Not anymore," I fight back, rubbing the old tattoo and the teensy spot of blood with my forefinger. "Life Sentence," I remind myself. "Seriously, all of this over a little blood draw?"

Trying to stop all of the chatter going on in my head I get dressed. Rattled, I lecture myself out loud, "I'm sober now, is being around a needle and a cotton ball really going to make me come all unhinged?" I throw my bag over my shoulder to leave, "Yes, obviously," I reply to myself. "You're ridiculous, Kristen," wafts through my mind. Noticing that I sound exactly like my mom in my head, I'm even more annoyed. "Quiet," I tell myself. I try to shake it all as I head for the door and with all of the chaos stopped momentarily; I make a mental note to get the tattoo removed.

·Chapter Six·

I look at all of the people seated around me, distracted like most of the world is now, half are on their phones. Some quietly catch up with friends or their sponsors, while others are here, but not here, vacant eyes meeting mine, but not connecting. "Hi, I'm Kristen. I am an alcoholic and a drug addict." I try not to sound too enthusiastic, but I am. I'm happy, I feel upbeat and I'm proud to be here. Right now, for me, in this moment things are good.

The lackluster response is automatic, "Hi, Kristen", textbook actually, for a substance abuse meeting. Greeting, introduction, move on to the next person. The customary opening continues, those who care to participate sound in, most defining themselves in one short, self-condemning and, lifelong sentence, "Insert name, I am an alcoholic."

The overhead fans click away, the only enthusiasm in the room as they do their best to circulate the warm air over the stuffy little group. This is my Friday Night. I'm in an old Community Center and I'm surrounded by my current peers, alcoholics and drug addicts. Like me, most are here in hopes of finding support and against most odds, overcoming addiction.

A tiny woman, weathered and rough, is leading tonight's group from behind an old card table. After reading something that's supposed to be encouraging, she jots a few things down on a notepad, looks up and in a scratchy, smoked too many cigarettes kind of voice, asks if anyone wants to start us off and share. I always want to share. The voice in my head chimes in, "except the part about your dad."

I ignore it. It's right though, apart from that I am an open book, willing to share it all, the good and the bad. I want people to know everything about me, everything I've been through and everything my family and friends have had to go through. I survived and I'm alive when so many others aren't. I'm sober and coherent; I made it out of a nightmare life, not only of addiction but all of the other degrading things that come with it; the seedy lifestyle, the lying, stealing, hustling for money, constantly disappointing people, jail, and in general living without any integrity, or even purpose. The fact that I feel good and have a decent life now, with a family of my own and a million reasons to live, compels me to raise my hand.

"I'll share," I say eagerly. "But not that part," says the voice again. I instantly try to sink the thoughts of my dad, burying them as I have for so many years. Losing my train of thought, I stand up and slide my own phone into my pocket, introducing myself once more. "Hi, I'm Kristen and I'm an alcoholic." I leave out addict this time, as I start to rummage through the thousands of files in my mind, trying to figure out what to share before I lose my window of opportunity with my already distracted audience. "So, I have almost six years sober."

They come to life to clap and cheer. I look around the room, hoping I can inspire or encourage at least one person. The fanfare has everyone temporarily paying attention as I continue, "My first intervention wasn't great, some of you know about this right?" I laugh nervously as I look around, most in the room nodding their heads, in quiet agreement. "I was eighteen and I had already been into my addiction for close to five years. I wasn't interested in sobriety. Not at all, I thought I was in love with my lifestyle, at the time I thought drinking and using was all I had."

Gaining confidence with the now attentive audience, I get real and honest, opening up as I go, "Unlike the people in my life, they, the alcohol and drugs, were always there for me. I mean I would wake up and smoke weed, drink all day and take pills until I passed out every night. That's how I lived. For me, it was my comfort zone. It's weird but I could count on them. I mean, I did count on them to keep me free from reality, from knowing how sad and miserable and alone I felt all of the time." My heart flutters, a tinge of sadness stops me. I try to catch my breath remembering how painful my life was, how lonely I used to feel, empty even. I tell myself it's okay, it's not like that anymore as I continue "I didn't stay in rehab after my first intervention, I wasn't ready.....

I think back to my first intervention and the intake process at The McDonald Center, I thought it was a joke, planning my escape as I was being admitted; I had no intention of staying. After the initial assessment, the hospital prescribed a treatment plan then my parents left me there, turning their backs on me, in hopes that someone with experience in dealing with addiction could solve my problems. That someone else could save me. That's when my life really took a turn for the worse.

In less than an hour, I had a friend out front ready to get me out of there. More than a friend on occasion, Cameron was the boy my mom caught me with. The one I had been cheating with when I was with Justin. He was great-looking, a little taller than me and had the whole bad boy complex going for him. Attracted to him, I was a bit apprehensive too, almost afraid, knowing that something about this one was dangerous. With my current situation screwed and zero for other choices, I decided to make the most of things, no matter what happened. I checked myself out, as an adult. At eighteen; I was my decision maker now. I walked away from the help I so desperately needed to a person I barely knew and the unknown, impatiently waiting out in a car I had never been in.

Our first stop was a liquor store where I lifted a bottle of Jack while Cameron bought a pack of smokes and some lottery tickets for good luck. My new life began as we drove east; away from everyone and everything I knew and loved. Already missing my life and feeling sad, the voice in my head quietly asks, "Why?"

Officially cut off from my family, my parents ignored my calls. My dad never there for me anyway wasn't surprising, but my mom was a different story. My mom, standing her ground and following through on her threats not to be there worried me. My friends too, wanted nothing to do with me, accepting my calls only to tell me "I was a lost cause" and to "stop calling." Under the guise of business, I'd say I was calling about "Red Eyed," only to find out that under the circumstances they were letting it die. "Screw them," is what I would tell myself, getting mad. I could definitely handle being mad better than I could handle feeling hurt. I knew not to reach out to Justin; I left him alone to move on. Deserted and alone, I binged on drugs and alcohol, a small part of me praying I guess that at least at some point my mom would give in.

Staying twenty miles east of everything familiar to me I was too close for comfort to the Women's Jail, in an area called Santee. I moved into an awkward situation with Cameron at his parents' house. Out of options, I was determined to make it work though. They made up a room for me, a room of my own; preferring for me to stay in there rather than share with their son. It was fine, I wasn't in there much, but whatever made them happy. I didn't need more people to hate me. I tried my best to make myself invisible, again.

With nothing to do, I'd go to work with Cameron every morning out in Temecula. During the week, he worked in construction, an hour north of where we were staying. I was left trying to find things to do all day until he finished. Without a job and having no money, I would literally drive around in his truck for eight hours while he worked. Most mornings we'd stop at Starbucks and while we were waiting for our coffee, we'd help ourselves to cases of their whip cream cartridges. This was a highlight, meaning I could start the day with "whip it's," inhaling nitrous oxide for hours. That combined with the drug and alcohol intake, sometimes I'd just sit and space out all day. Other days, Cameron would give me a little cash, many times all of his unwanted change and I'd be able to go to the Casino and gamble.

Most days I would steal beer and drink all day or smoke weed that I had pinched from Cameron's stash, I'd park somewhere so drunk and so stoned, I'd just sit and wait, unable to do much else. I really was a loser, wasting my days waiting for someone else to make me happy or plan something for me to do. I felt like I was a crazy person. Always, asking myself, "Why didn't my life matter to me? Why didn't I care?" I never could find the answer.

Each day when Cameron got off work we'd get really drunk and smoke pot together. Day after day the same routine, after being lit all day, I'd start over again with Cameron. I'd end up so drunk and so high that I would pass out, waking up wondering where I was. Thankfully, the majority of the time I was with Cameron. Sometimes I wouldn't be able to wake up in the morning and Cameron would go to work without me. I'd have to leave his parents' house while he was gone, so I would hang out with his best friend Jason who lived down the street. Jason, an out of work Construction Worker, also lived with his parents and was addicted to meth.

No stranger to meth, I started using it regularly, so much of it that my nose would swell and bleed. If that happened, I'd have to shoot it instead. Needles were never a problem for me, I actually liked them. I was now a "tweaker," using meth all day, every day, while also getting drunk and high. I was so wasted all the time I barely had a heartbeat, my life not mattering to me or anyone else, or so it seemed. Once Cameron was off work it was a total repeat of what I had done all day, it's a wonder I didn't end up dead.

Months into this life-wasting routine, I received a call from Cameron's mom that he had come to their house in a drunken rage, broke a ton of pictures, got into a fistfight with his dad and that we were no longer welcome there. Strung out and paranoid I spent the next few hours with Jason obsessing about what would happen to us. Cameron came for me later that afternoon, still drunk and angry, screaming obscenities and basically taking it out on me that we had no place to go. Just like that, we started living in his car. I was nineteen and now a homeless drug addict and alcoholic.

If I thought I was uncomfortable in other people's homes, not having a place to go was a million times worse. We'd stay in the car for a few nights, then get a motel so we could shower and clean up. I felt dirty and even more loathsome than ever, unable to bathe every day and having to find places to use the restroom, resorting many times to going anywhere I wouldn't be seen or stopped by the police. The motels, always seedy and filled with "tweakers" weren't much better. Blood splatters all over the walls and carpets, everything yellowed and dingy, smelling of old cigarettes and sweaty bodies, literal filth had become our refuge. Regardless, of how disgusting they were, I started looking forward to staying in motels, instead of having to be pent up in a car. It was a relief to have a restroom and a shower, knowing we could use freely and do whatever we wanted all night.

The uncertainty of not having a place to live was taking a toll on us and our already strained relationship. In desperation, I reached out to some friends to see if we could stay with them for a few days or until we could get our own place. Thankfully, they agreed to help us out and Cameron and I moved in with them, both of us grateful and thrilled not to homeless anymore.

Their house was in Clairemont, just minutes from Pacific Beach and everything familiar to me, everyone I missed. It was like a new lease on life, I had never felt so appreciative. The couple we stayed with was unbelievably kind. They were the only ones willing to offer us a place to stay when we were in such a bad way. We had our own room and felt welcome and comfortable. They even let us stay rent-free in an effort to help us get on our feet. Cameron still went to work out in Temecula every day and I would either go with him or get dropped off to hang out with Jason. Cameron and I had started going to Tijuana, Mexico or T.J. as it was known after he finished work. We'd hit up several pharmacies to load up on drugs, which would become one of our new side jobs.

Parking on the U.S. side we would walk across the border to stock up on a million different pills, needles, syringes, and Nubain, which was like a synthetic version of heroin. Being in Mexico you didn't need prescriptions to buy anything, the only trick was getting it back across the border. Loaded up with all types of drugs and paraphernalia, I would stuff everything into my bra and underwear, and we'd make our way back into the states. Keeping half for ourselves and selling the rest, it was big business and we started making a lot of money. No matter how many times we did it and how routine it became, I was always super relieved to get back across the border without being stopped.

This went on for months, a regular weekday ritual, it became like a game to me, rewarding in so many strange ways. Loving the access to unlimited drugs, I was shooting stuff into my veins and popping pills all of the time, constantly needing to use more and more of both drugs and alcohol to even feel anything. I was hopelessly hooked on all of it. Gaining Cameron's approval had even become like an addiction, as long as I did what he asked or wanted, things would go well for me. In a lifelong pursuit of looking outside of myself for acceptance, I did everything I could in an effort to keep him happy, regardless of what it cost me. Like my addiction to everything else I also became addicted to the adrenaline rush of getting away with everything. I was an addict through and through, all of it combined, was now my high.

Like most things I seemed to like, the enjoyment wouldn't last. One night on our routine drive to T.J., Cameron and I had both been drinking, even more than usual. After stocking up at one of our favorite pharmacies, I took a handful of random pills, drank more alcohol and blacked out. Not uncommon, I had been blacking out for years. Regularly consuming massive amounts of alcohol, using all kinds of drugs, shooting all sorts of mixes into my veins and asphyxiating myself with dust off computer cleaner and the "whip it's" from Starbucks, it was a wonder I even woke up every day. This time when I passed out, I woke up completely beaten. I had two black eyes, several cuts with dried blood, along with bruising and swelling all over my body.

"Cameron, what happened to me?" Shocked and disturbed that I couldn't remember, I looked to him to solve the mystery. "We got into a fight," he said plainly, not even looking up from what he was doing. At first, I thought he meant as a couple we got into a fight with other people. Confused by his reaction, I kept looking at myself; I couldn't believe how sore I was. I started opening and shutting my mouth, hoping my jaw wasn't broken, as I continued to look for answers. "What do you mean we got into a fight?" I asked, hesitating. I'm afraid of the answer I'm going to get as it dawns on me that he may have been the one that did this to me. Cameron, sounding irritated finally looks at me and says "We got into it, we, you and me, got into a fight."

It's a strange feeling to be beaten up by a man. Especially, someone, you think you love, and someone you think loves you. I stare at him in disbelief, feeling sick to my stomach. Now, forever afraid, I'm nervous as I ask, "So you basically beat the crap out of me and I can't remember a single thing?" Trying not to cry, it's useless. My voice is shaky and my tears start spilling over, stinging a small gash on my cheek. "Yep," Cameron replies.

Eventually, he told me he was sorry, promising that it would never happen again, but wasn't that always the case. We came up with a great story to tell everyone, keeping the truth a secret, only our secret left me more confused than ever. I was sad and felt alone, I missed my mom and being at home. Deep down I was frightened, my inner voice begging for me to get away. Quieting the voice and trying not to think about it anymore, I stay. All the drugs, the alcohol, shooting up, inhaling toxic chemicals, blacking out, and now I was going to let someone beat me? Like always, believing that making a change would be too hard, nothing changes.

Over time, I did make a small change; I got a job of my own. I couldn't believe it. I knew from the start, it wouldn't last, but even if it was temporary, at least I was able to get a job. I was proud in a way; I mean really, I was unreliable, hooked on drugs, an alcoholic, and a thief. While interviewing at Acapulco, a Mexican Restaurant near where we were staying, all I could think about was all of the free alcohol I would get, how I could give away food and drinks to all of my friends and how with tips, I would have my very own cash. I knew they must have been desperate when they hired me, but regardless, I was super excited.

I started off as a server and loved it. I was great at interacting with people, got along well with my co-workers, served my friend's free food and unlimited beverages and best of all, helped myself to bottles of booze all the time. Cameron, of course, was one of my regulars. He'd come in after work and have dinner and I'd serve him free beers until my shift was over. The strangest thing is no one was the wiser, either that or everyone was up to no good, so no one wanted to rat anyone else out.

Between Cameron's work, our pharmacy runs, and my new waitress job, we had saved up enough money to move and got our own place in Pacific Beach. I eventually quit my Restaurant Job and went back to my Nanny Job, taking care of the little Autistic Boy again. For some reason, everyone believed that I was doing better, even thinking that I had gotten sober. Since no one really asked, I wasn't going to explain. His parents dropped him off at our apartment early every morning and he and I would spend the day together. He had turned three and was fairly easy to take care of. I'd take him everywhere with me, even down to Mexico. We went so often, everyone there knew him by name, playing with him and giving him Mexican Candies while I loaded up on drugs.

He was a sweet little boy and I made sure he was always in my sight, in my estimation taking good care of him, keeping him safe and happy. My days were pleasant; I had freedom and money and was enjoying my job and little sidekick. I continued drinking, most day's high as a kite too. His parents had no idea of any of our whereabouts or what we did every day. Stories of parks and libraries, naps and playing kept them content. After all, my original referral had come from Baldwin Academy and with that recommendation, I was golden.

While my days were pleasant enough, my times with Cameron when he wasn't working had become torturous. He was more and more violent and aggressive. The domestic abuse was real; it was serious and very scary. He was always pushing me, choking me, hitting me, and grabbing me by the hair and smashing my head into things. Along with that he constantly yelled at me and called me horrible names. I was always swollen and covered with bruises, cuts, and scrapes. Coming up with excuses, people must have thought I was a walking accident. Already emotionally void and in a deep state of despair, the real damage was what it was all doing to me mentally. I stayed as drunk and as high as I could most of the time, having no self-respect or thought that I deserved anything better.

Cameron, already an alcoholic and addict, was now an abuser, forcing me into being his slave. He was a huge thief that became addicted to stealing too; most of the time, having me do all of his dirty work for him. Afraid of what would happen if I didn't obey, we'd spend most evenings going from liquor store to liquor store, and big grocery stores like Vons and Ralph's, stealing bottles of alcohol. We literally would clean out huge inventories of Jim Beam, Jack Daniels, Jose Cuervo, and more, then head across the border and sell it to all the bars in T.J.

It didn't stop there, some nights we'd go through Coronado stealing every bike we could find. These would also be delivered to Mexico, selling them for cash. Stealing and selling liquor and bikes was another "job" that we had on top of our normal paying jobs. We ended up being pretty blatant. I don't even remember being afraid of getting caught. I was always more concerned about Cameron beating me up if I wasn't on my game.

Finally, one night while we were stealing bikes in Coronado, we got pulled over. With the giant bolt cutter we used hidden, I thought we were going to get away with everything. I had a warrant out for my arrest though, most likely for not showing up to a court date, or skipping out on a traffic fine, so I went straight to jail. Cameron was free and left me to figure things out for myself.

My mom bailed me out, but wouldn't come and get me. She didn't want me in jail, but beyond that, I was on my own. Ashamed and disappointed in me, that was all she was willing to do at the time. I tried to reach Cameron, but he was probably off getting drunk in some bar. Unable to find a soul that was willing to pick me up and back to feeling alone and deserted, I resorted to calling Cameron's parents.

Our parents did get involved from time to time, trying to get us to change, especially my mom. Once she was speaking to me again, she started to like Cameron and would try to guide us onto the path of the straight and narrow. She continued to push rehab, but really had no idea how bad things were or that I was being battered. My Mom would not give up on me. If something happened, she would try to act like "this was the final straw." Or she would get mad and tell me, "You're on your own." This happened a lot after an arrest, court hearing or other trying situation, but she was always there for me when I needed her. I was in too deep now, Cameron and I both, using massive amounts of drugs, drinking all the time and getting easy money from stealing things. From our corrupt lifestyle, the straight and narrow path looked too hard. It seemed like too much effort, at least to me. I also thought it sounded boring; I wasn't interested in a so-called "normal" life, hourly pay or a salary, a nine-to-five job, a daily routine, and an average life. None of it interested me.

During this time my mom actually took the two of us to Hawaii on a vacation. Trying to get us to see the value of hard work and what we would be able to do, see, and experience if we were normal, we were inundated with sightseeing, the great outdoors and all sorts of physical activities. Loaded up on pills, I functioned as best I could, while thinking I might die. Kayaking, paddle boarding, and hiking were like extreme sports for me at the time. It was beautiful, no doubt, but I remember wanting to get home and back to business and back to using. I can't speak for Cameron, but I craved the adrenaline rush just as much as the drinking and drugs. There was a thrill that came with getting away with all of the things we were doing; I didn't want it to stop. Outside of the abuse, I thought I was enjoying my life.

We had been together for over a year and Cameron and I had reached the point of danger, he was so verbally and physically abusive that I worried all the time that he might really kill me. Once when he broke my wrist, he even had me believing it was my fault for blocking him from hitting me. Insanity, I no longer felt like we were in a relationship, most of the time believing I was just his pawn. I did whatever he wanted me to just to keep the peace, which rarely existed. It was a sick and depressing situation but I couldn't see a way out. The strangest part was that my dad and I had been back in touch. If his wife and my sisters weren't around he'd reach out, even to the point that Cameron and I would hang out with him on occasion.

One night we went to my Dad's House, while Marianne was out of town. He had invited us to come for dinner, and then relax in his Jacuzzi. Worried about my dad staring at my body, the Jacuzzi part concerned me. Besides that, my dad always let us drink, even though we were still underage. Not trusting the situation, I brought a giant shirt to hide myself and tried to limit my alcohol and drug intake. Of course, it was no use, Cameron chugged beer after beer. Every time he went into the house for more, he'd pound one inside, and then bring each of us another one when he came back out. This went on for a while until he was so drunk he couldn't walk or talk. I wasn't much better, but my dad was ready for us to leave.

That was my dad, send us home drunk, expecting us to drive all the way home to Pacific Beach from his house, which was at least thirty to forty minutes west. I never thought much about it but, in hindsight, my dad has been another man in my life that didn't really seem to care about me. Sure I was great to hang out with, drink, smoke weed, go for a bike ride, but beyond that, it seemed like I never really mattered to him. My relationship with him, for as long as I could remember, was always very confusing.

Beyond the issues with my dad, that ride home with Cameron would ruin us, our relationship or whatever it had become, would be over. Forced to drive, I was behind the wheel, completely out of control. I was so drunk that I was swerving all over the place skidding back and forth through the lanes, barely able to hold onto the steering wheel. Scared out of my mind, I was screaming, "Please don't make me drive, I shouldn't be driving. I'm too wasted."

Cameron started yelling at me to "Shut up," calling me filthy names and punching me until I pulled over. Swearing at me and threatening to kill me, he looked possessed as he took over and we headed back onto the freeway. Like some kind of demon seething with anger, he started hitting me in the head while driving down the freeway. Punching me, scratching me, pulling my hair and continuing to call me names, he would pull over and scream at me to get out. I'd start to get out then he'd yell, "Where do you think you're going, whore?" I'd get back in and he would start calling me vulgar names and beating me, bashing my head into the dashboard again and again. Drunk, feeling sick to my stomach and unsure of what to do, he started telling me, "Wait until we get home, you are really going to get it, I'm going to kill you bitch."

As horrible and abusive as Cameron had been in the past, I had never seen him like this. He was alarmingly out of control. I had never been so scared in my life. I believed he would really hurt me, possibly even kill me if we made it home. I was starting to hope we wouldn't make it. Would it be better to die in a car accident or for him to beat me until I was dead? The thoughts going through my head were insane. The next time he pulled off of the freeway to try and make me get out of the car I decided I was going to make a run for it. Pulling up to a red light at an off-ramp in an area called El Cajon, which is between Alpine and Pacific Beach, Cameron was stopping to get gas. I knew it was my chance.

I opened the car door and started running as fast as I could. Barefoot and stepping on pebbles and glass I didn't care, I just ran for my life. Within a few minutes Cameron was chasing me in the car, I was cutting through parking lots and jumping over fences. Crying and scared, I just kept running until I saw a truck at a red light and grabbed the handle on the passenger door, hoping to let myself in.

Thankfully, the door was unlocked; I jumped in and shouted "Drive," as a terrified woman, asking no questions stepped on the gas. I was a huge mess. Beaten and bloody, sweaty from running, my face and eyes were swollen, I couldn't stop crying. Hysterical, I begged her to just keep driving. "Look," she finally said, taking a deep breath, "I got to meet one of my boyfriends at the gas station back there, so what's going on?" I begged her to keep driving and told her about Cameron beating me, confiding in her that I thought he was going to kill me. She made a turn at the light and started to circle back to the gas station. "I have to meet my boyfriend," she said calmly pulling into a parking space. "If you want to wait in the car I'll take you to the police station when I'm done." What were the chances, I was in the car with a Hooker?

Cameron who had been following me closely, came screeching into the parking lot seconds later, pulling up to the truck I was sitting in. The woman and her man were taking care of some cash business but stopped to threaten Cameron and try to scare him off. I locked the doors and sunk down on the passenger side floorboard, hoping he'd leave. Within seconds, there was a loud crash as Cameron threw a huge rock through the windshield. With my heart pounding through my chest, I covered my head and crouched into a ball, knowing he was now crazed enough to actually kill me. Instead, I heard his tires squealing and I poked my head up just in time to see him driving away.

Now contending with the furious woman, she got in the car and drove us straight to the Police Station, complaining all the way. Mostly self-talk about how she always got into these "crazy ass" situations and how she was "just minding her own business." Then warning me "Girl, ain't no man worth this kinda bullshit." Once we were at the Police Station the officers in charge took her Police Report and she left me there.

Alone, battered and bruised, I had blood all over my feet and the bottoms of them were full of glass shards. I called my Mom begging her to come and get me. Even though I didn't want to press charges, I was informed that in Domestic Abuse situations, the State pressed charges now. Too many women over the years were scared to follow through and press charges, allowing the abusive men to get away with this type of behavior, so the State took over.

Still terrified for my life, my mom and I stayed in a motel that night and a hotel for several nights after that. Traumatized, and unable to sleep, flashes of Cameron's evil face wouldn't leave my mind. Days later we went to the apartment while he was at work and collected my belongings. He never even tried to contact me after that, it just ended. For me, fight or flight syndrome took over and I was paranoid for weeks, ready to run or hide no matter where I was. The oddest part is that it wouldn't be the last time we saw each other, or even the last time we would be together.

I hesitate a bit, looking out at my audience, "Like I was saying, for me, my first intervention, I wasn't ready. I thought my life was okay the way it was, I liked it, most of you probably can relate to what I'm saying, right?" Everyone's eyes are on me now, I feel like they're waiting for me to say something magical that will help change their thinking or somehow touch their lives. It's probably just me though, I want to help. "I mean, you have to be ready for sobriety, you have to really want it." I don't know why, but I start to tear up, "It's up to you really, no one can want it for you." Trying to be more positive, I add "Look, there isn't really a magic formula for sobriety, but it is possible. Just want it, want it with all your heart. Want it for you, because when you do, you'll be able to master it and then, then your life will be amazing, your life will never be the same... "Except for that part Kristen, you left out the part about your dad," whispers the voice in my head.

·Chapter Seven·

"You don't have to invite them. I mean really Kristen, if it's going to stress you out they shouldn't come." My mom looks at me as if she's waiting for an immediate decision. She's so practical, not concerned about hurting feelings, people getting mad or being left out, instead, not wanting any controversy, she's ready to ax people from Jordan's first birthday party without hesitation. Not just any people, but specifically my dad and Marianne.

I was bigger than that though, wasn't I? I could handle an afternoon with them, or could I? Just in the planning stages, my mom and I were having a Minnie Mouse themed party at Fanuel Street Park, which was around the corner from her house. She loved planning parties and had, of course, offered to host the entire event. It wasn't that she didn't want my dad and his awful wife there, although she wasn't a huge fan either, it was more about me and the anxiety it was already causing.

I was six months pregnant with my second child and whether it was the hormones or the real me, I continued to be torn between wanting my dad and my sisters in my life and the rejection I constantly felt from all of them. Marianne was another story, I knew I didn't want her in my life, I still couldn't stand her, but somewhat of a package deal, there was no way to have a relationship with the others and not her.

I was a wife and a mother now, my entire life was different, was I still going to let my Dad, my evil stepmother, and my sisters make me feel uncomfortable at my own child's party? Was I going to keep letting all of them make me feel inferior? Yes, was my answer, yes I was, but why? Why did I keep inviting that into my life?

I tried to reason with myself, thinking over and over that it would be a few hours at a Birthday Party; couldn't I do it for Jordan? Didn't she deserve to have family in her life? As much as I tried to talk myself into being okay with it I really wasn't. The party was months away, and I was completely stressed out at even the thought of inviting them, and what might happen. All of them being there together judging me and actually not just me anymore, but now my husband and daughter too, it was insane.

Maybe my mom was right, why invite them if it was going to cause so much tension. I guess I was an optimist; I wanted everyone to be there. I idealized myself fitting in and being part of a bigger family. I longed for the big holidays, the birthdays, celebrating the little milestones, summer barbeques, that whole extended family thing, the aunts and uncles, cousins, the grandparents, everyone getting together like in the television commercials. I wanted something that just wasn't a reality, at least not for me. For me the reality was awkward, always uncomfortable, trying to fit in with people that didn't like me or even care about me. So why did I keep trying? I wish I knew.

Like most things in my life, the party became an obsession. From the time we started talking about having it, I was consumed, on Pinterest day and night looking at cakes, decorations and searching for the perfect Minnie Mouse dress for my soon to be one-year-old. I wanted Jordan's very first party to be perfect. With my mom's help, the event itself would be amazing for sure but leaving it to me who to invite or not invite was too much pressure. So consumed, I knew I had to just make a decision and go with it. The guests, though especially a certain few could make or break the whole thing. Either way, invite them or not invite them, I was screwed. Would it always be such a battle for me?

Allowing my dad back into my life had already been a continuous struggle. Resolving to put the issue with him out of my mind, at least for now, we had stayed in communication; I just made myself a little less available. Burying the issue though was definitely easier said than done. Impossible really, keeping him at an arm's length didn't help get rid of the thoughts, they popped into my head routinely no matter how hard I tried to get rid of them.

Then there was Chase's Family as if dealing with my own family and what was going on with my dad wasn't challenging enough, my husband's family, while caring and kind, came with its own interesting dynamics. Without sharing too much personal information, Chase also grew up in a so-called "broken home," probably much worse than mine. His parents divorced when he and his sister were very young. His father worked most of the time, not able to see his children that often.

In his later years, he married again, a wonderful, kind woman that I fell in love with right after meeting her. She was a force of nature in a tiny package, beautiful and strong she had her own past but was all about being present and set on making the most of each day. We meshed from the start and became close. She accepted me and made me feel loved and important, which was rare for me so I treasured our connection. Chase's Dad and Chase, because of their history were a bit more disconnected. My husband tried though devoting every other weekend to making the two-hour drive north to Long Beach to watch football together, and have dinner. I'd join him, looking forward to some girl time with his stepmother who had become my close friend.

Chase's mom and stepfather lived closer, his sister too, just minutes away, so it was easier to get together with them. Like me, with my family, Chase and his family had been estranged off and on throughout the years, so getting involved with them was new in a sense to both of us. We initially spent a lot of time together, and I made every effort to get close to them, always so desperate for any kind of family I tried my best to gain their love and approval. For me, relationships, regardless of being sober and feeling better about myself weren't going to be easy.

Because of my own insecurities; I'd worry and overthink almost everything. Although I tried, taking the time and making an effort to build relationships as a sober person was still new to me. Communicating, initiating getting together, and putting the energy into getting along and getting over things that didn't go smoothly were the things I was only beginning to learn how to do.

Chase and I both, because of our backgrounds craved being surrounded by family and good friends. We both made it a point to be social, especially at the start of our relationship; the whole approval thing was in full force, both of us wanted to make good impressions on the important people in each other's lives. Over time though, we realized that the two of us were a family now and our love and friendship with each other was and would always be the most important.

One of the great things about both of our families was that in spite of divorces, personal issues or, even dislikes, everyone was usually able to come together temporarily for an event without a lot of drama. So to have both of our families with all of their complexities at the same place didn't seem to be an issue. The issue was with us. Both Chase and I had to figure things out, what made us comfortable or uncomfortable, who we were able to tolerate and what efforts we were willing to make in order for our children to grow up having extended family members be a part of their lives.

Chase was much better than me at navigating family, although he had an easy out since he worked all of the time and didn't have the freedom to get together as often as me. If his mom wanted to see Jordan, usually it was up to me to meet with her, the same with his sister, or any of my family. Again, for me, having a million issues, combined with being a first-time parent, made managing life and building relationships more complex, especially in-laws. Being a lifelong and chronic worrier, I also didn't feel comfortable leaving Jordan with anyone, including even my own mom, so that too could get complicated.

Relationships, in general, seemed more difficult than they had to be, at least for me. There were too many expectations. I think that was another reason I started spending so much time with my dad. My dad had no expectations of me. I think it was mutual; I really had no expectations of him either. Our relationship as adults, for whatever reason, was uncomplicated and easy, a bike ride, lunch or even a few hours at the beach. Someone to spend time with then we'd go our separate ways. It was the murky past rearing its ugly head that was complicating things.

The hardest part was that as much as I believed my dad had done something to me, I still wanted to spend time with him. For the brief time, I had stopped seeing him I missed him and even felt sorry for him. That alone would trigger panic attacks. Why would I feel sorry for someone that may have sexually abused me? That couldn't be normal, what was normal though? There wasn't anything normal about the entire situation, but that didn't change how I felt. Confused and once again resolved not to think about it, I invited him, I invited all of them. The entire group of people that constantly caused me to feel bad about myself, the ones I was never good enough for, the same people I had grown up excluded from even though we lived, at least part-time, under the same roof were now invited to Jordan's first birthday

Thinking of all of us living together made me shudder. It never mattered to me where I lived; I had always been uneasy or uncomfortable. I was only starting to become comfortable now. Throughout my life living situations always seemed to be temporary at best, at least for me; I guess a hazard of the way. I was raised. Writing out the Birthday Invitations and filling in everyone's addresses had me thinking about the past again, wondering would I ever feel comfortable or at home anywhere. So far the answer had been no.

Even after my mom rescued me from the explosive situation with Cameron, and helped me get my own apartment, it was never a home to me. As crazy as it sounds, and as much of a risk as it was for her, she felt at the time, it was the best decision. There was no way I could go back to her house, not with my lifestyle. I was so far gone and she knew better, I was an addict, the most horrible kind of addict, the kind that didn't discriminate. If it could take me out, make me forget about life I would ingest it some way, inhale it, shoot it or swallow it and, I wasn't beyond stealing, lying or cheating, even the people I loved, including my mom.

She tried again to convince me to go to rehab but I had no interest. Instead, I did what I was best at, I partied. My life continued to careen out of control and I loved it. I was brazen and shocking and answered to no one. I went where I wanted; I did what I wanted and literally took every kind of drug known to man. Wasted day and night, I could hardly decipher one day from the next. I didn't care about anything least of all myself. My mom continued to pay for my apartment, every month using the excuse of bringing the rent check to see me and sadly, make sure I was alive. Month after month she tried to intervene, pushing rehab as a solution, often threatening to stop helping me altogether, I didn't care. I banked on her caring enough about me for both of us, believing she would continue to pay for the apartment just to keep me from being homeless along with all of my other issues.

News of Cameron robbing the local Nordstrom Department Store, with a shotgun, although disturbing, only reminded me that the type of life we were living was exciting and adventurous. I thought about him and the robbery for days convinced all the more that I didn't want a normal, boring life. Accountable, responsible, and having to measure up wasn't for me. I missed him in a way, minimizing the worst parts of our relationship and now glorifying all of the exciting times and experiences.

I needed to move on though, so I started dating again and within a few weeks had connected with Jason, Cameron's friend from Santee. Now a Meth Dealer, he and I had already been close, and with Cameron in jail, it was almost a given that we would become more than friends. Having nothing in common outside of Cameron, drugs, and alcohol, it didn't seem to matter. Lit all the time I could barely speak anyway and I definitely wasn't one for talking about the past, the present or even the future. All of it took too much thought, and thinking was becoming my enemy. I was moment to moment and just wanted to stay high and have fun not think, about anything or anyone.

Within a few days, Jason was staying with me, living in my apartment and selling drugs from the place that my mom was paying for. We would stay up for days at a time shooting, snorting and smoking not just Crystal Meth but anything else we had at our disposal. I was either up for days at a time or completely incapacitated, never knowing if it was night or day, passed out or in a stupor, most of the time not even knowing who came or went. I had no purpose and rarely if ever, was aware of life outside of my apartment. It wasn't until I missed my period and I had to venture out for a pregnancy test that I was coherent enough to realize what a lost cause I had become.

Scary thin, scabs and pick marks covered my body like a dot to dot puzzle, pale and weak; I dragged myself to my car and drove to the neighborhood drug store. Walking down the Feminine Hygiene Aisle I laughed at the words, Feminine Hygiene, as I lifted the test off the shelf and stuffed it under my smelly three-day-old shirt. I tried to remember the last time I showered or even brushed my teeth. Stumbling into the bathroom, I locked the door ripped open the package and peed on the stick. Several minutes later the positive sign popped up, I tossed it in the garbage, threw up in the sink, rinsed it out and left.

Now what? I sat in the car wondering what to do. In somewhat of a fog, I knew I couldn't go through another abortion. Keeping it was impossible too though, out of the question really, there was no way I could take care of a baby, besides, it would be born addicted. I couldn't do that, for me, it didn't seem right, it would be cruel. The thought of inflicting addiction on a harmless baby made me nauseous; I opened the car door and threw up in the crowded parking lot. Looking up I caught the eye of a yuppie mom, disgusted by me, she averted her child's eyes and made her way towards the store. I felt low, I was scum, a dirty strung out druggie, obviously disgusting to most people and now I was pregnant. I started to cry, unstoppable tears, I sat in my car feeling broken and alone asking myself, again and again, why and what was wrong with me?

I wiped my face on my shirt and started the car, numb, I pull out into the oncoming traffic as a car swerves and lays on the horn. I give the obligatory bird and rush through the yellow light needing to get home and self-medicate before I decide to kill myself. "Bleep, bleep...," a police siren shakes my brain fog. I look in the rearview mirror, "Shit, double shit, why was this happening to me?" I think about trying to ditch them, but there's too much traffic and I know from experience it's too tough to lose them in the daytime. I pull over but I can't even manage to come up with an excuse. I'm under the influence, and I have drugs in the ashtray. I think about eating them, but I'm too slow, the cop is already at my window.

I watch my car being towed as I sit on the hard plastic seat of the police car with my arms cuffed behind me. What used to scare me isn't as alarming now, I guess once you've been to jail it's no longer terrifying, or an unknown, only a hassle and a time waster. I think of who to call as we make our way out of the beach, east towards Santee where the women's jail is located.

It's at least a twenty-minute drive; twenty minutes to listen to a cop give me a pep talk about changing my life while I was still young. I tune him out, just like all of the others who've had me as a captive audience in the back seat of a car, thinking they can save me with some "better way of life" verbiage. I don't want to call my mom, my dad is always a no and there really isn't anyone else I can think of that isn't going to make me feel worse than I already feel.

After processing, with my options narrowed down, I decide to call Jason, he promises to be there as soon as he can post bail and make his way through the traffic. In less than four hours I'm in his car heading back to the beach, pounding a beer and ready to light up a joint. I blurt out "I'm pregnant" as I flick the lighter. He grabs the joint out of my hand and looks over at me, too serious and too caring, he asks "Really?" then ruins it by following up with "Is it mine?" As we continue driving I try not to feel hurt but feeling hurt is my default setting. I did hurt, my life hurts, and I was still unable to see the way out. Jason, who I have no feelings for, wants us to clean-up and keep the baby, he wants us to be together. I laugh at the thought, but inside I wonder if it could save me. I answer no. Nothing can save me, I couldn't stop. I didn't want to stop, I wasn't ready for reality. Reality would mean sobriety and if that was the case, now it would mean a baby. Way too hard.

Within days we were both strung out, I had used so much meth that my heart felt like it was going to burst right through my chest, I hadn't slept in days and I still hadn't made any decisions about my pregnancy. Subconsciously, maybe I thought that by using such a massive amount of meth, not eating a thing, and staying up for days at a time, it would all cause my body to naturally reject it, but so far, physically nothing changed. Jason called Child Protective Services on me for using while I was pregnant, and of course, the police became involved, all of it eventually causing us to be evicted from the apartment.

My mom, having no idea I was pregnant came to beg and plead for me to go to rehab, "Please Kristen, you can't keep living like this, you're destroying yourself." Looking at her, seeing the desperation in her face, and trying not to cry, how did I tell my mom that it was too late? I was already destroyed. With no desire to live without drugs or alcohol, I turned down her offer to find and take me to rehab. My mom, in somewhat of a last-ditch effort gives me an ultimatum, insisting if I don't go to rehab she can't stay in my life, sadly threatening, "I refuse to keep watching you do this to yourself." Not usually the emotional type, seeing her begin to tear up is heartbreaking, she continues pleading, "I can't do it anymore, please Kristen, please at least try it, please try to get some help." Not wanting to look at her, I load most of my stuff into a giant black garbage bag, I'm hearing what she's saying and I don't want to keep hurting her, but I know I can't go to rehab, not now. I don't want it; I'm not ready.

"My poor mom," is all I can think as we parted ways, once again I choose drugs and alcohol over everyone and everything, even her. I drive away and as soon as I'm out of her sight, I start sobbing. With nowhere to go, I head to a friend's house out in Santee, a friend I met in jail, someone I'm hoping will let me stay. I'm homeless again. What has me thinking about that? Why am I thinking about being homeless? I take a deep breath and look around my house, it was small and cozy, comfortable for me and my family, I felt safe and happy, I could almost say I felt secure for the first time in my life.

The thoughts of being homeless were in the past, foreign to me now. Security came with sobriety and as long as I was sober I knew I would always have a home. Trying to stop thinking about the past, I finish writing out the last invitation and seal it in its cute matching envelope. Happy to have finished, I stack it with all of the others on the corner of the table, making a mental note to swing by the Post Office later that day for stamps and to drop them in the mail. It's still strange to me, but ever since having Jordan, I thought about the past a lot, not by choice, it just seemed like random things would pop into my head reminding me of something, someone or even a certain time period, maybe it happened to everyone and mine was just disturbing because of my sordid background.

I look at the cheery envelopes, pleased with myself; I was now the so-called "bigger person," inviting everyone, including my dad and his wife, my sister Taylor and her husband, and my sister Katie and her fiancé. "You didn't invite them yet, you can still change your mind," I remind myself, looking back to the stack of envelopes. "I'm not going to change my mind," I reply to myself proudly. "No, you're just going to obsess for the next two months wondering if they'll bother coming and if they do what it will be like having them there," I say under my breath.

Of course, I was right, it was true, I would obsess not over just my family and how that situation would end up but over every detail associated with the party. Chase thought I was losing my mind, and I agreed, even starting to be consumed with why I was so consumed. Why did I care so much about what people thought of me? I even started worrying about being bipolar, thinking maybe that strange therapist was right, one-minute caring and obsessing so much over what people might think, and then moments later changing to "Screw it, who cares."

What was wrong with me? It was seriously worse than my wedding, why? I don't know if I'm trying to prove myself or if I'm still looking for acceptance, feelings both good and bad come and go, from time to time I blame it on the hormones, but I know it's mostly just me, this was how I have always been, never feeling good enough, never getting things right, I was never comfortable or able to just be me. I was like a crazy person, I just wanted to live and not care about what other people thought, especially my dad, a predator, Marianne, who sabotaged my entire childhood and my sisters who had never taken an interest in me, even as a sober person.

I'm realizing that sobriety only changes the fact that I'm sober, it doesn't magically erase all of the reasons I was choosing addiction. What did I do about that? How did I get rid of all of these feelings, these memories, how do I clear out a lifetime of issues? I want to stay sober; I want all of these thoughts to go away so I can live my life and be free. "Life Sentence" comes to mind again yes Chasing Sober is my "life sentence," I can accept that. All of the issues holding me back from enjoying my life, enjoying being me, NO, that I will not accept. It's over; the past is over, why can't I just let it go?

·Chapter Eight·

I wake up and hear Chase in the shower, so reliable; he's promised we'll be early to help my mom set-up for Jordan's party. I yawn and stretch, looking over to the baby monitor on my nightstand. My little Birthday Girl is happily babbling away, standing at the railing of her crib, waiting for one of us to come and get her. I lay back and sigh, listening to the water running and random singing, Chase is probably excited, a proud dad moment, his baby girl is one today.

I'd like to be excited, but I've been awake for all of two minutes and I'm already stressed, obsessing about my dad and the others being there today. Mad at myself for thinking about it first thing in the morning, I try to replace the thoughts with all of the wonderful things, instead. My sweet baby has made my life amazing, her first year one of the best years of my entire life. I couldn't love her more, Chase too, I really feel grateful, and gratitude a feeling I never used to understand, is a feeling I now have most days.

Chase comes into the room with his towel tucked around his waist. He's grinning from ear to ear, "You better get up Bub, get cracking, game time," he laughs, "it's on; today's the day you get to connect with your family." I roll onto my side and bury my head in the comforter, "Why did I invite them," I whine, joking, but not joking. I've been driving Chase crazy for the past two months, constantly dwelling on the topic of my dad, Marianne, and my sisters and of course the entire party "situation." It's a bummer that my baby's first party has now been relegated to a "situation."

"Come on Babe, you know it will be fine, it should be all about Jordan, don't let all the stuff with your dad and your sisters ruin it for you." I get out of bed and put on my bathrobe, Chase grabs me and hugs me, "Remember, no one coming to this party today is any better than you." The baby hears us and starts fussing, most likely wondering why neither of us has come to get her yet. Chase pulls on his jeans and whips his towel at me, "I'll get her Bub, you better start getting ready."

He leaves to take care of Jordan and I go to the kitchen to make some coffee, my thoughts are immediately back to Marianne, and my sisters, why am I so worried about them and what they're going to think? It isn't new; I've always been this way, I'm only recognizing it more now that I am sober. I've asked myself this question a million times. I've always worried about what people might think about me, especially them, but why? Why is it that some people could care less about what people think and mine was on blast? Was I that desperate to be loved and accepted?

I don't even like these people, they have made every event in my life stressful, they've made my entire life stressful and now I have no way to numb myself or make them less important, I don't know how to handle them sober. Chase and the baby come in just in time to keep me from having a meltdown; Jordan so cheerful and cuddly wants me, reaching for me, always happy for me just to hold her. She is my life now, she and Chase love me and that's all that should matter. I play with her, hugging and kissing her she's healing to me, reminding me of the million reasons I need to pull myself together and take charge of her party.

The three of us get ready and head to my mom's together; I'm finally able to push my obsessive thoughts aside and am starting to get excited. Caring for Jordan and helping host the party will keep me busy and for that I'm thankful. The weather is perfection and when we arrive all of the balloons and decorations are in place, the venue is amazing. The food looks delicious and the cake, candies and party favors are all magical, I'm thrilled, my mom outdid herself. Roughly fifty people show up, a mix of family, close friends and a few neighbors.

When my dad, Marianne, and my sisters arrive, I instantly change; I feel it happen, my heart races, my stomach is queasy, and my demeanor instantly goes from bubbly and enthusiastic to self-conscious and heavy. I'm dark now like a light went off, I'm no longer myself. In my head, I know I need to keep busy, look busy, and be busy, whatever I can do not to have to interact with them. Chase, so self-assured goes over first, shaking my dad's hand and talking to them, I'm sure he's welcoming them, telling them to help themselves to food, showing them where the drinks are, and finally pointing over to Jordan who is with my mom having some lunch. I feel bad for my husband, the issue with my dad has been hard on him too, he loves my dad, my dad was a good friend to him and now we're all disconnected, in a way we're all in limbo, because of me, because I'm not sure, or am I?

"Kristen you have to go say hello," the voice in my head pushes me. "I know, but it's going to be awkward," I complain. "Why did you invite them, then?" I try to calm down and breathe. I tell myself to be quiet. I know it doesn't have to be awkward but it will be, Marianne has been a lifetime of awkward, my sisters too, it's always uncomfortable now. I try to be funny, make it lighthearted, and then resort to small talk. Just thinking about talking to them is exhausting.

I walk towards them, reluctantly, hoping Chase notices me making my way over, and stays. My hero, he does, he stays, putting his arm around me protecting me, I won't have to hug my dad. Marianne and I are cordial, while my sister's take turns hugging me, limp and lifeless; void of feeling, they've morphed into their mother, only not outright mean to me, but there's no warmth. Standoffish, better than me, they both seem to size me up, looking me over from head to toe. I think they're judging me and my heart sinks, all of the awful things they've said behind my back, shared with me by my "gossip girl" father, come flooding into my mind. "Stop Kristen, stop," I tell myself, I stand up, straightening myself, remembering what Chase said this morning, "No one is better than me." Excusing myself, I feign having to check on Jordan and walk away.

The party really only lasts a few hours, but it seems never-ending now that my dad and his entourage are here. None of them ever branch out. Clumped together, not only better than me, they're better than the party itself, and the other guests. Under scrutiny, I try to enjoy myself; but it's different now, everything has changed with all of them here. I'm like a prisoner; I'm confined, my moving around freely restricted, only I've imprisoned myself by listening to all of the garbage in my head. I'm my own prisoner, but I blame them.

My sisters are cute, I watch them together from across the grass, chatting, laughing, and enjoying each other. I'm staring, sad that I'm not a part, sad that I don't get to have that. My sisters are normal and I'm not, but why? What happened to me, did being molested make me different from them? Vivid thoughts flash through my mind and I fight for them to leave. Why would my dad only molest me though? I'm anxiously watching them, did Taylor get molested? All of those years of her wanting to sleep with me, sometimes clinging to me, glued as if trying desperately to stay attached until we woke up in the morning. "Stop," I tell myself, "Don't do this," but I continue in my head, the alarms are sounding, "But she was alone there, all those times you were at your mom's."

"What about Katie Girl," I look at her, she was the sweetest thing, quiet and soft, delicate like a doll, I used to love her so much. Until Marianne turned her against me, then we drifted apart, now we were basically strangers. She would have been alone also, alone with my dad after Taylor and I were both gone, did my dad molest her too? Should I ask them? I mean could I? Is it okay? Is that what you do when you think your dad molested you? Do you ask your sisters? Would they even tell me? How would I ask? I need a rule book; I need to know how to do this, how I'm supposed to handle all of this.

I look away, but it doesn't stop my thoughts, wild now, a million questions are darting around in my head, do they have memories too? Did he molest all of us or just me? I need to know. Thinking of my sisters as possible victims, I'm sickened by it all, I start to feel dirty and used, why would my dad only molest me and not them, what was wrong with me, that he would choose me to ruin. Was I that worthless, so worthless that I didn't matter? He couldn't have molested them, my life was ruined, but their lives weren't, I look over again, trying not to cry, they look so normal, so not ruined.

"You're not ruined, look you're fine, you have a good life now, a husband who cares about you, and a family," I look around as the voice in my head, the same one causing all of this in the first place, is now reasoning with me. Before I'm aware of it my mom is standing next to me, "Kristen?" she looks at me, "Kristen, what are you doing over here?" I stare at her blankly, not sure what to say. I mean do I tell her I'm trying to figure out if my sisters got molested too? No, that would not be a good idea, not here, not now. "Why, what's up? Trying to sound casual, calm even, I ask, "Are we ready to sing and cut the cake?" This woman knows me, "Yes, but what's going on with you? It's like you were in a trance or something?" She looks at me, always mindful of "triggers" now, she asks in a hushed voice, "Are you okay?"

My mom is valiant, a fighter, never giving up on me. I can't help but love her, the strongest and most reliable person I know, she too is everything to me, I wouldn't be here if it wasn't for her, and I don't know what I would do without her. Although she and I had parted ways several times throughout my addiction, she never once gave up on me, always keeping her finger on the pulse of my life, knowing where I was and what I was doing, always ready and waiting for that one instant that one glimmer of hope when I would hit my "Rock Bottom," that one instant when I would finally surrender. My mom would be there, waiting, ready for the tiniest window of opportunity to help me get sober.

I think back to the million times my mom thought I was at my "Rock Bottom," and sadly the same million times I wasn't. The day I drove away from her in Pacific Beach and made my way out to Santee was just one of those times. Pregnant, broken and alone, my "Rock Bottom" was still a long way off. Once I arrived out there, my friend's house was welcoming and receptive, a drug house, I wasn't alone; there were others there too, strung out, passing the time by using more drugs and smoking. I sat on the sofa and shot a syringe of speed into my arm waiting calmly to feel its warmth spread over my chest, waiting for the cough, it hits so hard and fast it usually causes you to cough, then you know it's a good shot, you'll be high, at least for a few hours. Desperate, I wait, I cough.

After explaining my situation to my friend, she tells me I can stay in exchange for helping her with her kids and housework. Coming through the door with all of my worldly possessions, thrown haplessly into the giant black garbage bag, I have a twinge of sadness, lonely for the familiar; wanting to belong somewhere, momentarily, I long for a purpose. I shoot another syringe full of speed into my arm waiting to be relieved of all of my feelings. The house was bleak and everything going on there was criminal. The small children being there was depressing to me, they were surrounded by addicts, cigarette smoke and wayward people, not having the choice to leave or do anything better. Within days, with no money and needing drugs, my friend decided to show me the ropes on robbing people.

We'd head down to La Jolla and ransack people's cars, usually finding open doors or windows left "cracked." I guess they had never seen a "Tweaker's Arms," bone thin and twig-like, I could fit my entire arm, up to my shoulder through the tiniest opening. We'd find wallets, credit cards, checkbooks, jewelry, sunglasses, and on occasion, goodies, like drugs or guns. I loved it, like a treasure hunt, I got a high just from the excitement of what I might find. I had no shame, I was ruthless, now involved with fraud, using the credit cards to buy gas, alcohol, and things to sell like, gift cards and cartons of cigarettes. So enthralled with my new "opportunities," I had little interest in housework or babysitting, so within a few weeks, I was forced to move on.

Packing up my garbage bag of belongings, I spent a night in my car before finding a friend who agreed to rent an apartment with me. Home to me was Pacific Beach; it's where I belonged, so she and I rented a place on Oliver Street, in the heart of the little beach town. Never a home, only another short-lived place to stay and get high I was content. Being back in the beach area I cleaned up and went to see about getting my nanny job back. Within days the little boy was being dropped off at our apartment. I was either up for days, strung out or in bed not able to move or function.

My friend would help me out, often meeting the family in the morning and playing with the child until I could get up. She was only an alcohol and weed person, so she'd bring me a handful of Soma's, (muscle relaxers) and a joint to help ease me out of bed. Once I was up I'd shoot some speed to get going. Better than coffee, it was my daily routine; quick fixes were what I was all about, that and tuning out to all of the reality constantly reminding me of what a low-life I was.

Oliver Street lasted all of six weeks, until my friend and I had an issue and she moved out. Unable to afford the rent on my own, I found another friend and moved to Ocean Beach, the drug capital of San Diego, at least the seedier parts. Within days of being down there, I woke up to excessive bleeding and cramping, my pregnancy which I had shelved, was now reminding me that it hadn't gone anywhere. Not wanting anyone in my "Drug Circle" to know, I reached out to my friend Erica from Baldwin that I rarely, if ever saw. Within twenty minutes she was at my apartment, ready to take me to the hospital. Out of my mind worrying, bleeding everywhere and in the worst pain, I was such a major drug addict that on the way to the Emergency Room I forced her to stop at a 7-11 so that I could buy a pack of cigarettes, some candy and Lottery Tickets for Good Luck.

Admitted into the hospital, I really thought I might die. Praying to a God I didn't know that I would live; I promised him that I would get my life together if I could please just make it through this. It was one of the most horrifying experiences of my life; I ended up going through a miscarriage and suffering from the effects of drug withdrawal at the same time. In excruciating pain and bleeding profusely, they took blood tests and then pumped me full of "legal" drugs to try and help until I could be scheduled for a "D&C Procedure," later that afternoon. Erica, worried that something serious could happen, called my mom and when I woke up she was there. Predictable, the second I opened my eyes she started pushing rehab, begging for me to get help.

"Kristen? Hey Kristen, what's happening, what's wrong with you?" I'm back to Jordan's Birthday Party, my mom is still looking at me; wondering what my problem is. I can't tell if she's annoyed or worried. "I'm fine, let's do this, let's go sing so we can have some cake." We walk towards the center of the party to the Cake Table and my mom gathers the group around to sing "Happy Birthday." Chase is holding Jordan; she's as precious as can be in her little Polka Dot Minnie Mouse Dress. She has been amazing all day, wonderful really, so personable and funny. She seems to love all of the people and the party, and just like her parents she's obsessed with the food.

My mom lights the one little candle and carries the cake over to where Chase and I are standing with Jordan. As everyone starts singing to our sweet little one-year-old, she burst into tears. Chase blows out the candle and I take her, hugging her and letting her know she's okay. My mom saves the day by bringing over her very first piece of cake. In the moment, I forget about all of the troubling thoughts, for a brief time I'm able to let down my guard and be totally present. In this very moment, I'm not ruined, I'm normal. In this moment I'm just an ordinary mom, enjoying a very happy and very normal life.

·Chapter Nine·

The lights are off, it's dark, and the room is cool. I try to sit up, but the pain across my abdomen stops me causing me to wince. I look around, still groggy, not immediately recognizing where I am. The noise coming in from the door is busy, hurried; people walking, talking, carts rolling by, bustling, beeping, phones, and indistinct chatter. It's too much. I feel weak as I lay back, remembering I'm in the hospital.

The curtains open to a view and the sun is slowly making its way up, the sunrise, a soft glow, gives just enough light for me to look around. Where is my baby? I force myself to sit up, suddenly aware that my baby isn't in the room with me. My baby is missing! My heart drops and I feel sick, I'm so uncomfortable I can hardly move. I try to get my legs over the side of the bed to pull myself up, but a wave of nausea washes over me and I have to lean back again against the pillows.

I'd had my second C-Section with no drugs, at least not the good kind. In the proud stage of my sobriety; I refuse to touch anything remotely related to a narcotic or opioid, instead, I'm taking a sad replacement drug called Toradol, that doesn't work. Panicking, I don't understand why they'd take my baby. I start crying out, "Where is he, where is my baby?" I stand, feeling faint; exposed, my hospital gown barely covers me as I search for the intercom to call for help. Finding it, I push the button and get a voice on the other end, which is uninterested at best, "Yes? What do you need?" I know as I speak, that I'll sound crazy crying out for my baby, but I do it anyway, "I need my baby! My baby is missing! Where is he?" Unreactive, the same voice tells me she'll send in a nurse and hangs up. "What is wrong with this place?" I whisper to no one.

I'm scared, but I'm mad now too and I really need to use the restroom. I can't understand it. Why would anyone take my baby out of the room without asking me? Is there something wrong with him? Where is he? Starting to sob, I rummage through the bed, now looking for my phone. I hated that I was alone. Chase slept over but left early to go work out and shower before picking up Jordan from my Mom's. Was the baby missing then? I'm freaking out, I can't handle it and am becoming more distressed by the minute, especially since no one seems to care or seems to be helping me. I start yelling out again, worried that no one is answering, "Help me please, I want my baby. Where is he? I need my baby, please, someone bring me, my baby," still sobbing, I'm desperate now, I have to find him.

I make my way to the bathroom; every step torture, the pain continues and my heart is racing. I'm nearly there when one of my close friends, family really, comes in as planned with our Starbucks in one hand and a Gift Bag brimming with sparkly ribbons in the other. I'm so happy to see her. The relief I feel to have someone that can help me find out what they've done with my baby sends me into uncontrollable tears.

"What's wrong? What's happening to you?" She asks. Concerned, she puts everything down and rushes to my side, at the same time another woman comes into the room, overly casual and oddly comfortable, she looks like a visitor, only it's six-thirty in the morning. She pushes the privacy curtain between the bed and the door all the way open. Inviting all of the chaos and noise from the hallway into the room it causes me to freak out even more; this and I still have no idea who she is.

In the bathroom, I can barely sit, miserable with pain, I leave the confusion briefly, still not understanding what's going on or where they took my baby. Standing up I wash my hands and face, trying to pull myself together, I hear my friend ask the woman in the room who she is as I come out. I don't believe her when she answers that she's the nurse. Always on high alert, and overly protective, I'm insecure about strangers being in the newborn area of the hospital, especially people in "Street Clothes." Already skeptical and hypersensitive to anything not as it should be, it doesn't compute that a nurse would be in workout attire, or more specifically LuluLemon Leggings and a matching jacket. Taking it all in I even have a mental picture of her shoes and socks, Gray Addidas and white ankle riders, just in case something happens. It's bizarre to me; she has nothing, no hospital badge, no stethoscope and she isn't carrying a chart or anything that even remotely identifies her as a nurse.

Moments later, my baby is wheeled into me, safe and sleeping in the little rolling bed. Relieved, I start crying again, so happy to see him, "Why did you take him away from me? No one asked me or even told me, I was worried sick, I thought someone kidnapped him!" The nurse, that could or could not be an actual nurse laughs, thinking I'm joking. I'm upset now, pissed really, the last ten minutes have been hell for me, "Look, I'm not joking, what happened isn't cool and now you're here, looking like you walked in off the street or out of an exercise class, with no evidence that you're an employee, trying to tell me you're my nurse, it's not right, not okay. It's not acceptable to take my baby away without my consent. I don't think any of this is right. I mean, I'm a paranoid person, to begin with, I'm in recovery and now I'm upset, which isn't good for me or my new baby, so really not cool."

I take him out of the little bed, looking him over to make sure he's okay, he's sound asleep and I kiss and hug him, holding him close. He's so beautiful to me, I'm so grateful that he's back and he's fine. My friend gently takes him and knowing me well, calms the situation by putting all of the attention on the new baby and the excitement of seeing him for the first time. I'm happy she's here, only I'm still rattled and I can't make sense of what happened. It isn't right.

I find my phone and call Chase, who, like me, can be a chronic worrier, he says the baby was in the room with me when he left, sleeping in the little "cart thing," next to my bed. He follows up, "That's weird Babe, you need to get to the bottom of this they shouldn't be taking babies away from their parents like that. Do they think something's wrong with him or what? You need to ask them what they did with him." He's concerned, maybe even a little upset, I try to get him off the phone; he's making me feel worse, nervous, now I'm obsessing about it. Is there something wrong with our baby? Was it us? Did they judge me because I was in recovery? Did they take him for drug tests? Is that even legal? What was going on? The more I think about it the more anxious I get.

Aside from the incident of him being taken from my room without permission, Ryder Cole Campbell is born on May 25, 2015, and we couldn't be happier, he's gorgeous, a mini-version of his dad, and from the moment we first meet him we're all madly in love. Unlike his brunette sister; he's fair with blond hair and sky blue eyes, and I can already tell he is going to be an easy and good-natured baby.

Although the hospital and my experience are different from when I had Jordan, stressful really, I try not to let it outweigh the joy of having a new baby. The nurse ends up being very sweet and helpful apologizing and showing me her Employee Identification, explaining that because of the Holiday it's a bit more casual than normal. It's Memorial Day Weekend, my Personal Physician is out of town, there's a very limited staff and everyone we need has taken the weekend off, which normally wouldn't matter, but my baby, perfect to me, according to the skeleton crew of doctors and nurses has several problems that will require ongoing treatment and more than likely, several surgeries.

While the prognosis is good, one of the Primary Doctors on duty that weekend matter-of-factly shares with Chase and I that we should be prepared for our child's first year to be challenging, full of Doctor's Visits, hospitals, and surgeries. I'm devastated, heartbroken; I don't want any of it to be true. I'm not sure how other parents feel or react to the news that their child isn't perfect or healthy or that they'll require invasive and painful treatments and surgeries, for me, I was sick about it, terrified, not wanting to think of any child, especially my child, having to go through anything painful or even being away from me for an operation.

Both Chase and I were overwhelmed with having to make so many weighty decisions and make them so quickly. It was shocking, certainly unexpected and my emotions were all over the place, one minute trying to be brave and stoic, looking at our options objectively and then the next moment completely falling apart, in tears asking why? Why does my tiny baby have to suffer so much?

Sometimes, when I would get down, I'd guilt myself into believing I was responsible for everything he was going through. Unlike my first pregnancy, with this one, I had taken a medication for morning sickness. I wondered if I hadn't taken it would he still have these issues, wishing I would have just toughed it out as I did with Jordan. Other times I would have vivid flashbacks to all of the years of massive drug and alcohol abuse, wondering if that could be the reason. Thinking that I could have in any way caused my child's suffering really traumatized me. All of it was just too much to take.

Ryder just a few days old came home with us scheduled to see a hip specialist within a few days. One of his diagnoses was Hip Dysplasia, a disorder where his tiny leg wasn't connecting properly at his hip; his particular case would require surgery, possibly more than one. Sent home from the specialist in what was called a Pavlik Harness, I was crushed. Knowledge is power though and once Chase and I were aware of his condition and what it was called, we went to the internet and with all of its information; we were able to research and learn much more about it.

Looking at photos, reading other people's stories and identifying with dozens of families going through similar situations really helped put us at ease, knowing it was fairly common and that we weren't alone was in itself a huge relief. To see evidence too that Ryder would eventually be fine and be able to function normally was freeing, taking a huge weight off of our minds and hearts. All of this though didn't mean it was going to be easy.

That was the part that scared me, the not being easy part. Throughout most of my life, when things were too difficult for me, as a learned behavior I immediately turned to drugs and alcohol. Now though, as a sober person, I was expected to handle disappointments and challenges routinely, like everyone else, drawing on my own personal strength and resilience. Did I even have those? Initially, I was so consumed with making sure my family was okay and that Ryder and his treatment plan became our priority, there was no time for me to dwell on old habits or even think about an easy way out.

This wasn't about me, this was about my child who needed me and, he needed the sober me. I found strength being in this role; in fact, we never missed or were even late to a single appointment. I followed every instruction in detail, (OCD), and when it came time for the surgeries, I was able to handle each one, not allowing myself to be overcome emotionally. Instead, I reminded myself to stay strong and focus on being the parent my child needed to get him through this. Even though it was all bigger than me and one of the most difficult situations I had faced since becoming sober, when I faced it one day at a time, I was able to master it, never even thinking of falling back to drugs or alcohol for support.

To be clear, there wasn't a single day during this time period that was easy, not one. If anything, as Ryder was growing and changing, the challenges increased. Meeting all of his needs medically, making sure both he and Jordan were happy and thriving, encouraging myself to be playful, fun and attentive, instead of tense or dwelling on how hard this was or focusing on the negatives made it more bearable. It seemed like there were a million other things too that were required of me to keep my family and household functioning and it became intense. The now famous phrase "It takes a village," is one of the best ways to describe our lives at this time and not just me and the help I got with my children, but in a broader sense, people just being there for other people, loving and supporting each other in whatever they're experiencing, both the good and the bad.

I was not without a village and my village was strong, I could count on them and my family could count on them. My husband and I were both amazed by all of the support we received and not just in the initial stages but all the way through. My mom, our pillar of strength and life coordinator, never once let us down, also, other family members and close friends were there, sometimes just spending time with us and being involved was enough to strengthen and encourage me.

There were days though, even with the help that were unbelievably hard, days when things were just crazy and extreme. One, in particular when Ryder with a cast from his waist to his ankles and only a tiny square cut-out for diaper changes had diarrhea. It was everywhere and cleaning it was impossible. To keep him and his cast clean was a full-time job in itself. My friend who came regularly through it all kept reminding me that it was temporary and I could get through it, even trying to help me see everything as funny and laughable, sharing with me long after It was all over, that she used to cry on her way home wondering how in the world I was ever going to get through it.

Those were the days I would feel the pressure, the enormity of my situation. Those were the days that I would completely break down only now in my sobriety, I had to be sure I didn't stay broken but could regroup, bounce back, the fighter, the Mama Bear again determined to get my child through this no matter what came my way.

What could break me at this time and I was honestly concerned, was my relationship with my dad. We had been in a strange space for a while now, months really and I think he was totally unaware. I mean, I could see why; apart from going out to lunch there wasn't a lot I could do while I was pregnant and our time together naturally became more limited. Keeping him at a distance was something I had established for myself, at least until I figured things out. I never really discussed it with him or let him know, in fact, I'm pretty sure he had no idea. He would text me, not regularly, but here and there and on rare occasions we'd talk on the phone, oddly the same tired conversations, him complaining about his wife or sharing hurtful things about my sisters. Then when Ryder was born he came, unexpectedly, to see me in the hospital.

That day I knew, in my heart of hearts, I remembered him touching me, more than ever that day I believed that my dad molested me. I cringed when I saw him come into my hospital room, instantly insecure. I didn't want to be alone with him. In bed, wearing a flimsy hospital gown with nothing else, I felt bare and vulnerable, the visitor in that moment, wasn't my dad, but a predator, his presence made me feel threatened and alarmed, in that moment I was fearful. I wanted him to leave, in his presence I wasn't safe and like when I was a child, there was no one there to protect me.

This wasn't new. Not being comfortable around my dad wasn't new. As I've said, for years I would cover myself; wear loose or high collar shirts, sometimes even baggy sweatshirts, regardless of the temperature. What was new was my awareness. Even when it came to nursing around him I would panic. Never feeling comfortable nursing in front of most people, I was very modest about it, covering myself and even going into a different room depending on the situation. Most of my friends were so liberal and comfortable with it, easily breastfeeding in front of anyone, wherever and whenever it was needed. Not me.

When Jordan was little if I had to do it and we happened to be around my dad, it was always a problem, definitely my problem, but my dad was uncomfortable with it too, he'd step outside, or leave for a while, coming back when I was finished. It could all have been very innocent and even courteous on my dad's part to leave, in my head, though it was something so natural and normal, why were we both so uncomfortable? I would question myself, wondering if under ordinary circumstances and not thinking I had been sexually abused, would it be the same?

The real question, would any of my life have been the same? As a mother, reflecting on my past had started when I was pregnant with Jordan and now with her and a new baby, I couldn't stop reliving it all, reviewing, sorting and trying to make sense of everything, I tried to convince myself it was because I wanted to be sure my children never had to go through any of the experiences I went through, but now it wasn't that clear. Maybe the memory of what I believed happened to me was resurfacing so that I could protect them, having an awareness I could be more vigilant, keeping them from situations that wouldn't be safe. As sad as it was, protecting them from my dad was what kept resurfacing the most.

My past was consuming me, burying me in one memory after another and even though I put up a fight to get it all out of my head, the more I fought, the more my past kept coming to life, some of it like it happened yesterday. The miscarriage was one of those things. Spending so much time in doctors' offices and hospitals had me thinking of that time period and what happened to me after my miscarriage, what happened after being discharged from the hospital. It was the beginning of some of the lowest times of my life.

The timing couldn't have been more coincidental, only now, in real time I left the hospital with a beautiful living baby and returned to a home where I was wanted and loved. Being discharged from the hospital back then, years ago, I left with an emptiness and loneliness so severe I didn't know if I would survive and I returned to a world that could care less whether I did or not.

Back then, I was beyond low and oddly grieving the loss of a baby I never wanted, I was also suffering from a mess of whacked-out hormones and trying to keep all of the feelings I was having hidden away from everyone. The only thing I wanted at the time was to get back to my apartment and self-medicate. My mom, my poor mom, always at the ready for me to hit my "Rock Bottom," and finally agree to rehab, sat in disbelief as I refuted her offer for the hundredth time, instead, asking her to take me back to Ocean Beach.

She sat next to my hospital bed begging and pleading for me to reconsider, trying to paint a picture of how different my life could be in just a few short weeks if I would just try. She would never give up without a fight. I knew how desperate she was for me to go, she was tired and the battle for me was taking its toll on her. It was taking its toll on me too, but I couldn't see far enough ahead to believe it could be better. I could only see in the now and, in the now I needed a fix.

My mom eventually dropped me off knowing there was nothing she could do to help me, especially against my will. Painful for both of us, I got out of the car and couldn't look back, a part of me wondering if I would ever see her again. At this point, not caring whether I lived or died, within minutes I had a tie off around my arm and a needle full of meth shooting through my veins, following it up with several shots of Jack Daniels I could finally feel myself relax, I could blot out the past few days and everything that had happened.

Taking several of the painkillers sent home from the hospital for good measure, it was only a matter of time before all of it was out of my mind, my thoughts warm and fuzzy, nothing left to even think about, no more miscarriage, no trauma, no grief, no mom or rehab. This was the life I wanted, I needed this life; it was the only way I could stop the thoughts. I eventually passed out and even if it was only temporary, at least for a time, passed out and unaware felt better.

Aimless and wayward I continued to lie, cheat and steal my way through life, constantly drunk and spun out on Crystal Meth and an arsenal of pills, I was a shell of a person. I rarely ate, barely slept and had hooked up with a well-known drug dealer in Ocean Beach that kept me completely out of it, literally handing me an unending supply of free drugs in exchange for a 'friends with benefits' situation. Hollowed of feelings and devoid of emotion, I was in the habit of using people, using my body and doing whatever I had to in order to get by.

Often one-sided, I was indifferent to relationships, my priority continued to be my reliance on alcohol and drugs. This proved to be true with my drug dealer friend, nice enough, I just wasn't interested in him the way he was interested in me, this even after he gave me the most beautiful light brown Pitbull Puppy as a gift. She was a sweet girl that I named Baby and she became my life, she went everywhere with me. I lived for that dog. Obsessed from day one, in a strange way she may have been a distorted replacement for the baby I lost. Even when I think of her name, unintentional at the time, in hindsight, it's subliminally eerie. Regardless, once she became mine, I couldn't live without her.

Apart from having Baby the puppy in my life, it was a very dark time for me and even though I could put on a brave face or an exterior of being okay, I was alone. So alone and afraid I could hardly bear it and still looming over me anytime I was even remotely aware of life, there was the same deeply disturbing question, why? I continued to keep myself drugged and drunk, always trying to avoid thinking or feeling anything. Numbing the so-called demons inside and the waste of a human I had become hurt though. So, hurting and alone, I drifted through life pretending that I was alive and well, in control of me, when I was just patching myself up enough to get through each day, controlled by substances and never really knowing what was next or thinking I could have, be or do anything better.

One of the sad truths is that I wasn't as alone as I may have thought. Most of the people in my life, active addicts and alcoholics, recirculating friends and acquaintances that I had known from Junior High and High School, as well as, a handful of new people, all seemed to be battling their own deep dark secrets, their own demons. At the time, none of us ever talked about our "reasons." We never talked about why we were all junkies and drunks, what happened to each of us individually, what we were escaping from. Desperate to feel better and anxious for the next high, all of us on some level were looking for a reprieve from reality. In a way, most of the "reasons" were similar, something so painful from the past, so damaging, that staying numb and escaping was all we could do to survive.

Unable to identify my reason, for years, the looming "why?" was unrecognizable. I only knew that I wasn't right, that there was something wrong with me, something so uncomfortable that I had to escape by getting and staying obliterated. It seemed to take a lifetime, but now, whether through sobriety or being a wife and mother, whatever the reason, I am aware now, I know.

Over the past few years, it had become increasingly clear that my personal demon wasn't just something from my past but was a current part of my life. My "reasons" for years of agony, addiction and self-destruction were most likely caused by someone I loved and trusted, someone I thought valued me and cared about me. The memory of what he did to me may have been in the past, but my personal demon, most likely my own father, was very real and very present.

·Chapter Ten·

To say life was busy after having my second child would be an understatement. In life, I had never been a fan of busy people, especially the ones that made it a point to let you know how busy they were, out-busying you like it was a contest, wearing busyness like a badge of honor. To me, busyness was a hiding place, an excuse, a way for people to avoid things that made them uncomfortable, things like their past. As much as I hated it, I had to join the club though; I was bust my ass busy when Ryder came home. Not that I wasn't busy before.

Again, in my sobriety, I had to make it a point to stay busy, planning and organizing my days, weeks and months strategically, making sure there was never time to lean back towards addictive thoughts, behaviors or people. This, what I was experiencing with Ryder, was different. It wasn't social and fun, scheduling time with friends and family or walks at the beach, bike rides and lunch, this was about my son, my precious baby boy and scheduling our lives to the tee in order to keep him on a trajectory to wellness. It only intensified over time, managing him and his numerous appointments and procedures became a full-time job.

With Ryder recuperating from his second surgery in as many months and still requiring a cast from his waist to his ankles and Jordan a very active and inquisitive, toddler, I had very little time for anything outside of caring for them, Chase and our household. It wasn't that I couldn't do anything else; it just took a lot more effort and planning.

With everything I had going on I guess I wasn't as excited as I should have been when our mailman delivered a beautifully embossed envelope. Not immediately recognizing the return address and name, I knew when I pulled it out from the pile of mail that it was a Wedding Invitation. Bulky and oddly shaped, complete with a LOVE Stamp, I turned it over to find my baby sister's initials glittering in italics on the back. As happy as I was for her, I couldn't help but feel deflated, my sisters, me, and weddings have never been a match. I can't imagine with things the way they were now, that Katie Girl's wedding will be any different.

The last time I saw my sisters was a few weeks ago when Ryder was born, both of them came to see me just after we were home. They came together, which, whether real or imagined, left me feeling like the outsider again. The two of them arrived full of life, energy and excitement, their bond evident, close and connected, complete with inside jokes and the ability to finish each other's sentences. I tried not to be jealous, but I couldn't help it, I wanted that, I wanted to be that kind of sister too, I wanted to laugh and joke and finish sentences.

Instead, I was awkward like always, excusing my baby weight, explaining Ryder's deficiencies and, justifying Jordan's wild behavior, which by the way, made me feel even worse. I mean these were my sisters, why would I have to make excuses, couldn't they accept me and now my children as we were and love us anyway? Mad at myself, especially for minimizing my family, I wondered silently why this always happened. Was it me? I always felt so inferior to them. I surrender to it being me, maybe the pressure of facing the perfect girls with their perfect lives, planning the perfect wedding made me feel less than perfect and now in addition to me not being perfect, even my baby wasn't perfect. Nothing in my life was perfect, but wasn't that okay? Life wasn't perfect, so why did I let them, and their visit, get the best of me?

I looked at the invitation again, apart from deep and lifelong issues with my step sister and half-sister, to me, just my sisters, there was now the issue with my dad. Was it just an issue though? Could what he did to me and the trauma of it, most likely causing my descent into years of addiction, really be summed up as succinctly as an "issue?" I thought about my dad, saddened, knowing we would never be the same again. How could I go to a wedding with my dad there? Not only would he be there, but he would be the Father of the Bride, I feel sick just thinking about it. I'm back to the outsider, ruined, the one my dad molested and of course, I'm left wondering again if it was only me.

I think of him and immediately start second guessing myself, what if he's innocent, what if he didn't really do anything, what if it's all in my head? With no time to confront him, I was back to faltering, excusing, wondering? I needed to confront him, but I was scared, I didn't know how to do it, just like asking my sisters if my dad had done anything to them, how did I do that? Funny, now that I believed I found the ever-elusive answer to years of questioning "why?" I was such a mess, "what now?" was left in its wake and it was just as confusing.

Oddly enough, my dad had stopped by the house recently too. Uninvited, and unexpectedly, he came right before lunch to see me and the kids. It was busy, I was busy and, the timing wasn't right. I thought about it though, I thought about telling him that I may have been molested just to see his reaction, to look at his face, to see if it made him uncomfortable, but it was my dad, I felt bad. I couldn't bring myself to do that to him. I mean I could literally be trying to cover my breasts to keep him from staring at them and, at the same time thinking he's a loving and caring father. That's how disturbing it was, or how disturbed I was. The entire time he was at the house I would think about different ways to get it out there, to make it a discussion, but I didn't really have the tools, I didn't know what I was doing, so instead, I visited, pretending like I always have, that everything was normal, all the while hiding myself in one of Chase's oversized sweatshirts.

I guess if I did decide to go to Katie's wedding, confronting my dad could wait, I mean it had waited this long, there wasn't any hurry or was there? Would time diminish the memories or the clarity of what I now believed happened to me? With everything that Ryder was going through and Jordan not even two-years-old, I was busy, but was I really too busy to get to the bottom of all of this? Was I busy or was I avoiding the issue?

The voice in my head with its constant duality now cautions me, "Maybe there's a reason you keep avoiding it, maybe you should just let it go. It happened so long ago and look it's over now, you're okay, you're better, why do you want to dredge up the past and cause a huge problem?" Not new, this is what I had been going through for the past two years. I was always back and forth, talking myself out of pursuing it, trying to get it out of my head, trying to forget about it all. I couldn't though I knew now, I was almost sure of it. "Almost doesn't count you know," the relentless voice chimes in.

Katie's wedding, I already know, will be uncomfortable for me, regardless of the situation with my dad. Sure, it was easy to use him and the "issue" as an excuse, but there were a million other reasons I was already apprehensive just thinking about her wedding and what it would take for me to get through it. To start, remembering my sister Taylor's wedding the previous year, was a wakeup call to how horrible and out of place, it would make me feel. From the Engagement Party all the way to The Big Event itself, there wasn't a moment that I wasn't tormented by age-old feelings of not being good enough. I was honestly more nervous about her wedding than I was about my own.

I kept telling myself that it wasn't about me and that not feeling good enough was my problem, but from beginning to end, every moment I spent with my two sisters I was crushed and heartbroken, knowing that no matter how hard I tried, I would never have the kind of relationship they had. I would never be one of those kinds of sisters. From the onset, with Katie as Taylor's Maid of Honor, and me as one of the Bridesmaids, I was already the outsider. How could I not be? They shared the same mother, grew up full-time under the same roof as true sisters do, had similar features and characteristics and now even had matching tattoos. Believing I was only included in the Wedding Party out of obligation, on top of everything else, I tried my best to ignore the old feelings and buttons that were being pushed and stay positive. The new me, I tried to rise above it all and focus on all of the good aspects of at least being a part of things, when there were so many years that I wasn't. The trouble was that it wasn't good for me, it pushed me back into the dark place of not mattering, a place I couldn't handle, I didn't want to handle and now, I could choose not to be a part of.

Taylor's wedding was beautiful but uncomfortable. Maybe it would have been different if I wasn't a part of the Wedding Party. I was exiled by my own status, my sobriety. Somewhat of an outcast in most of the activities and events that led up to the wedding, and the wedding itself, not drinking with everyone, only separated me more than the already existing divide between me and my sisters.

It wasn't really just my sisters, or my dad, there was also all of the time spent at the same party, in the same group or even the same room with Marianne. I could hardly look at her without feeling the years of hurt and anger welling up inside, sometimes holding back tears for the horrible way she treated me as a child. I would look at her in her arrogance and wonder what was worse, or what had caused more damage, what she did to me or my dad? I couldn't imagine ever treating a child as terrible as she treated me and never apologizing or feeling that she played any part or had anything to do with my self-destruction.

I was no longer a child though, I didn't have to allow her to treat me abusively, I was an adult and I could choose to be around her or not. Attending a wedding was one thing, committing to being in a wedding was another? If Katie asked me to be in her wedding I didn't think I could accept. I couldn't take the next few months, with Bridal Showers, Dress Shopping, Rehearsal Dinners, and of course, the big day itself, all the hours spent with people that didn't really seem to give a rip about me was less than appealing. Choosing to do the right thing would be easy if I was choosing to do the right thing for me.

As if I didn't have enough reasons to send my regrets, I was insecure too. I wasn't wedding prepared, stressed and overweight, I knew it was shallow and selfish, but I couldn't help it, I wasn't comfortable with how I currently looked. I had gained close to a hundred pounds with my pregnancy and had only lost roughly twenty-five or so in the past month. My sisters, were petite and adorable, thin and fit, like living Barbie Dolls, they were beautiful to me.

 I was a long way from that, most days showering, throwing my wet hair into a ponytail and pulling on leggings and a T-shirt, I couldn't remember the last time I even put on mascara. I spent my time going from one appointment to the next and, when we weren't busy with that, I was chasing after Jordan and entertaining Ryder, not to mention keeping my house clean, tending to the mounting piles of laundry, grocery shopping, cooking, and a million other day to day tasks, not really able to carve out much "me-time."

I loved it though. I loved the "Mom Life," so why was I questioning myself again? Never changing, whenever I thought about any of them I felt ashamed in a strange way, never measuring up, no matter how much time passed or how much I changed. I was never good enough, but why? I'm sure I was responsible, after all, they were my feelings, my twelve steps had taught me that, I was in control of them, or supposed to be anyway. Obviously, I would have to work on it. In the meantime, the idea of being so involved with all of them in just a few short weeks definitely seemed like too much. I didn't think I could pull it off. All of these thoughts, combined with what Ryder was going through and the "issue" with my dad had my anxiety skyrocketing.

Whenever my anxiety was high I would worry about my sobriety. I had been sober for over seven years and I had seen other women go back to a life of addiction for things far less sensitive and far less stressful. Not that I was comparing, I just needed to be realistic. I needed to remember that no matter how many years of sobriety I had, I was in recovery, an addict, I would always be an addict and I did have to take that into consideration, especially in dealing with "triggers," like stress, anxiety and emotional upsets.

I literally had no time to devote to working my program. In fact, I really hadn't done much of anything since becoming pregnant with Ryder. I wasn't even exercising as I should. Exercise always helped clear my head and keep me determined. So, no exercise, no program, no meetings, no reading the "Big Book," I had no sponsor and I wasn't really even working the steps. I wanted to do it and I thought about it, almost every day, but I seriously had been too busy. I knew that I needed to work the program first, become anchored in what I knew would help me the most. I needed to make my sobriety a priority.

My support through the people and the program were what I needed to help me get through confronting my dad. I made a promise to myself to find the time. Just thinking of recommitting to the twelve step program made me feel better; maybe it would help me in deciding what to do about my sister Katie's wedding too. Taylor's wedding and all the angst that came with it was before I knew about my dad, at the time of her wedding, I was having memories but all of it was still new.

Believing now that something happened to me, it was no longer just a memory, but to me a reality. The worst part was that now that I believed I had been sexually abused, I had more memories than ever and with so much time alone with my babies, my thoughts were spiraling out of control. There was a movie of my life that seemed to be constantly playing, reminding me of just how screwed up I used to be. I spent ten years of my life heavily using, a hardcore, seemingly hopeless addict and alcoholic. During that entire time, I saw my sisters, Marianne, and even my dad four or five times at the most.

While I was using I was away from them, but how they treated me and the shame and rejection I felt growing up with them, stayed with me, continuing to affect me and my behaviors. My years spent in addiction were spent believing I was worthless and deserved nothing better. Now, having memories that I was molested by my own father, along with everything else, I stopped wondering why I was the way I was, for the most part, I knew.

My experiences, of rampant drug and alcohol abuse, dysfunctional and violent relationships with men, homelessness, arrests, time spent in and out of jail, not respecting myself or my body and using it in trade, even becoming a massive thief and habitual liar, all of it cemented the fact that I didn't matter. For years, I was less than, less than everyone I surrounded myself with and although I wasn't an expert, I now believed nearly all of it could be traced back to my dad and the sexual abuse, Marianne and years of her humiliating and shaming me, constant family abuse, including my stepsister and half-sister, always being treated better than me and of course, Sam my Stepbrother, being sent away as a child

In times where he could have made a difference, I can visibly picture my dad just walking away from me and the terrible suffering that I was going through, turning his back on me, not willing to get involved. In my mind and heart, even now, years later I have the same feelings, unloved and unwanted, especially by my dad and his nightmare of a blended family. I think he knew all along that he was at least part of the reason "why" I was so screwed up.

Thinking back, to some of the lower points in my past, Ocean Beach always came to mind. The beginning of the end, in so many ways, the miscarriage and hospital experience exposing that I was more vulnerable and alone than I ever wanted to be again, I decided to check out, desensitizing myself all the more to life and reality. Baby, the Pitbull became my lifeline, such a loving and beautiful dog, she was all I had and the only thing I let myself care about.

In fact, I cared so much about her, I often felt guilty that she was stuck with me, a useless addict and alcoholic. Months later, abandoned by the low life drug dealer that gave her to me, I was a pulse, in a skeleton of a body, with more meth than blood likely swirling through my veins, I looked like death. My appearance, grooming, and conduct, along with my bright red Jetta, erratic driving and growing PitBull hanging out the window screamed addict and I routinely started getting pulled over by the cops.

Initially stopped for minor offenses, like speeding or not making a complete stop at stop signs, under normal circumstances I would get a ticket, but because I never took care of anything, I'd have outstanding warrants and would get arrested. I got arrested or ticketed for different things, not having insurance or registration, an expired or suspended license, DUI, possession, you name it I got written up or arrested for it. I got pulled over and arrested so many times that with all of the constant fines and fees involved, I couldn't pay the rent and eventually got evicted. With nowhere to go, somehow it was decided that I could live at one of my dad's rental properties, an apartment in his complex on, of all places, Park Avenue.

Within days it became known as the "The Shooting Gallery," a place where everyone was welcome to come, hang out and, literally "shoot-up," drink, smoke weed, use drugs and, party all day and night. It was during this time that I was reintroduced to Skinheads. Many of them convicts and felons, ruthless and unafraid to break the law or go to prison, even referring to going to prison as going "Home" and being out of prison as "On Vacation."

Most were big guys, tough and scary, covered from head to toe with Anti-Semitic and White Supremacy Tattoos, they were intimidating to most but not to me. I easily became influenced by them and quickly became preoccupied with spending time with them. Shortly after being reconnected and encouraged by a friend, I had started visiting several of them that I had known from High School, in both the County Jail and State prison.

I was so messed up that I reconnected with and started exclusively dating a Skinhead named Adam who was incarcerated at the time. Arrested for murder and not just an ordinary murder, but a grim and grisly murder, he was in County Jail getting ready to do life in prison on the Three Strikes Law. In my state of mind, it didn't matter, to me he was larger than life, aggressively masculine and unbelievably sexy, not to mention he showed an interest in me. Built from working out all of the time in jail, he was strong and muscular with a shaved head and covered everywhere with tattoos, one of the most obvious being a Hitler Tattoo. I would do anything for him and that wasn't my biggest problem.

In love with his lifestyle more than I was with the man himself, I started spending time with him whenever I could, visiting him on a regular basis in prison. I also started visiting other Skinheads while I was there, considering them all a "part of the family." I loved the idea of being "connected" to these people, obsessed with everything about them I even started to look like one of them. With their "Doc Martins, Fred Perry Shirts, Khakis and Wife Beaters," most had flagrant and varied tributes to White Supremacy, including Hitler's Picture, his mustache, Swastika's, Iron Crosses and worse. I wore the clothes, started getting insane tattoos and outfitted myself with belts, jewelry and other items that identified me with my new group. They were all murderers, thieves, drug dealers, rapist and worse. Racist and intolerant, I was so attracted to "belonging" or being a part of something, that none of it mattered to me.

The County Jail and Donovan State Prison became my playgrounds. Constantly at one or the other, I made a life out of visiting inmates in both places, often visiting several prisoners each week. When I wasn't able to be there in person, I was at home writing every one of them or at my apartment waiting for hours just to be able to accept their collect phone calls. I was even willing to risk my own freedom, melting Crystal Meth and letting it dry on cards, then making them look like they were drawings from children, to avoid suspicion. I'd mail them and they'd be able to tear them up and eat them, allowing them to get high in Prison.

With nothing better to do and Adam leaving money on his "books" for me, I was able to get by easily, always had gas money and constant access to all of the drugs I wanted. Dedicated to my newest pre-occupation, I lost myself in living my entire life for Adam, a man I could never physically be with or have any type of real relationship with. Bizarrely, I absolutely loved prison and was drawn to the environment, the armed guards and the hardened criminals, the sounds of the buzzers when the doors opened and shut, I even loved the dreary gray of the fluorescent lights.

Under Adam's spell, I never hesitated to do anything he asked me to do, including things that I could go to prison for. I never thought about it at the time, but what was wrong with me that I would put my entire life on the line for a man I barely knew? He was a Violent Murderer who had made a habit out of assaulting people and for whatever reason he and his comfort and happiness became more important than my own. Scariest yet, was that I had started seeing another Skinhead on the outside at the same time, which could cost both of us our lives.

I met Aiden when he came with some friends to "The Shooting Gallery," my apartment on Park Avenue. He had just gotten out of prison which was perfectly normal, everyone getting out of prison seemed to come over to my house and almost everyone I was spending time with was a convict. Aiden had come over to get high and brought his own giant bag of meth. We crushed the meth with alcohol and soaked it into a cotton ball, then took turns using the same needle to shoot up. I would shoot up so much meth and alcohol that my veins would disappear. When that happened then someone else in the group would have to shoot me up, sometimes between my fingers and toes and many times straight into my neck.

Immediately attracted to Aiden, to me he was beyond sexy, with a shaved head, huge build, dark brooding eyes, and a rough exterior but kind heart. Overall, he was just super attractive to me. He was literally covered from the very top of his head, (a Swastika), to the bottom of his feet, (an Iron Cross), in tattoos and, he was menacing, always carrying a huge knife and a small gun. Notorious in the "Skinhead World," he also carried huge wads of cash and bags of drugs, he was untouchable and that to me was irresistible.

Our attraction was mutual but in front of others, we hung out as friends, only hooking up on occasion, when people weren't around. We really liked each other though and would have "fun nights" where we would shoot-up, hook-up and with all of the lights off in the house, peep out the bathroom window to the busy street below for hours. If you're unaware, that's what "tweakers" do, paranoid, passing time peeping out windows and doors, worried that someone or something was out there.

Seeing both Aiden and Adam at the same time was exhilarating, the thrill of getting away with stringing these two tough guys along, my fearlessness fueled by massive syringes full of Crystal Meth flowing through my body made me feel invincible. With Aiden on the outside, it was much easier to spend time with him and have a real relationship. Adam on the other hand, being behind bars was definitely limiting and between the two I had to choose the person that I could physically be with. During this time I went to jail myself a few times, in a way, I became numb to it. It became sadly familiar. If I had to stay in for any length of time I knew I'd go through withdrawals.

Withdrawals in jail, also familiar to me, were the worst. They were scary and uncomfortable, like having the flu, only in jail there was nothing to help, nothing comforting, not even a blanket to keep warm. Usually, my withdrawals were from both drugs and alcohol, which made them even more intense. I'd feel like I had the flu, lethargic and nauseous and, then on top of it I'd start having tremors and seizures. No one there cared, they were used to it, I'm sure it happened all of the time, all of them apathetic to inmates and especially addicts. The only thing that made it more horrible was getting on the "Jail Bus" like that and going to court.

Like going to jail, I had been on the "Jail Bus" several times too. Every time, without fail, I would look out the window and watch the sea of people in their cars going to work or wherever they were going and I would be so sad. I'd watch all of the normal people with normal lives and normal jobs, families, homes, and pets. I'd think of Baby, my PitBull and the crap life she had because of me. I would start crying about my miserable life and wonder, just like always, "why?" promising myself, like I did every time, that when I got out of jail, this time I would really get sober.

I would wish so badly that I was normal, but then I'd get out and get my Trolley Token and head straight back to trouble, drugs and my old way of life. It was a vicious cycle that I couldn't get out of. I continued to get arrested for the same things, drugs, DUI, shoplifting, you name it I got picked up for it. Again, I think just looking like I was spun out on drugs caused the police to pull me over. Sometimes they'd take me in and sometimes they wouldn't. It was always a crapshoot.

Back at "The Shooting Gallery," Aiden and I, over the past several months had been getting closer and I started to really have feelings for him. One day he was driving home from a Casino, (which fun fact; many addicts are also addicted to gambling, with the lure of easy money, including betting, Casinos and, especially The Lottery) and he got into a car accident. On parole, carrying weapons, with no license or insurance and a huge arsenal of drugs, he got out and ran from the scene, calling me to come to pick him up. I rushed out there, but by the time I arrived there was already a Helicopter and a dozen Cop Cars, I was too late. As I pulled up, Aiden had been arrested and was in the backseat of one of the cars being driven away, he looked out at me and said "I love you," through the window. Once he was locked up, I started spending all of my time visiting him in the South Bay Jail.

Once men get behind glass they can really talk the sweet talk. Aiden was no different. I hung on every word, at the time believing he cared about me and that at some point we could have a future. I constantly sent and received sexually explicit cards and letters and kept them in a box under my bed. Still living at Park Avenue, I was so bad into Crystal Meth that I could barely function. I had horrible track marks all over my entire body, dark circles under my vacant eyes; I smoked like a fiend and was pin thin. I would go to visit Aiden and half the time my car wouldn't start. I'd have to find someone to drive me down there and drop me off. One day, feeling low after getting dropped off, I was obsessing about how I would get home when Aiden asked me if I would marry him. High as a kite and thinking that he was joking, I agreed.

After becoming so involved with Aiden I stopped communicating with Adam, which meant I also lost his support, including money, drugs, and protection. Now with Adam out of my life and Aiden in prison, I was completely on my own. In the midst of figuring things out, I got an "out of the blue" call from Cameron who had recently been released from prison. After serving three years for robbery, he was lost, feeling alone and looking to reconnect, unsure of how to resume his life. Oddly, I was excited that he reached out to me and although the memories of Domestic Violence scared me, there was something about him that I was drawn to, maybe the familiarity, that and I needed cash, drugs, and someone to drive me back and forth to visit Aiden. The thing is when you're an addict, you don't just use drugs, you use people too. For me, Cameron and me reconnecting was perfect timing.

Aiden was waiting for me to marry him before being sent to Donovan State Prison and although I tried to avoid the topic, each time I went to see him he would bring it up. Finally, I scraped the money together and found someone who was willing to marry us in prison. Of course, spun out on meth and wearing a flannel, leggings and flip flops, there was no ring, no flowers, no kiss, nothing special. I was married in jail. I never thought that's how I would be married. There was no one there, no family, no friends, not even a single picture was taken and I couldn't even touch my new husband. Saying "I do" with a glass partition between us, under the gloom of the humming fluorescent lights, it was a sad day, not "Rock Bottom" sad, but I was getting there.

I was a married woman, miserable and alone, but married. In the back of my mind wondering if it was only because someone wanted to use me for conjugal visits, I felt like the worst type of lowlife, always desperate for love and approval. The most degrading part was that the one who actually consummated my new marriage was Cameron, who was waiting out in the car with Baby, my PitBull, to take me home.

Lower than low, I was disgusting, even to myself. I never slept, shot, snorted and swallowed huge amounts of meth and continued to be an alcoholic. I took loads of pills too, never even bothering to ask or find out what they were anymore. There was never a time where I was not high. I lied all of the time and stole from everywhere and everyone. I wore filthy clothes, sometimes picking them up off the floor and putting them on. I was full of pick marks and track marks, having to constantly wear long sleeves and pants to cover myself. In order to get cash, I had started stealing tons of clothes and accessories from big department stores and returning them for money, over time paranoid that they were on to me, I'd have to find people to do the returns for me and we'd split the cash.

I was to the point that I would shoot up every twenty to thirty minutes sometimes twenty to thirty times a day. I was beyond obsessed, I loved it and I loved the needles, the way it made me feel and how fast it could change me. I would hate myself and my life, feel despondent and rejected and within a few minutes of shooting up I would be on top of the world, rid of thoughts and feelings that bothered me, I'd be up and ready to go again. My neighbors hated me; the police came constantly, sometimes spending hours in the alley outside watching my apartment but really never doing anything. I was a complete and total train wreck, still getting pulled over and sometimes arrested for drugs, I would swallow most of it before they'd get to me, so there was never enough to really sentence me.

I felt like a scumbag piece of garbage and I was. Still there, on the sidelines, waiting for that glimmer of hope that I was ready to change was my mom. She kept in touch with me but barely, just enough to make sure I was alive. She was brokenhearted about the life I was living, still using every opportunity she could to try and convince me to go to rehab and get sober. Completely destroyed by the Skinhead affiliation and choices to hate other types of people she'd often tell me she didn't even know who I was, I could hear her crying softly sometimes, reminding me that she loved me and would be there when I was ready to get help.

Although she paid for my cell phone and most likely gave my dad rent money for the apartment, I think it was just to ease the pain of worrying about whether I was overdosed somewhere, homeless and dying on the streets as a nameless drug addict. I'd see my dad around the apartments from time to time, doing maintenance and repairs, part of having an income property, I guess. He'd see me surrounded by Skinheads, knowing they were a rough crowd, he just stayed clear. We never really communicated much. I'd look at him so sad and desperate, wondering why he, unlike my mom wouldn't bother with me. He never tried to get me to stop or go to rehab, he never even acknowledged me. I believed even then, that I didn't matter to him.

I put the Wedding Invitation on the counter, reeling from the memory of my dad. With this memory, there's no doubt and there's no confusion, sadly this memory is painstakingly real. It's so real, I can picture it, vivid in my mind my dad is turning a blind eye to everything going on in his very own apartment complex, all of it. Everything, out in the open and right under his nose and he did nothing. The memory of him watching me, his own daughter, filthy, strung out and, covered with track marks, I was surrounded by hardened criminals, drug addicts, and Skinheads and he just watches. He's watching me go into my apartment, only I don't go in. I stop and turn around at the door, but he's not there anymore, my dad is just walking away.

·Chapter Eleven·

"Pops," shows up on the Bluetooth just as I'm turning into the parking lot, my heart sinks as I push decline and pull into a spot, wondering what my dad wants and why he keeps calling. It's the second time today and it dawns on me that we haven't talked in several days. We haven't been in contact since Chase and me, with Jordan, FaceTimed him and he accepted our call with pornography on in the background. Of course, it took us a second to figure it out, the perverted sounds and then the flash straight to it while he got up to shut it off, left no doubt to what my dad was doing.

Unruffled, like he had to shut off the news or a sports channel, he stammered "Hang on, hang on, one second," a few times, until the noise stopped and his face came back on the screen. Shocked and beyond disgusted, Chase and I couldn't understand why on earth he'd answer, instead of just calling us back later.

My dad tried to carry on a normal conversation afterward as if nothing happened. Repulsed, I grabbed Jordan, who was crying to see "Pop, Pop," and took her into the other room, leaving Chase to take over the whole embarrassing scene. I actually was relieved that it wasn't me, by myself, facing another troubling behavior of my father, alone. With Chase as a witness, I didn't have to doubt whether I really saw and heard what I did, wondering forever if I had imagined it, or believing it was all in my head and that I was crazy. Chase was upset afterward, asking me "What kind of sick person answers a FaceTime call from his daughter with that going on?"

I couldn't answer. I didn't know, I only knew that I had a problem too, because instead of ousting him from my life, we were still in touch. Shaking my head, wanting to forget about it, I get out of the car and head inside, wishing I had just answered the phone instead of having to call him back.

Confronting my dad was always on my mind, always and even more so after the pornography incident. For whatever reason, though I kept avoiding it, so much so, that he had crept back into our lives, in a weird way. Things definitely weren't normal, but we were in touch, phone calls, and texts, before the incident, there was Facetime, mostly for the kids if he wasn't able to stop by, and most awkward of all, he would stop by. On occasion, the kids and I would meet him for lunch. The best of all plans, meeting prevented him from coming to the house, we'd be out in public, with a time frame and people around and it wasn't as strained or uncomfortable, at least for me. I couldn't imagine that he wasn't picking up on any of it, that he wasn't aware.

The most confusing part for me was that I was so hot and cold, when he was with us, in person, I would literally be cringing on the inside almost the entire time and, when we were apart, I was sad, feeling sorry for him, wishing things were different. I think I allowed it to drag on; knowing in my heart, that once I confronted him it would be over for us, more than likely he would no longer be a part of my life. We were all living in limbo, almost as if someone was sick and dying, spending time together, until the inevitable last goodbye. It was so heavy and heartbreaking; I knew it couldn't go on like this forever, I knew I had to make a decision.

Rushing through the door, I make my way to the back row, checking my phone for the time as I slide into the metal folding chair, it's familiarity comforting, "meeting chairs" are now a longstanding and repetitive part of my life. I feel a sense of accomplishment that I made it and with three minutes to spare, I'm technically early. I breathe a sigh of relief and put my bag down, pulling out my notebook and pen, ready to be wowed. In a few short months, I had changed my routine and habits, the Weight Watchers Meetings, among other things, had been a big help.

I had been part of the program on and off for a few years, but with Oprah taking over it was amazing now, so positive and encouraging, not just about food issues anymore, but more about your emotions and "why," you were eating. Oprah changed the way it was done and I can't speak for anyone else, but it was working wonders for me, I learned to make better choices about food, deciding to eat well and eat only when I was hungry, I now took the time to stop and think about what I was eating and why.

Taking control of my eating and making better decisions, made me feel better physically, mentally and even emotionally. It honestly helped make my life better. I had lost over sixty pounds in the nine months since Ryder was born, thanks to Weight Watchers, exercise and mindful eating. It was so good, I felt so much better about myself, inspired, and encouraged to, as Oprah would say "live my best life." Embracing change was the new me and I was really enjoying it. I would leave on such a high, my heart light and humming, the magnitude of my life and dealing with it no longer scary or overwhelming, but manageable.

Along with Weight Watcher's, I had also returned to my Twelve Step Program, which I promised myself to make a priority. I knew that without sobriety, I would truly have nothing, so grateful and thrilled to have survived and to be alive, I never wanted to forget how important the program had been and would continue to be in my recovery. My life was so good now; I didn't want to do anything to jeopardize it.

Making time for both meetings was important and kept me in a good place. The interesting part was that in so many ways they were similar, only one centered around addiction to drugs and alcohol, while the other focused on food. In both programs people shared personal stories of successes and challenges; everyone applauding afterward. Tokens were handed out for sobriety at one and for weight loss at the other and the fellowship and encouragement at both meetings was always supportive and positive. In addition, for me, each provided a community of people in similar circumstances, a reminder that I wasn't alone and that like others, I could, by making the right choices always be successful.

In my Twelve Step Program, I was so committed that I even reached out to a sponsor, one that was perfect for me. She was real and matter of fact, staying in touch and keeping me accountable. With a similar background, I was able to share some of my more personal issues and she could relate, easily offering tips and advice on what had helped her. I was also back to working the actual "Twelve Steps," and reading the "Big Book." Getting my life back together felt good and I felt good, not perfect but definitely improved. I think all of my changes were good for my husband and kids too, I was aware now, that my feeling good about myself affected not only me but everyone around me. Feeling good was my new addiction, which wasn't a bad thing, but it was definitely preventing me from confronting my dad. I didn't want to go through the feeling bad parts that I knew were lurking under the surface.

Instead of confronting my dad, I spent my time "Chasing Sober," improving myself and focusing on the loves of my life, my family. Ryder, my sweet baby boy, with his cast off and moving around on his own, was almost ready to walk, which was no small feat for my little guy after being immobile his first nine months. Jordan, my heart, had started preschool, a giant hurdle for both of us, but especially for me with my background of school issues and dark memories of it not being a good or happy place. Bringing her in and leaving her, I had to keep reminding myself that she wasn't me, her life wasn't anything like mine. Jordan's experiences with school could and should be wonderful.

Walking back to the car in tears the first few weeks, I was ridiculous, especially because it was only two mornings a week and she loved it. My hero, Chase, was on top of the world and had recently started a new job with a great salary, bonuses, and paid vacation. Hired in Human Resources at a big sports outfitting company, it was a huge accomplishment considering his background and everything it took for him to get there. I was so proud of him and so grateful that all of us were doing well and in a good place, but was I really? Could I really be in a good place when all of the issues and problems with my dad and his family were still unresolved?

By far, addressing the issue with my dad was my biggest concern, but more recently, there was a newer issue with my little sister Katie, a problem between us that I didn't think we'd be able to overcome, at least not anytime soon. Unfortunately, it happened before she got married, our conflicting feelings and beliefs about the past caused such a huge rift that in the end; I didn't even attend her wedding. I tried, I really did. Going in, I was all in; I wanted and had agreed to be one of her Bridesmaids. Determined to be there for her, I put all of my own doubts, fears and insecurities aside, wanting to do my part to make sure my Sister's Wedding was beautiful, the perfect event, everything she wanted it to be.

Sadly, at her Bridal Shower, I was seated across from the triple threat of Marianne, with both Taylor and Katie next to her. When the conversation started revolving around what a fabulous mother Marianne was, complete with both sisters sharing tender memories of how loving and involved she had been, always there for her daughters and the best mom a girl could have, blah, blah, blah. I couldn't take it. With both of them elaborating and Marianne starting to get emotional, I just couldn't stomach it any longer so I excused myself and went to the restroom.

I had to at least get away from it. I wanted to leave, I knew I shouldn't have put myself in this situation, I knew I had made a mistake. It was horrible, too much for me, like always there was no way that I could be with them, their lives and recollections were all so different than mine, they were so different. They were a "they" and I was just me, alone, the outsider. I feel mad, believing they intentionally did this kind of thing to make me feel bad, to punish me, reminding me that I wasn't one of them, they were better than me, the real sisters, and the perfect daughters.

"Kristen, what's your problem? What are you doing in here? We're in the middle of a party, in case you didn't notice." Katie in her bride to be tiara and matching sash looks adorable but sounds hostile. Now standing in the kitchen, I'm caught off guard and feel trapped. I look around wanting to have a reason. "Water, I was looking for water," I answer, picking up a water bottle from several that had been set out for guests on the counter behind me. "Really, because it seems to me like you have an attitude," she says. My little sister, stands in front of me, staring at me, only I don't know what to say, is it a question? Is it a statement? Is she scolding me? Am I supposed to go sit down now with my "attitude." It's not like I can go back now, not after this.

The old me is pissed, wishing I could take her out, but instead, I try to answer her calmly, knowing as my words go out, they sound more defensive and reactive than I want them to. "You know those aren't my memories, you know how I was treated by her. It's almost like you and Taylor say and do those kinds of things in front of me on purpose, trying to make me feel bad, or sad, it's like you want to upset me. I mean, do you guys enjoy making me feel like the outsider because you constantly do it." My adrenaline is rising; I'm hurt and angry, trying to tread lightly on how much I say about her mother, I continue, "All I'm saying is that you guys don't have to do that in front of me, you know what it was like for me. I mean, I can't even watch Cinderella because of the three of you!"

I close my eyes wishing I hadn't added that last part but it was too late. What did she want from me anyway? Honestly, couldn't she have just given me a few minutes to collect my thoughts, pull myself together? What did she care if I was in the kitchen getting a drink, why was she policing me anyway? I didn't have to stay and listen to her put her mother on a flipping pedestal.

Wanting this to stop, go away, just disappear, it only gets worse. Katie laces into me, "I'm sick of you! I'm sick of the way you treat my Mom, she isn't as evil as you'd like her to be, and she isn't a villain." Trying to keep a hushed voice and failing, she continues her neck and cheeks flushed with anger, "We're all sick of you! Everything is always about you. What about us? All of those years, do you think none of us were affected? Do you honestly think none of it affected us, that we weren't hurting? You're so selfish. Do you ever think about any of us, what you put us through? I'm over it, I'm over you, I don't want you in my wedding if that's how you feel about my mom, I don't want you to stand for me, I'm serious, I'm tired of tiptoeing around you and all of your issues, we're all tired of it."

Her truth was out, it was out and it was real. Her true feelings, so big and painful, so unexpected, I couldn't breathe. In her life, she didn't have room for me, to understand me or my feelings. She had already decided how she felt about me, only she never told me, not until now. I look at her trying not to cry, I want to hug her, I want things to be different, I want us to start over, but it isn't the time. I can't change it, not here, not now, most likely not ever.

I wanted to throw the water bottle across the room and scream that part of the reason I turned out the way I did was because of her and her evil mother, the same one she just sainted, in the living room, but instead, I try to breathe, setting the water bottle on the counter. Looking at what used to be my sweet, baby sister, all I see now is a mini version of my stepmother, like a sponge she soaked up all of the hate and animosity that her mother had for me over the years and it was hers now, there was no use in fighting it. It was too late. I had to get out of there before the tears came. "It is how I feel Katie, I hate your mother and that will never change, so there, I guess that settles it, I hope you have a nice wedding." I turn to leave and catch everyone in the other room quietly watching me go. "Don't cry, don't cry, don't cry," I keep telling myself, willing for my tears to stay put until I get to the car. I pick up my bag from a bench by the front door and leave, shutting the door quietly behind me.

I got into the car and the flood of tears I so desperately held in, all spilled out. I pulled on my seatbelt and drove around the corner and completely fell apart. Sad, mad and in a strange way relieved, I let it all out. There were so many underlying feelings, so many years of no one ever clearing the air, so many years of my dad pitting us all against each other. Marianne too, wedging us apart by playing the innocent party to all of them. For years I had threatened my dad that I was done with Marianne, I never wanted to be around her, but now I was realizing it was all of them. They were all the same; they envisioned me as the bad guy and they were all innocent.

They believed it was me, in my addiction that made things uncomfortable. How could they not know that it was all of the horrific treatment and abuse, the shaming, and withholding love, always treating me less than everyone else? They all witnessed it for years and over time, joined in and now it was all me? I had made their life uncomfortable? I was done with them, all of them. My dad was the worst; I blamed him for all of this. I wanted them; I loved my sisters and wanted them to be in my life.

My dad ruined it. Continually destroying any chance we had for a relationship by dividing us with gossip and lies. Maybe over the years, I could have even learned to be okay with Marianne, if my dad didn't destroy that too. Again, it was too late; they weren't good for me, being around them, thinking about them, all of them, I was done. I pulled myself together and drove away; I couldn't help but think that on top of it all, I ruined the chance to ask my sisters if my dad did anything to them. I guess I could still try at some point, I mean, could it really get any worse?

Still upset, and feeling the need to talk to someone, I wrestled with whether to call Chase or my Sponsor. Chase would be at work and me crying and upset would make him worry, I knew he'd feel bad for me and wouldn't really be able to do anything to help. I didn't want to do that to him so I called my sponsor. I filled her in on parts of what just happened and she offered to meet up for a cup of coffee. It's weird though I wanted and needed advice only I didn't really want to share bad things about my family. I loved both of my sisters in spite of everything, my dad too.

I don't want things to be like this. I don't want to lose all of them. As difficult as it was and as much as I didn't want it to be this way, it already was though. We were over, all of us. I couldn't put off confronting my dad any longer, I had to find out. I needed to know, to hear him confess, I wanted him to apologize. I wanted him to be sorry for what he did to me and what he let his wife do to me. I wanted him to be sorry for all of it. I take a deep breath, wondering if what I wanted was even possible. Here I had been working so hard to improve myself, to stay sober, to be positive and keep my life running smoothly and in one afternoon with my Cinderella-like Family, I felt like it was all ruined. No matter how hard I tried, I felt like I would always be ruined.

Meeting for coffee helped. I left Starbucks with a better feeling about myself, focused and more determined to do what I needed to do to move forward. Feeling stronger and more empowered, I hoped it wasn't just the coffee. My sponsor, on target, reminded me of what was important, which was everything I had been doing, especially staying sober and attending meetings. She also suggested a therapist. The weirdest thing was that in the past, I would have definitely pooh-poohed the therapist idea, but something about my situation made me believe the time was right. The issue with my dad was big, huge really, and combined with my sisters and Marianne, it was all bigger than me. Too big for me to take on by myself, I knew I needed help, I was ready.

Just thinking about making an appointment, I was already obsessing over what I was going to say to her, where to start, how it would work, I wasn't sure whether to start with now or the past. The recent memory of my dad, walking away from me in my addiction, stuck now in my head, scarring in a sense, would have to mean something. Driving home, I think about it again, it wasn't long after that incident that I hit my "Rock Bottom," wouldn't that be telling? Leaving Starbucks that day, I start questioning all of the things my sister said.

Years ago I would have listened to her, made her truth my own, without question. I would have believed her; I would have thought she was right. Not now, not anymore. She was wrong, her belief that "I was selfish," and "all of those years, what I put them through?" What could she possibly know? I mean, most of that time she was a child. I shake my head. I'm back to my dad walking away that day, I wouldn't think that they, any of them, my dad included, had any idea of what I was going through, I think they believed that I was choosing addiction, that I chose a lifestyle of torture and hell for myself and somehow now, to hear my sister, they were actually the victims. My sisters most likely only knew what my dad shared with them and my dad, the day he walked away, had no idea how bad things already were. So how would he know that things were just going to get worse for me, I was only going to get worse.

From that point, I was on a crash course of self-destruction, like never before. Watching my dad walk away back then, I felt more worthless than ever, I pushed past any normal limits, using more drugs and alcohol than I thought was humanly possible, surprising myself that I didn't die. I lived for the constant high, that and my dog, Baby. Those were the only two things in the world that I cared about. Stuck in a useless marriage with a convict, life for me was one huge disappointment after another. I didn't know what I was thinking, marrying a prisoner, allowing my life to revolve around him, what he wanted and needed becoming more important than anything else. This included providing him with what he felt was his right, the dreaded "Conjugal Visits." As much as I didn't look forward to it, there was a strange part of me that was oddly excited for the rare prison experience.

I drove myself down to Donovan State Prison, where I was set to have my first one. My car barely started, which should have been a sign for me to blow the whole thing off, but instead, I tried and tried until the engine turned over. I was filthy and disgusting, not caring or believing that it mattered, or that I mattered, I went as I was. With old makeup smudged under my eyes, dirty hair, day old clothes, chipped polish on my hands and feet, flip flops and chain-smoking for days, I'm sure I even smelled like a giant ashtray, or worse. I had been shooting up every thirty minutes in anticipation of what I was facing and my inner dialogue was consumed with the same questions as always. "Why?" Why was I willing to do this? What was wrong with me?

Taking the freeway exit for the prison, I look around, scouting the area for cops. Pulling to the side of the road, in what seemed like a desolate area and with the car still running, I push up my sleeve and tie off my upper arm. Flicking the veins all the way down for good measure, I take out a baggie of meth, melting it on a spoon. I soak it up in a used cotton ball. Beyond the need for hygiene at this point, I fill a dirty syringe and try to find an agreeable vein, only they're all exhausted, tired and used. I can't find one, they've all disappeared. Instead, a flick my wrist and gently and slowly push the needle into the tiny vein there. I'm scared, trying to be careful not to push the needle too far; the vein is so tiny I could blow it out.

I'm scared, looking around nervously, as the murky liquid goes all the way in. I remove the tie off and shove everything into an old Doritos Bag off the floor of the car and put it into the glove box. I try to relax a minute, waiting to feel the shot hit me before I continue driving. Feeling anxious, I wonder again, as I wait for the warm feeling to burst across my chest, what is wrong with me? I'm on the way to a prison, to have sex behind bars, with someone I don't see a future with and now I'm blatantly pulled over on the side of the road where a million police patrol the area, giving myself a "fix." Then in an instant, the warm sensation fills my body and, just like magic, all my thoughts vanish, my feelings are numbed and I carry on.

Arriving at the Prison a few minutes later, I'm lit, enough to get me through I hope. Required to arrive an hour ahead to check in, I get in line for the long wait with dozens of other people. Most of them I've seen before, the diverse group surrounding me, waiting to see their own prisoner's, are interesting for sure. Better than a Reality Show most look like hookers and crack heads, some are sad, mothers with children, others cleaned up, most likely parents coming to see their wayward, adult children. I start to think about my own mom but force myself to stop. I can't help but stare, watching everyone, wondering what their stories are. I want a cigarette, but there's no smoking, and before I know it there's a policeman asking me to step aside.

He starts asking me a million questions about Aiden, how long I've known him? Did I know about his past? Did I know he was a murderer? Drug Dealer? Why was I visiting a Notorious Criminal? Not volunteering that we were married or any other information, I listen, aware of most of it, but I had no idea he had tried to stab someone in court earlier in the week. Joined by another officer at this point, he tells me they have probable cause to search me and together they walk me out to my car. Taking my keys, one of them watches me, as the other searches the car.

Minutes later, a woman cop pulls up, gets out and comes around to where I'm standing, pushing me against the car, she roughly starts frisking me. Sick to my stomach I feel like I have to use the restroom, thinking this is it for me. I'm sure of it when they pull the Doritos Bag out of my glove box. I'm so sad, I know I'm going to jail and in a few days, I'll be back on The "Jail Bus" to court. Most depressing of all, I know I'll have to go through withdrawals there over the next few days and I know it will be awful. They put me in handcuffs and read me my rights, loading me into the back of the female cop's car. Bummed too that my car will be impounded, the impound yard, like everything about being arrested, is going to be expensive. I hate this, but I can't even cry. If I started, I wouldn't be able to stop. Besides, crybabies and jail don't mix.

Just like I expected, I'm off to Los Colinas Women's Detention Facility, a nice way of saying jail, where they take another round of Mug Shots, search my Netherlands and lock me up in a very loud and unruly environment. Dreary and cold, within a short time, I will undoubtedly begin the withdrawals. I know that Cameron will take care of Baby, my dog, while I'm here, other than that no one will miss me. I don't even call anyone. Who is there to call anyway, one of my many winning friends or acquaintances? Or there's my loving father, who could care less? Then there was my mother, whom the thought of disappointing again is almost as bad as being in jail. I definitely, don't want to call my mom. To go through her begging me to go to rehab for the millionth time would be a definite downer. Instead, feeling depressed and alone, I wait it out.

Within a week I'm completely detoxed and coherent, with a first-class ride on the "Jail Bus" to court. Looking completely emaciated, pale, scabs covering my entire body and dark circles under my eyes, it's the same old story, as I look out the windows at all the perfectly normal, happy people on the road, heading to work or school or somewhere that had to better than heading to court for drug charges. I promise the inevitable promise that this time I'll do it, I will get sober when I get out of jail, but I know even as I think it, it's a long shot.

Led into court, I'm approached by a hurried man in a fancy suit that asks, "Are you, Kristen?" I answer, "Who's asking." He laughs, calling me a "Joker," then introduces himself, telling me he's been sent there to help me. The miracle of miracles is that Aiden, somehow getting wind that I had gone to jail that day, had his Attorney find me and show up at my hearing to represent me.

Not even aware of how the attorney managed it, I was convicted of possession, sentenced to time served and, unbelievably, I was free to go. The Attorney was such a kind and caring person, telling me in a sincere way, that he didn't want to see me again, reminding me, like every authority figure always did, that I was young enough to get my life together. I don't remember ever being treated that compassionately in my life, he even gave me money to get something to eat, take a cab and, get my car out of the tow yard. Unlike my own father, he held me by the shoulders; looked me squarely in the eyes and made me promise to get help, get clean.

I was so touched that a perfect stranger would treat me so humanely, so warmly with so much understanding, that I actually thought about staying sober for a minute. Sadly though, like any true junkie with a wad of cash, I called Cameron to come and get me, we picked up my car and within the hour, even with several days of unintentional sobriety under my belt, I'm back at "The Shooting Gallery," resuming my same old way of life.

Happy to be out of jail and back home, I was on a Meth Binge for days, constantly craving the euphoric rush, only now it was taking more and more meth to get it. There was so much drug use and shooting up going on in my apartment that there was a Red Box for dirty and used syringes, along with supplies like tie offs, sterile wipes and clean needles. Compliments of The Needle Exchange Program, they provided everything needed to use and use wisely, I had even passed my first free Aids or HIV Test. If only it was as easy to get drugs.

In order to get free drugs and make money, Cameron and I had ventured back to Mexico, buying large amounts of every kind of drug and reselling it stateside. It was my new hustle and I loved it. I was so out of my mind that I even started going alone. Wanting to keep all of the profits for myself, I even started buying and reselling steroids to bodybuilders, cutting it with another substance, for an even bigger payout. I honestly started thinking of myself as a Business Woman, only the easier it came the easier it went, at least for me. Cameron, busy stealing copper and reselling it, had several of his own money making side jobs, so I didn't feel bad about going without him. Donovan State Prison, just minutes from the Mexican Border was a perfect stop, I'd swing by and see Aiden, on the few days I was allowed and then keep heading south to load up on my resale drug inventory.

The best thing to come from my most recent arrest was that I was no longer eligible for the "Conjugal Visits," I guess an arrest record was fine, a conviction wasn't. I was relieved, for many reasons, the main one being that I had been hooking up with Cameron in exchange for favors since Aiden's arrest and incarceration. I just figured a girl had to do what a girl had to do. I had started bartering sex and other acts, for random things, never thinking much about it. Money was actually one of them, but I never thought of it as prostitution, in my warped thinking it was more like a trade-off. If my car was running Cameron would give me gas money and I'd drive the forty minutes south to see Aiden on my own. If my car wasn't running, he'd drive me, willing to wait in the car, while I went in for the hour. He'd also share drugs and alcohol with me and, on occasion, when I needed to eat; he'd buy me some garbage food like a burrito or Jack in the Box.

One day, more trashed than ever, I drove down to the border after stopping by to see Aiden behind glass. Parking my car at The Park and Ride, on the United States side, I biked over to the pharmacy in Tijuana, by myself. Feeling freer than ever, I always had a bike with me, usually to take Baby, my dog out, letting her run while I biked, but now it was for my business ventures. It was a fun vibe and I loved it. Delusional, like I didn't have a care in the world, I had stocked up on a huge assortment of "goodies" and was riding like a crazed person back to the border. With my headphones on, music blaring in my ears and believing I was home free, I didn't really notice that there was a police siren "bleep bleeping" behind me.

Finally noticing they were after me and knowing the reputation of the Mexican Police, I hopped off my bike and ran, ditching it and trying to ditch them. Realizing I would never be able to get back across the border being chased, I tried instead to find a place to hide. I ran into the courtyard where I bought all of the drugs, only when I did the police ran in after me, rolling down the metal doors so I was stuck. Hoping someone would hide me, instead, everyone in there who had known me for years, my dealers really, all now pretended they had never seen me before in their lives. Scared and shaking, having no idea what was going to happen, I thought I would crap myself. I thought about doing it just so they wouldn't want to touch me, but the idea of rotting away in a Mexican Prison with diarrhea all over me was too repulsive, so I tried to contain myself and follow their instructions.

There were two policemen, corrupt and evil looking, shouting something at me aggressively in Spanish. I put my hands on my head, guessing, I didn't speak any Spanish and they didn't speak much English, but with the universal law of authority, they threw me forcefully against the wall and frisked me inappropriately, finding all of my obvious hiding places and seizing all of my drugs. After they finished feeling me up and taking liberties in sensitive areas, they handcuffed me and pushed me into the back of their cop car with another person, an old Mexican Man, who groped me further and kept grabbing my leg.

With the policeman going through my backpack and speaking to each other in Spanish, I broke into tears, finally asking the groping man, what was going to happen to me? In Broken English, with his hand now on my thigh, he told me that after they were done with me they were going to kill me and hide my body. The police finally got into the car and drove around the corner, picking up my bike and putting it haphazardly in the trunk. With my bike partially hanging out and not telling me a thing, they drove me and my creepy companion, who was a Sexist Lech, to their "fake" Mexican Prison. With my cell phone ringing the entire time, I felt heartsick, wondering who was trying to reach me. With no thought to the seriousness of my situation, I was hoping of all things, that I would get to call them back.

Letting my imagination get the best of me, before long all I could think about was that they were going to do all sorts of horrible things to me and then murder me. Pulling up to an old building in the middle of town, they took me out of the car and pushed me through the front doors. Passing another Policeman sitting at a desk, I'm shoved and locked into a dark, cement holding room.

I stood and looked through the tiny window, watching them dump all of my drugs out on the desk, while they sorted through them and laughed. They start going through my backpack next, I can hear my phone ringing again, I watch as the man sitting at the desk answers it. Barely able to speak English, I can hear him say something about two hundred dollars before he hangs up. I watch as he walks back to the holding room I'm in and opens the door, still handcuffed, I stand there while he starts searching me again, fondling my breasts and private areas, I want to cry, but something in me is too proud. It isn't until I have a shadowy memory of my dad touching my breasts that I start sobbing and completely break down. Startled, the man stops and backs away, leaving the room and shutting the door behind him.

All in all, I spent five hours held captive, in what most likely was a sham Mexican Prison. I don't think the men were legitimate police or their shady set-up a real police station. Regardless, after a few hours, they let me make a call, telling me that it would be two hundred in cash for me and another hundred for my bike. To think I was only worth double my bike, was disturbing, but I wasn't going to argue it. I called Cameron and explained the situation, begging him to come and get me. After hanging up, they took my phone and left me sitting in the holding room alone.

Waiting, desperate for drugs, I hoped that Cameron would show up before I crashed. With nothing to do but think, I reviewed my life, I'd made a mess of it so far. It was meaningless really. I was an alcoholic, junkie always on the lookout for new and exciting ways to get, stay and, remain completely blown out. I had no desire to change and definitely no desire to stop. If anything, I was always ready for more, eager for the next level. Married now, the wife of a hardened criminal, a Violent Murderer, with no real life of my own, I spent my time satisfied to just visit and wait. I never knew or cared about what might come next.

I couldn't even count or remember all of the times I had been arrested or how much time I spent in jail. I was a drug dealer, a prostitute, I used people, like Cameron, until something or someone better came along and to me, saddest of all was my poor dog, Baby, and the one thing I really cared about couldn't even count on me. I'd be away for hours or even days and she'd have to rely on other people to take care of her when I wasn't around. I was a loser, my life deplorable and apart from Baby, I didn't really care. I started reasoning on whether or not this latest episode could be defined as my worst or my "Rock Bottom."

This definitely had "Rock Bottom," potential. Being arrested and thrown into a holding cell or "prison" in a third world country with three corrupt men that could have raped, tortured or even killed me. Also the thought that no one knew where I was and that they could have kept me hostage for years, murdering me as my lecherous friend so kindly reminded me, "after they were done with me." It all could have ended so tragically, instead, like always, I was fine. I was going home. So this couldn't be it, this couldn't be my "Rock Bottom."

I knew at some point it would come, I had heard about it for years, mostly rumors, people who had experienced it and tried to get sober, even some of my friends. No one I knew had been successful yet. I thought about my "Rock Bottom," wondering when it would finally happen. Part of me, the voice in my head, the one kept hushed and buried away, faintly whispers to me, "I hope it happens soon."

It wouldn't happen soon. Cameron, after rescuing me and my bike from the supposed police headed straight for the same pharmacy and same people that had vanished during my arrest earlier. Not one to hold a grudge, I went in like I always did, laughing and visiting (I even have pictures with some of them). Cameron and I stocked up on every drug imaginable and more, before heading north to the safety of the United States. Stopping at The Park and Ride to get my car, we sit in Cameron's truck and share a bottle of Jack Daniel's while prepping our meth. I'm already so happy and relieved to be free that I feel invincible, the fact that I was still able to get all of my drugs after being detained all day was so rewarding. "I win," was what I thought.

Tying off, I look for a vein as I load the meth and Jack Daniels concoction into a syringe. Multi-tasking, I think proudly of how good I am at this and wait for the shot to hit. Tasting the alcohol first, once it blazes across my chest I get out of Cameron's Truck and into my own car and head home. Intoxicated beyond belief, Cameron and I race each other up the freeway, maneuvering our way through traffic to the presumed "safety" of "The Shooting Gallery." When we arrive we have company though, friends I guess, only what kind of friends bring heroin?

Leaving Weight Watchers, I walk to the car feeling troubled again. I'm mad at myself; I spent most of the meeting dwelling on the past instead of interacting and being encouraged. It's been weeks and I still haven't followed through with any of the promises I made to myself that day at Starbucks, the promise to see a therapist, to contact my sisters and finally, to confront my dad.

Constantly being reminded of how awful things were back then, or of how bad I was, all of the memories of using drugs and alcohol couldn't be good for me, in fact, I knew it wasn't. It made me feel stressed and anxious, uptight even. I hated all of these memories, I wanted them to stop, go away. That wasn't who I was anymore. I wanted to be present and focus on now and how wonderful my life was. What happened? Why did I back down again? I was so determined that day, I felt empowered and courageous ready to face what I needed to. The longer I avoided the issues, the more my past was free to reign over me. Recommitted to move forward, I pull out my phone to call and get an appointment with the therapist, and at the same exact moment my phone lights up. "Pops," is calling me again.

·Chapter Twelve·

I lay lifeless, except for my thoughts. I can't breathe, I'm gasping for air only it isn't real, it's all in my head. In my head, I'm trying to breathe, but my body remains motionless. I try to move but I can't. I struggle to sit-up, to breathe, to open my eyes, but I can't, nothing happens. I'm scared. I'm dying, this time I'm really dying and there's nothing I can do. I'm sad, I don't want to die. I knew this could happen, I knew I could die, but I didn't care, I did it anyway. I do care though, I'm not ready. I want to live, I want another chance. I'm suffocating and there's nothing I can do, this is dying, this is my overdose.

My body, like cement, is heavy, weighed down. I'm on the floor, helpless only someone's there. They're pulling my hair, tearing at my shirt, they're touching me now. Is it real? Who is it, who's touching me? Are they trying to save me? I can't open my eyes, I try again to breathe, but it's too hard, the air hangs in front of me, stale and stuffy, too thick, just out of reach. I try to inhale, but it's shallow at best, I need more, I need air, fresh air, clean air, normal air.

I can't get any air. I give up; I'm really going to die this time. Paralyzed, I feel like I'm already dead, but if I'm dead would I be trying to breathe? It's quiet, I can't be dead, my heart is beating, I can hear it, I can feel it pound, one troubled and tired thud every few seconds. I must be alive. I listen, it's slow, too slow, my heart is giving up too. It needs air, I need air, someone help me, please help, I don't want to die. I try again to breathe, to sit-up, open my eyes, but I can't, nothing is working.

Again, I feel someone there, it's real, only they're not helping me, they're hurting me. What they're doing doesn't feel right, their body weight on mine scares me, I can't breathe, they're yanking my hair, they're grabbing me. "Stop, please, can't you see I'm dying!" I say it in my head, but it doesn't move from there, I'm thinking it, but it won't budge, I can't make it go to my mouth, I can't speak. Under my shirt now, someone's hands are on me, moving up, over my stomach, rough and scratchy, too rough. "Stop, what are you doing? Please stop, leave me alone." I'm panicking, but nothing happens. In my head, I'm fighting, flailing, screaming, I'm saving myself, but my body won't move, my mouth won't speak, my eyes won't open.

The hands are on my breasts now, I start to cry, I hate it. I don't want to die, not like this. "Please stop, leave me alone," I beg, but there are no words, the thoughts strung together in my head stay there, jumbling up, hopeless. They're going to rape me, I feel sick like I'm going to throw up, again, nothing happens, my body refuses to do anything. "Who are you? Why are you doing this to me? Please, I'm begging you to stop, I don't like it." Nothing, the words never come. I feel my hearts last beat, I stop thinking, the fight in my head is over, I stop breathing.

I gasp for air. Opening my eyes, water beats down on me, my heart like I've just finished a marathon is pounding out of my chest. I'm in the shower, my shower, crying and distraught. I look around, trying to get my bearings, it wasn't anyone I knew, it definitely wasn't my husband, this time it wasn't even my dad. I turn off the water and stand there in a daze, shaken. It was so real and came on so quickly, another dark memory, a scary memory from when I was on heroin, so much heroin that I passed out, I couldn't move. I actually thought I was dying while some burned out druggie was attacking me. I wrap myself in a clean towel feeling dirty, the memory so clear, was years ago. Why was this happening, every seedy, disgusting and horrible thing from my past kept resurfacing, bubbling up, drowning me in memories, making me feel like I was crazy? I wasn't even safe in my own shower now.

I towel off and put on my bathrobe, questioning my sanity and wondering how I'm going to stop this from happening. It was here and there at first, occasional memories or flashbacks, some vague and others, like this one, so real, it was as if it was actually happening. Now it seemed like every day I was fighting off memories, fighting off the past.

In my mind, I keep thinking the solution is to confront my dad but can confronting my dad really change everything? I mean is all of this going to magically disappear when I tell him that I have memories of him touching me. I think to the appointment with the therapist, can meeting with her really get rid of how I was feeling or the things I was thinking. She would have to be a miracle worker at this rate. I guess secretly that's what I was hoping for, I haven't even met the poor woman and I have so many expectations of her. In my mind, she is the one person I'll be able to completely confide in, the one that's finally going to help get rid of everything troubling me. More realistically, I think things will improve if she can at least help me sort it out and somehow find a way to move past it all.

My appointment with her is later today, only this time I'm not dreading it, this time I'm ready or at least I'm convincing myself I'm ready. Still trying to shake what just happened, I silently ask the Universe or God, or whoever there is to help me, to please let this therapist be the perfect one for me and my situation.

I can hear the kids in the other room, Chase is playing with them, laughter and little feet padding around on the wood floors, they're so happy and carefree, the way it should be. The sounds calm me and warm my heart. Jordan just turned two and Ryder will be one in a few days, my precious boy is walking now, running really, everywhere he goes he's in a hurry, making up for all of the time he was sidelined and in a cast. I think of them and feel happy, they're everything to me. Chase too, we have our moments but for the most part, he's a great husband and a really good dad. Unlike my own father, he's involved and loving, taking time and wanting to do things with both of the kids on his own.

I smile thinking about him playing "Barbie's" with Jordan, trying to cram the tiny shoes on the doll's feet for her while making funny voices and doing his best to keep her entertained. Of course, trucks and football with his son were more up his alley, but he honestly was more than I could ask for as a father. He was easy about it, even giving me time to devote to myself and the things I wanted or needed to do, my meetings, exercise, lunch with friends. We had a relaxed way of allowing each other their own time while still making us and our family our priority.

I still haven't shared too much about what I was going through with him. Afraid to open up and put it out there just yet, apart from my dad answering FaceTime with porn on and my reaction, he doesn't know the details. I feel bad, but I don't know what I would tell him anyway, at this point I'm not sure of the details myself. There's nothing to share, not yet anyway. My family dynamics have always been so screwed up he most likely thinks it's the same old things, my relationship with my father strained because of what's been going on with my sisters and Marianne.

Even with everything going on, my dad had recently stopped at the house for a visit. He called first, catching me off guard; I told him it was okay to come by. He came after lunch and naps and we sat out in the yard talking while playing with the kids. It was warm out, a beautiful day, peaceful until I mentioned therapy. I don't know why I told him, I don't remember if he was trying to make a plan with me and the kids or if he wanted to do something with Chase, somehow the topic came up. It came up like a match on dry brush, a blaze that started and quickly grew out of control. He had a million questions and concerns; he was almost flustered, angry about it.

In an instant, my dad was an interrogator wanting to know everything there was to know about why I was going, what I was going to talk about, who I was going to and, whether or not they were legitimate. As if that wasn't enough, then he tried to devalue it, almost trying to talk me out of it, scaring me into thinking I would most likely be sorry and that it was just going to open a huge can of worms. It was wild; his conversation was intimidating, making me feel like I was doing something against him personally, something wrong, that my planning to see a therapist was in some way going to cause problems for me or for him, for us.

I think about it as I dry my hair, my dad seemed almost agitated about it. Why would he care that I was going to a therapist? I had been to therapists off and on throughout my entire life, I would hope he would want me to find a good one to help me stay on track, stay sober, be a good wife and mother and have a good life. Instead, he kept questioning me about it repeating that "I should leave well enough alone," and that, "I seemed okay to him." When I was able to diffuse the situation by telling him that I was going mostly about marriage stuff and parenting and that I was just trying to figure some things out, he calmed down. Regardless, his reaction apart from being surprising was also unsettling.

Like always though, I excused it, reasoning that maybe he felt bad that his daughter still needed therapy, that somehow it was a reflection on him, that he wasn't a good parent. My awareness that everything was always about my dad and never me was troubling. Our entire relationship centered on him and what he wanted or how he would feel, but instead of recognizing it for what it really was, I was left feeling guilty. In my mind, I was upsetting my dad by going to therapy.

Instead of recognizing it for what it really was? The scene plays out again in my head, what was it? Why was it always about him? Not only that, why was my dad so worked up about my seeing a therapist or better yet, not wanting me to see a therapist? Was he worried about the past? Did he have something to hide? I turn off the hairdryer and look in the mirror, what is wrong with you Kristen, I ask myself. Why am I always excusing my dad and his screwed up behavior? I look at myself again trying to figure out what's wrong with me. Lost, I try to decide whether or not to put on makeup. I decide not to, just in case I tear up today and as I put my make-up bag away, a weird conversation we recently had pops into my head, another creepy moment with my dad that for whatever reason, I just dismissed.

We were talking about happiness and I mentioned that I thought that I was finally happy, that Chase and the kids and having a family of my own was something that really made me happy. He didn't say anything at first; in fact, there was an awkward silence which made it uncomfortable, making me question myself for being too honest with him. I think in an effort to break the silence, I asked him what made him happy. Without even thinking about it, he looked at me and said "You. You and the kids and cars make me happy. What doesn't make me happy is between five and five-thirty every day when Marianne gets home."

Wondering why he would say that, I'm creeped out. It's confusing, I think it's weird and then I start to feel bad for him, sad that he feels that way about his own wife or his life. I'm back to the mistress thing, I don't know why but his comment makes me feel like the mistress, in these moments, I am the mistress, not the daughter. To me, he's saying things a father shouldn't say, sharing too much personal information about his odd relationship with his wife and how he feels about her.

I hate it. I hated that we weren't normal that he wasn't really like a dad to me, he was too open about strange and intimate details between him and Marianne, too private, and then I start to doubt myself. I hated that he involved me in his twisted way by saying weird things like that but maybe I'm wrong? Maybe it isn't weird? I get dressed, trying to excuse it again, talking myself into believing it's all normal, we're normal and things are fine, only I stop myself "No, it isn't normal Kristen, none of it is normal, stop making excuses for him!"

I head into the other room to find my family, quiet now; I wonder what they're up to. In the kitchen, everyone is having breakfast, content. Chase and I are able to sit and have a cup of coffee while the kids finish eating. "Are you sure you guys are going to be okay on your own today?" I ask him. He's taking them to visit his mom for a few hours while I go to my appointment, and then dropping them at my moms' so she can take them to swim lessons while he goes to work. He holds his hand out to the kids, proud of how happy they are with him in charge and answers, "You worry too much Bub, we're going to be fine, I just hope you like this therapist and get things worked out. You haven't been yourself lately."

He hugs me, kisses me on the head and leaves to shower and get ready. I clean up the kids and the kitchen and then start to get everyone dressed. I think about his comment, knowing he's right, I haven't been myself. I feel happy though, my family really does make me happy, I am happy. I try to convince myself as the voice in my head starts to remind me like it always does, "Except for the part about your dad." Feeling more optimistic than ever I think to myself, "I know, but not for much longer."

Within a few hours I pull up to the therapists feeling anxious, heart attack anxious. I start to wonder if this first visit I should just get to know her and she can get to know me before I delve into such a "big" topic, a warm-up session, I tell myself. "An avoidance session you mean," the voice in my head chimes in, "No Kristen, there's no turning back now, you're here for help, get help." The voice is insistent today, I think as I walk to the front door, how I'll start and what we'll talk about still unresolved as I ring the bell. She works out of her house and I'm relieved, hoping maybe it will be more relaxed than meeting at an office where it's similar to a doctor's appointment, sterile and clinic-like. I'm still looking for warm and fuzzy, comfortable, someone who cares and is compassionate, someone who can help me without judging me or making me feel crazier than I already feel.

I wait, the door opens and I jump, a tiny middle-aged woman with giant, thick-rimmed glasses greets me with a laugh. She's very cute with a strong New York accent that instantly makes me feel at ease, warm and friendly I like her immediately as she welcomes me in. She shows me to a cozy room set up as an office, with two big armchairs facing a desk that she slides behind. "I'm sorry, but I have to use the restroom?" She looks at me with so much understanding; I think she already gets me. "Down the hall on the left, take your time," she smiles then starts jotting something down as I head to the bathroom with my nervous stomach.

Returning, I sit down in one of the chairs facing her, as she very kindly reminds me, "Breathe Kristen, you're going to be okay." I wonder how she knows as I take a deep breath. After introductions and a few minutes of small talk, I start to tell her about my life, my marriage really. In my head, I'm safe if I'm here to talk about my marriage. I tell her a little about Chase and his background and then me and my background and when I finish, she asks about my childhood. I freeze. I'm not ready. Why do they all ask about my childhood I wonder?

For weeks, I've been preparing myself and now here I am and I'm avoiding it all. I don't want to talk about it, about my childhood, more specifically, about my dad. I know I need to say something though so I start, "I think my dad hated me when I was a kid, he was always short-tempered, mad even." I realize I'm not making sense but I continue, "I mean my dad hated me when I was sick. When I was sick, he would always yell at me, to go take some cough medicine if I coughed."

It's quiet, as we look at each other. I think she's stunned. I'm stunned, where did that even come from, it was so random. "Really Kristen?" the voice in my head, "That was ridiculous, how is she going to help you when you share crap like that, tell her why you're here, tell her about the memories!" I look at Rosie, her name is Rosalie, but I guess everyone calls her Rosie. I look at her unsure of what to say or how to start. Sensing my hesitancy she gently asks, "Were you in danger?" Without thinking I immediately reply "No, not really, I mean, well..." I stop, I'm not feeling good, I feel sick. She looks at me through her big glasses and in her thick accent she shares, "For me, my childhood wasn't safe, it was dangerous, there was danger at home, abuse." She pauses and asks me again, "Were you in danger?"

Feeling nervous, I try to stay in adult mode, keeping it together as I wrestle with my answer. "I mean I don't know if it was danger, I mean I guess..." I hesitate again as my stomach knots up, only this time I force myself to share, "I don't know how this works or if I should tell you this right off the bat, but I'm pretty sure my dad molested me, that my dad sexually abused me." Shocking myself, I start shaking and I have to ask to use the bathroom again.

I run, barely making it, I'm sick, diarrhea, throwing up, shaking, sick. I'm crying and freaking out, all of the years of hiding from my reality in addiction and all along there may have been a reason. All along maybe it wasn't me just being a big fricken loser. I think of the question, was I in danger? "Yes, Kristen, you were." I try to compose myself but I can't. After what seems like hours but is really just a few minutes, Rosie gently taps on the door and asks if I'm okay. I'm not, only I answer "Yes, I'll be right out. "She tells me, like before; to take my time and I listen as she walks back to her office.

I don't know why I'm so upset, it's strange, I've been having these memories from the time I first found out that I was pregnant with Jordan, but it's almost like I'm surprised. Maybe saying it out loud made it more real than I was expecting, I'm not sure. I don't understand my own feelings, I'm not sad or depressed, I don't think I'm mad, maybe confused. I guess I'm confused, I've never said it out loud, I've never told anyone until now.

I think back to when I was a teenager trying to tell my mom, that was the last time I could remember talking about it and even then it was confusing, I felt ashamed and unsure. I finally said it, as an adult I was finally able to tell my truth, to say it and not be shamed or told that I was crazy. It was out, out in the open now and it was just as scary and uncomfortable as I imagined. I think "My dad molested me," was probably the most horrible thing I would ever say, the most horrible thing any woman would ever say, I start sobbing again uncontrollably.

Pulling myself together, I rinse my face with cold water, wondering what happens now, what's next. I blot my face dry with some tissue and check myself in the mirror before opening the bathroom door. I walk back to the office where Rosie sits waiting for me, trying my best not to fall apart again. I sit wanting to explain, "I'm sorry, I've just been having these thoughts and these awful memories and I've been pushing them aside for so long, I've never really told anyone." I take a deep breath and try to relax. It's funny but I feel so free, actually for the first time in a long time I feel relieved as if things will finally get better. The therapist, my therapist now, is so kind and caring, she smiles and reassures me, "You're going to be okay, you're going to get through this." The strangest part is that for the first time in a lifetime, I actually believe her.

I string together some other things about my dad, things that have been bothering me, other reasons I have to believe that he's guilty of sexual abuse. There's a work party I went to, just me and my dad, I was a teenager and after in the car, he was too touchy-feely. Of course the boob issues and the sports bras, years of hiding myself from him, while at the same time thinking he is a loving and caring father. I share a bit about feeling like the mistress and the fact that he never lets anyone know that he's with me, hiding me like a secret.

All of a sudden there are a million things, things coming to me that I hadn't thought of in years. It's all so disturbing. Heartbroken, the fact that he never said a word about Katie and I fighting before her wedding. I didn't attend my Baby Sister's Wedding and my father never even acknowledged it, not a word. So horrible, I couldn't fathom it. As a parent, if it were my children, I would insist that they patch things up, insist that missing an important event like that was unacceptable, something they would regret for the rest of their lives. As a parent, aren't you responsible to help mediate differences between your children? Wouldn't any parent do their best to encourage apologies and reconciliation, anything to help? I listen to myself as I speak, "My dad did absolutely nothing and what's worse, he never even mentioned it."

Rosie listens patiently, from time to time asking a question about what I've said or how something made me feel, never judging or adding her opinions. Speaking openly about my dad I really don't need anyone to explain it, the more I talk, the more I recognize on my own how strange our relationship is. I start to feel angry that I allowed it for so long. It bothered me for years and I thought it was okay, again I thought my dad was a loving and caring father. I stop myself, I need to stop now, it hurts, I feel crushed. I love him.

I look at my phone for the time, I've been here forever and I need to go, I promised my mom, I would meet her and the kids at swim lessons. Rosie and I discuss sexual abuse and some identifying signs for a few minutes and she suggests a book that will help me called, "The Courage to Heal." We set another appointment and she walks me to the door, telling me I can call anytime if I need her and then sends me off with a hug. She's so real and so normal, I feel excited to have found her knowing that she will definitely be able to help me.

I get in the car completely obsessed. Now that I'm at this point, I need facts, details, more information, I want to talk to my sisters, I have to know if my dad did anything to them. I call Taylor, my half-sister first, she wasn't even biologically my dad's, she would have been the most likely target. An awful thought, I'm bothered at myself for thinking it. After one ring my call goes straight to voicemail, I know by how quickly it happened she sent me there, not wanting to talk to me. I try to ignore the hurt, it's how she's always treated me but for some reason no matter how long it's been I feel a twinge of sadness. I'm never important enough for her to answer. I leave a brief message, a few niceties and a basic "Can we get together?" hoping that she'll call me back.

Katie's next but as I pull up her number I have a change of heart. I'm second guessing myself again, in my head I start doubting that my dad would ever touch her, beautiful Katie Girl, the baby, the sweetest most gentle child, he wouldn't, would he? As it drifts through my mind, I realize how screwed up my thinking is, was she above being molested because of her age or disposition? She was above being molested and I wasn't. Why did I think like that? It's crazy, I didn't deserve to be molested, no one did. I force myself to shake the thoughts and stick to task, deciding that I'd wait for Taylor to call me back and leave well enough alone with my other sister. We haven't talked since our fall out before her wedding anyway, would she even take my call, let alone be honest with me?

Desperate, I sit in the car and make a list of friends and neighbors that have known me through the years, people who might remember my relationship with my dad, if there was anything out of the ordinary, something I may have shared or that they may have seen that might not have been normal. I'm on a mission to find out whatever I can, a detective on a case, determined to gather evidence against my suspect. Only the suspect is my dad. Pained for a moment, it passes; I know I have to get to the bottom of this. In addition to opening my investigation, I order the book Rosie recommended from Amazon and download it onto my iPhone. She believes it will help me understand more about what I'm thinking and feeling, what I'm going through.

Beyond that, I'm hopeful there are strategies to help me get through it. Regardless, I'm dying to read it. I think ahead and plan on carving out time tonight, after dinner and baths, once I get the kids to sleep. I start the car wondering if I'm crazy as I quickly jot down another friend's name on my list of people to call. Crazy or not, someone had to know something. Crazy I guess, why did I need anyone else to validate what I believed happened to me? I will for myself to stop thinking about it and get into "Mama Mode," as I head down to the beach to meet my Mom and kids.

Swinging through Starbucks on my way I pick up an Iced Coffee and head to Murray Callan Swim School. I'm about ten minutes later than I thought which puts my mom and kids already in the pool and the lessons underway, the perfect opportunity to spy on everyone and see how they're doing. I love to watch the kids but once they see me it's impossible, so I walk around the building, push through the bushes and press my face up to the window. Peering in I find my mom and both kids, they're with a Swim Instructor, the two adults are waist deep in the pool taking turns sending Jordan and Ryder back and forth to each other under the water. My heart melts, they're amazing, they're so little and able to hold their breath, they're doing so well. I watch my mom too, she looks so happy and relaxed, so comfortable, it's not how I remember her. I was worried it would be too much for her to take them both, but she's fine, in fact, she looks like she's actually enjoying it.

I think about how I'm going to tell my mom about my dad as I watch the three of them in the pool, how she'll react, what she'll say. I remember her reaction when I tried to tell her before and I feel sad. I guess she did what she thought was right at the time, she would never think it was possible for my dad to do anything to me, but now? What would she think now? All of a sudden I'm sobbing again. Uncontrollably, like earlier at the therapists. I can't stop. All of this is too much.

Watching my mom with Ryder and Jordan, it hits me that this is what it would be like if I relapsed. Devastating it all plays out in my head. If I started using alcohol or drugs again I would lose everything. I would lose my precious family and my mom would be raising my kids. I feel desperate even thinking about it, I wouldn't be able to see them, I wouldn't be able to be with my own children, I most likely wouldn't even be allowed near them. I watch as they swim, tears streaming down my cheeks.

They're splashing around now, happy and having fun, so full of joy and laughter and here I am completely engrossed in all of this garbage from the past. I wonder again if I should just let it go, forget about it, the past and everything about it, they're triggers for sure, all of it could trip me up. I couldn't afford to let this ruin me; I couldn't imagine what would happen to all of us if I messed up. Like playing with fire, maybe my dad was right, maybe I was opening a huge can of worms. Can I just forget it all though, move forward like things were? Without hesitating, I know I can't.

I look again at my mom, composing myself, she's in her sixties now, I don't think she'd make it through again, too brutal, too sad and heart-wrenching, exhaustive, she'd be trying to find me, get me sober and raising two toddlers. She couldn't do it. My poor kids too, they didn't deserve a life without me, not if I could help it. I never want them to see me other than I am now, strong and stable the mother they needed and loved. I can't imagine them having to see me drunk or stoned, strung out, an eye-opener that cut to the heart, I wasn't sure of anything more than the fact that I needed to maintain my sobriety no matter what. I sit in the grass for a minute, reflecting on my life.

It's funny but for the first time, instead of feeling scared and powerless I actually feel strong and in control, I don't feel a draw to drugs. Maybe purging myself of years of carrying around the dark and dreary secret about my dad had freed me. Whatever it was I feel it, I feel so strongly that I never want to use drugs again; the fascination with them is gone. I don't feel that threat, as hard as it is to believe, my desire was lifted. My desire to use alcohol and drugs was gone. That person too, I don't know her anymore, it isn't me.

This is me, the wife, the mother, the sober woman with a sense of self-worth, I deserve this life and my family deserves this life. Nothing from my past is worth what I have now. I'm grateful to be alive, especially when so many others aren't. I never thought I would be able to say that about heroin, that the desire would be completely gone, for me, from the very start, "heroin had me by the balls; I knew I had sold my soul to the devil."

Thinking back to the first time, I remember being scared of heroin, beyond scared really. I had heard too much about it, too many people were overdosing, people I knew, gone too soon. I remember thinking to myself, "Don't do it, stay away from it." As much as a drug addict and lowlife as I was and as bad as things would get, deep down I didn't really want to be a statistic, I didn't really want to die. The first time I used heroin, I knew in my mind that it could be a death sentence; I literally knew I might die and I did it anyway. We all knew it, all of the drug addicts in my circle knew, all of us aware that each time any of us used heroin it could be our last. It didn't seem to matter. For me, I guess I thought like everyone does, that it wouldn't happen to me.

Hours after spending the day in a Mexican Prison where any number of terrible things could have happened, life went right back to normal for me. There was no epiphany, no miraculous change or desire to do anything different or to be better. Instead, Cameron and I raced up the freeway to "The Shooting Gallery," my apartment, wasted on pills, alcohol, and veins full of meth. With our own arsenal of drugs from the pharmacy in Tijuana, we would have been content to shoot up our own concoctions and drink ourselves into oblivion, but our friends showed up, convincing friends with heroin, everything changed.

I was definitely hesitant at first but enticed by the idea of something new, I was ready for a change, ready for what would be considered the next level. I had been using the same old drugs for years, so I convinced myself that I was ready for the "Wow Factor," that heroin promised. The allure of it and the high it offered, along with the little value I placed on myself and my life, when combined with the peer pressure of my group, I was left in a precarious situation. More than intrigued, I watched as the visitors pulled out a baggie full of this brown, murky substance and placed some on a spoon. Mesmerized, I watched as everyone took turns using, and then passing the heroin around.

Worried, I hesitate as it comes to Cameron and me. I looked on as Cameron went first, tying off his arm, then balancing the small brownish mass on a spoon while holding the lighter directly underneath. Taking a cotton ball, he soaked it and then sucked the muddy looking liquid into a syringe. Finding a willing vein, he slowly inserted the tip of the needle until a tiny bit of blood popped up, then slowly pushed it the rest of the way in and waited.

My heart was racing and I was definitely undecided as he pulled the tie off from his arm and handed it to me. "It's not too late to say no," my self-talk kept reminding me. Ignoring myself, I tied it around my arm while he started the process over again. I was next, I watched the flame under the spoon and the murky liquid melt, feeling fearful at the thought that I could die in a few minutes.

What was wrong with me? I barely knew these people and here I was about to shoot some disgusting looking liquid from god only knows where into my body just because they were all doing it? In a constant state of self-destruction, why would I hate myself enough to take a chance on losing my life? I try not to think about it as Cameron hands me the same needle they've all used, now full and while trying to ignore the constant pleas in my head not to do it, I slowly shoot heroin into my arm for the first time.

Within seconds I was euphoric, dreamy and light. Like never before, I didn't have a care in the world. I felt this strange sensation of total well-being and freedom that I had never experienced in my life. I instantly felt good about everything, including myself. The rush of euphoria was the best feeling I had ever experienced. I had rarely if ever felt joy or happiness in my life and suddenly with heroin, I had those feelings and sensations. I think that heroin actually changed my thinking, drugs, and alcohol numbed everything where I actually believed heroin made me feel happy, joyful, even ecstatic. I was immediately in love with the feelings I was experiencing and since it didn't kill me, my fear of using heroin was gone and I was instantly hooked.

The love that I had for heroin was real and instantaneous, shooting it was on a whole other level and in that moment, with my very first hit, I was a Heroin Addict. That day, it literally took over my life, every aspect of it. Heroin, in my distorted way of looking at things, made my worthless life worth living.

I catch my breath; it was hard to remember it all. I try to put it out of my mind, looking forward to being with my kids and changing my focus. I was so sick of the past and thinking about my dad, I hoped it would all be over soon. I push myself up off of the grass and peer into the window again. Swim School is over and the pool is empty. I walk back around the building to the entrance and head in to help my mom shower and dress Jordan and Ryder. As I do, I feel my phone vibrating in my bag, I forgot to turn it back on after the therapy session. Thinking it's probably Chase checking in on us, wondering when we'll be home, I pull it out to see. I was wrong; it's a text from my dad. Without reading it, I put my phone back in my purse and keep walking. I try to ignore it, I try to put it out of my mind but my stomach knots up and my heart starts racing. I pull my phone out and read his text.

POPS

How did the therapy thing go?

·Chapter Thirteen·

"This is a bad idea," I think to myself. "I should have asked her on the phone and been done with it," I'm already self-sabotaging. I want to stay calm, be composed, professional, I'm here to take care of business, but inside I'm a nervous wreck. I'm heading into a Coffee Shop around the corner from my house to meet my Sister Taylor. She returned my call after several days and agreed to meet me here. She lives about fifteen miles east, but big surprise, she's heading west afterward to her mom's house or I guess my dad's.

"My" Dad sounds strange now that he's a villain. Now that he's a villain, he seems more mine than hers. I don't know why he never was hers, not really, he was her step-father, and she had her own dad. Her dad wasn't really in the picture though, I mean, my dad gave her away at her wedding. Step-father sounds creepy now..., "Oh Kristen, stop, you're overthinking," I warn myself.

I find a table in the corner and take a seat, hoping it's out of the way and private enough for our topic. I'm watching the door, thinking of ways to bring it up, like, "By the way," or "Do you remember," only they don't seem right. Taylor walks in and pushes her sunglasses onto her head, I watch her for a minute as she looks around for me.

Confident, she looks sure of herself, I wished I looked confident. She's cute, casual in jeans and a sweatshirt; she sees me and heads over. I stand up and we hug, but I'm not sure why. In my head, I'm thinking, "This will most likely be the last time I see her or hug her, our last conversation." I hug her tight and we sit down as the waitress comes over. She orders something fancy, "Doppio," explaining, "It's Italian for Double Espresso," and I get an Iced Coffee, explaining, "It's English for ordinary." We laugh, light for a moment, like old friends, only we're not. "Our last laugh," I think as the waitress goes for our coffee.

There's small talk, weather, traffic, we stay neutral until the coffee comes. I wait for the waitress to leave, and without any set-up or explanation, blurt out, "Look, Taylor, I'm pretty sure my dad molested me." My heart hurts as I say it, I feel like I'm betraying him, I'm a traitor sharing classified information. I watch my sister sip her showy little coffee, wondering how something so small can be a double, while I wait for her response.

Superior, at least to me, she raises one of her perfectly groomed eyebrows and looks across the table, "What are you looking for Kristen?" she asks coldly. I watch her, looking for a sign, something in her expressions or body language, anything that will give me the answers I'm so desperate for. There's nothing. Stoically, she continues, "You won't get validation from me. You may have those memories, but I guarantee you that nothing happened to me!" She stares at me almost defiantly then asks, "Have you talked to him about it? Have you asked him?" She pushes her cup and saucer forward and puts her napkin on the table, she's getting agitated and I wonder if it's a clue as she glares at me and continues, "Because if you haven't, I'm telling him. I'm telling him on Father's Day, that gives you a week."

I sit quietly, not sure what to think. If my dad didn't do anything to her, why is she threatening to ruin Father's Day for the man? Why would she want to hurt him like that? Besides, if nothing happened to her, it's not hers to tell. Why would she want to be the one to do it? I'm shocked that she would be so cold-hearted and ruthless, so threatening. Oddly, she adds, "I believe you believe something happened to you, but nothing like that happened to me. I can tell you 100% that never happened to me." I look at her wondering why she's saying it again if it's some kind of subliminal confession.

"I'm not sure I believe you," I reply, "I mean, I just think all of those years, it was you, Taylor, you were the one wanting to sleep with me. You were the one there alone. I was at my mom's, I mean, why were you so afraid? You made me think it was me, needing you all of those years. I think you needed me, you needed to sleep with me so nothing would happen to you, at least if I was there." I'm mad now, I think she's lying. Am I mad because she's lying or because she might be telling the truth? Her truth, at least what she's saying is her truth, would mean my dad only picked me, I'm back to the ruined one, my dad only ruined me. I was worthless to him. I silently tell myself to stop, to focus, stay present.

"You're crazy Kristen," you'll never change, always starting trouble. Nothing happened to me, stop trying to convince me it did!" My sister's cheeks and neck turn pink as she speaks, she's definitely agitated. Obsessed with the truth, I think her reaction must mean something. "I think you're in denial," I say it calmly, sensing our meeting is coming to an end.

I'm right, she's leaving. Did I hit a nerve and she's about to cave, she can't take it, is she about to let her guard down, why is she leaving, why so quickly? She's been here all of twenty minutes. Taylor, with her cheeks and neck bright red now, gets up and pulls a twenty out of her wallet and throws it on the table. "You don't want to know what I think Kristen." She puts on her sunglasses, reminds me I have until Father's Day to talk to my dad then turns and leaves.

I stay, sitting alone finishing my coffee, trying to make sense of what just happened. Replaying it in my head, I'm overthinking again, wondering whether my sister was being honest or not. Why did it matter? Whether someone else was molested or not shouldn't make a difference, my sister was right, I shouldn't need validation from her or anyone else, why was I looking for it? Why was I always looking to others for validation? Because that's what I've always done? For as long as I can remember I looked to everyone else in my life for approval or validation, never trusting myself or believing that what I thought mattered. Worthless people don't matter and, worthless was how I had always perceived myself.

I thought it was just the old me, the alcoholic, drug addict me, but here I was with almost eight years of sobriety, giving my power away, trying to give my power to my sister, letting her decide, by how she responded, whether or not what I thought to be true was true, whether my memories of being molested were real or not.

The old me and the new me, as much as I want them to be different, are still basically the same. The old me relied on the coping mechanisms of addiction, while the new me was struggling, still trying to figure it out, how to do the more challenging things in life sober. Sure, there have been, in the last several years, a number of things in my life that have helped me feel better about myself or more worthy, I think even feeling loved has changed me, being a wife and a mother, but even in building up my confidence and self-esteem, for whatever reason being around my dad and his family tore all of it down, completely destroying it. Instead of feeling good and self-reliant, I would feel unlovable and worthless again. I didn't know how to be around them in my sobriety and not let that happen.

I try not to cry, thinking about it. I don't blame them for my addiction, I can't blame anyone, I know I have to take responsibility for myself and what happened. I do think there are people in our lives, at least there are in mine, that for whatever reason have the power to make me feel small, or I guess, I give them the power to make me feel small, however you want to look at it.

For me, from the time I was a child, it was definitely my dad and his new family. Believing I didn't matter to him, along with how he allowed his wife and my sisters to treat me, eroded any chance for me to have a healthy self-concept. My step-brother too, being sent away and how I viewed my role in my dad's family after he left, all of it combined, made me feel expendable and unimportant. I learned how to numb it all from an early age by self-medicating. Now self-medicating wasn't an option. So how do I handle them now?

I wipe away a few small tears and put on my sunglasses. Finishing my coffee, the allowable addiction, I think back to my days of using heroin. The memories of actually being a Heroin Addict are painful and scary, the things I did, what I succumbed to in order to feed that addiction, beyond dehumanizing. For a brief period of time though, when I used heroin, I wasn't small or inferior, I was happy, I fit in, For the first time in my life, I felt normal, the way I perceived everyone else was feeling. Heroin use, like a benevolent gift, let me experience all of those good feelings I had always longed for.

The downsides of Heroin Addiction were horrendous though. From the onset, I knew that I had literally sold my soul to the Devil, but to me, feeling good about myself and feeling happy, even if it was fleeting, was worth it. Heroin immediately took over my entire existence in exchange for a few hours here and there of not just numbing my pain and hurt, but making me feel good, excited and alive. The exchange cruel and costly left me desperate and willing to do anything for my next fix. The exchange, with all of its "costs," and "consequences," included possibly dying. I knew from the start, I would most likely die from a Heroin Overdose and, at some point that became okay with me.

The apartment on Park Avenue or "The Shooting Gallery," was already a Drug House, my instant addiction to heroin only made it worse. Dark and seedy, there were blankets over the windows and ratty furniture, collected from alleys in Pacific Beach, all haphazardly placed around the tiny living room. There was an old mattress on a cheap metal frame in the bedroom, complete with a never made bed and dirty sheets, the floor around it constantly covered with clothes and towels needing to be washed. Drug paraphernalia and drugs sat out openly on tables, while a continuous stench of pot and stale cigarette smoke layered the walls and ceiling, filling the stuffy, closed up apartment with a heavy, unpleasant odor. The overflowing and dirty ashtrays combined with the trash piling up everywhere made it almost unbearable. Home sweet home, the thought of it was repulsive, but that's where I lived, where my addiction thrived and druggies from all over San Diego came to use and hang out.

I started using heroin without giving up anything else, I just added it to all of the drugs I was already doing. Heroin became my first choice, but I was still a huge Meth Addict, constantly popped, snorted and shot a million pills, smoked weed, and cigarettes, drank heavily and had a needle obsession. I loved the needles. I loved shooting up, primarily heroin and meth, but I also experimented with shooting other concoctions, things like crushed pills and alcohol, or whatever I could find and put into liquid form. Any part of my body that dared to expose a vein was game.

Things had been bad for me for a long time; I was stealing, cheating and lying to everyone, just to get by. I was still being pulled over and sometimes arrested, depending on what they'd find and how wasted I was. My Dad's rental property was under police surveillance and all of the neighbors were sick of me and the twenty-four-hour drug activity going on in my apartment. Most had called my dad, their landlord, who shared with me years later that they were all, constantly complaining, and begging him to get rid of me. When that didn't work, they'd call the police who were already there watching the apartment, waiting for the opportunity or evidence to raid us.

It seemed like everyone normal hated me, including my parents. My dad ignored me, acting like I was a stranger or worse, invisible. My mom wouldn't talk to me unless I was calling her to go to rehab. Her phone would ring and she'd answer, "Are you okay?" Are you ready to go to rehab Kristen?" when I didn't immediately respond "Yes," she'd hang up.

Life around me was filled with dark and desperate people, squalor and filthy circumstances became normal to me. Outside of the initial Heroin Rush or several minutes of euphoria and the few hours shrouded in a sensation of calm and well-being, the rest of my life was in shambles. I felt heavy, weighed down, hopeless. My mind was clouded over with thoughts that nothing mattered except heroin. I spent hours convincing myself that I didn't care, but I did. My own voice deep within, faint like a whisper would appear out of nowhere like it had a million times before and, ask "Why? What is wrong with you?

I fought to ignore it, just like I always did, but the question would linger. No matter how horrible things were, I would use heroin and for a time believe that everything was okay. My Heroin Addiction convinced me that no matter what I had to go through or how bad things were that once it was flowing through my body it would rescue me, make me feel better, take care of me. It was a liar.

Most drugs I could go without to a degree, either that or substitute with something else, at least for a few days before the withdrawals came. Crystal Meth, weed, pills, even the alcohol, but with heroin, I was a slave. With heroin, you cannot go without. Within a few hours, I'd have the shakes, start throwing up, I'd ache and feel sick, then diarrhea. Heroin Addicts call it "Getting Well," and when I needed to "Get Well," I would do absolutely anything at that point to get heroin, anything. I was so desperate and depraved, a totally whacked out junkie that I resorted to doing sexual favors for money. I had used this tactic in relationships from the time I became sexually active, but now I was willing to sell my body to men I wasn't involved with.

It started with a perverted friend, willing to give me money initially just for sex, but over time it included sex with his friends too and then letting others watch. Repulsed, I hated all of it, but the more I was willing to do, the more money I would get. Enslaved to heroin, when I needed it, I'd call him, delivering myself to his house for $100. Driving to his place in Pacific Beach, the area I loved and grew up in, only made it more heartbreaking. I'd have to go in and close the door behind me, knowing that normal life, friends, and familiarity were all just outside; while I let people use my body for money. Humiliating, all of it was so disgusting and degrading, sickening. Lying there letting someone have sex with you for money was the most disturbing of all of the things I did, the shame and emptiness left me even more lifeless. I'd try not to cry, pretending I was anywhere but there, wishing I could be different.

Mentally it was so brutal; I don't think I could have felt more loathsome or worthless afterward. Many of these men were people I knew; some were friends, guys my same age. I was nothing but garbage to them, dressing afterward, and then putting my hand out for the money I was always so sad and repulsed. I'd reason, it was that or withdrawals and to me, in my sickness and addiction, withdrawals were worse.

I'd leave, trying to block it out of my mind, driving a few streets over to my Mom's House, where I would sneak in and shower. I wouldn't see or talk to any of them again until I needed money. Every few days the "Pervert," would call to see if I was needy, ready to come over again. I wanted so badly to be able to say no, but I couldn't I always needed the cash, I was always desperate. Over time it never got easier, I just got better at blocking it all out.

Desperate and Junkie are one and the same. You'll never meet a junkie that isn't desperate. To "Get Well," is what every Heroin User is after and, heroin doesn't discriminate. Most people have an antiquated idea that addicts are all lowlife scumbags, losers, choosing to waste their life away on drugs and getting high, but it isn't true. Even completely normal, decent, mainstream people, once they start using heroin, will do anything when they need to "Get Well," and anything is an understatement. Women sell themselves to men, men sell themselves to men, women to women, beyond desperate for a fix, people will murder, rob banks, hold up stores, steal, lie and cheat, even their own family and friends. There are no boundaries; a person who needs heroin will do practically anything it takes to get it.

Unfortunately, in my life, my past and some of the things I did carry over in complicated ways. With my husband, if I want or need something I sometimes barter with him. I know many people do. It isn't right and it's definitely self-deprecating, but I do it. My friends too, some of them in order to get money, to get their way in a decision, new clothes or shoes, a new bag. One of my wealthier friends, when going through her divorce would do favors regularly for her ex-husband in exchange for large amounts of cash. She "made" thousands of dollars while she waited for her Divorce Settlement. It isn't right, but it happens. It's real and it's an issue, at least for me. To my friend, if she needed a thousand dollars, she knew how to get it. For me, in my addiction, one hundred dollars was what I needed. It was enough for heroin and at the time, that's all I thought I was worth.

Along with my deplorable living situation, being monitored by the police, disowned by my parents and, selling myself for drugs, I started experiencing a lot of health issues, primarily respiratory and breathing problems. Already worried about dying from a Heroin Overdose, the health issues really scared me. I started having uncontrollable anxiety and paranoia. I knew that I was ruining my body, I rarely ate and when I did it was always cheap, fast food or junk food. I rarely, if ever, had anything healthy or live like salad or fruit. I had been using drugs and alcohol for over nine years, smoking cigarettes and pot for the same amount of time and rarely exercised or went out for fresh air.

On occasion, I would ride my bike so Baby, my PitBull could run, but she was pregnant now so even that fell to the wayside. In my early twenties, I was slowly killing myself. Using heroin and meth together, smoking and taking things that affected my breathing and heart rate were taking their toll, but I wasn't able to stop. Constantly short of breath and fatigued, I also had drug-induced sleep apnea. Not sleeping well, I was often disoriented, and had started falling asleep all of the time. The sleeping wouldn't have been a problem except when I slept; I stopped breathing and most of the time I wasn't in a safe environment to sleep. Trying to remedy the situation, I would use more and more meth after the heroin wore off in hopes of staying awake.

Over the next few months, getting worse and experiencing more and more side effects and reactions, I still couldn't stop. Sometimes shooting up would cause me to throw-up or I'd be nauseous, my entire body would itch, I'd be constipated for days, drowsy and lethargic, constantly passing out to the point that I couldn't function and almost always struggling to breathe. On several occasions, I honestly thought I was dying. If I stopped using heroin, even for a few hours, the withdrawal effects were even worse, agitation, tremors, shakes, diarrhea, vomiting, bone, and muscle aches, chills. They were extreme, unbearable really, either using or trying not to use, I never felt well anymore. So I kept using. I looked and felt horrible.

Over the next several months, my heroin use was insatiable, that and meth. Not feeling strong enough to venture to Mexico, I had to find and use drug dealers for everything I needed. My habits weren't cheap and I was always dirt poor, broke. I continued to do whatever it took to maintain my addiction. I could feel myself going under.

I think I was expecting my "Rock Bottom" to just show up, make itself known. Like an out of town guest, one that was coming in just to rescue me, clean me up, hug me and tell me I was going to be okay, piece me back together and show me how to have a good life. I was ready, looking forward to it, I wanted a good life, I wanted to be normal. Tired and not feeling well, I didn't know how much more I could take. Sad and broken, I waited, but while I waited, I used.

During this time, I bought a sack of heroin that was dark brown and thick, strange looking, at first I was apprehensive but I didn't have a choice, I couldn't care or worry, I needed it. Not knowing where it came from was the least of my problems, I didn't have a needle. Rummaging through my car at an out of the way, run down gas station, I managed to find one in an old make-up bag I kept in the trunk of my car.

The make-up bag, a decoy for hidden drugs, was filled with old blush, powder, and lipstick. The needle, buried underneath was dull, maybe too dull. I put it in my backpack, with everything else and went into the Women's Restroom, locking the door behind me. Pulling out what was left of my kit from The Needle Exchange Program, along with the needle and the scary heroin; I start melting it on the spoon and pulled out a cotton ball. Filling the syringe with a giant thick shot, I looked at myself in the rusted out, graffiti etched mirror and can't believe my eyes.

Barely recognizing myself, I was alarmed. I had been consistently shooting heroin, from several different sources, into my neck for the past few days. My neck was swollen, black and blue, covered with holes that mapped out my latest injections. The needle I had, old and blunt from overuse would only add to the awful mess on my neck. Still part of The Needle Exchange Program, this was all I had until the next time they came. I look at myself again, thinking about how bad I had become. I actually carried a card around that identified me as an active drug addict and someone who was allowed to carry needles.

Every Tuesday and Thursday, I would line up with all of the other drug addicts for my supplies. Like a Food Truck, full of Junkie Provisions, it pulled up on schedule every week in a seedier part of Downtown, San Diego, distributing everything you needed to shoot up, everything, but the drugs. You'd get five clean, sharp needles, cotton, little dishes, tie-offs, water, a purified tube, a shooting up kit and rubbing alcohol, all for free. They also tested for HIV and Hep C.

Standing in line for my kit, strung out, scabbed over and disoriented, I would look around and think that I wasn't as bad as all of the other addicts. Delusional, I was exactly like them, maybe even worse. When it was my turn at the window, I'd look in at the nurse practitioner, the same one every week, she was kind and pleasant, so clean, she'd smell like soap, and she was sober. I would look in, feeling so beaten down and dirty, wishing that I was clean and sober, or at least clean. I would feel embarrassed, taking my handouts with my head down, sad and lonesome.

I look back to the mirror and puff out my cheeks several times looking for a good vein, one down the side of my neck, less visible. Staring into my eyes, they're vacant, hollow like I'm not even there. My heart sinks, my stomach drops, I make a promise to myself to do something, something to stop, I need to stop, I don't want to die. Feeling crushed that I've allowed this to happen to myself, I can hardly breathe. As I make another empty promise that I'll stop after this, I jab the dull needle into my neck and wait to register, for the drop of blood to appear, and then push the muddy looking heroin into my body. Just like that, I switch into euphoria, happiness, I don't care anymore, no one cares.

Heading home, I wondered if Cameron would be there. Cameron and I were on and off, still undefined, more friends with benefits than anything else. My truest and most constant companion continued to be Baby, my Pitbull. I loved her, the most loyal dog, she was always with me at the apartment and whenever I could take her along, she was all I really I had. Living in a Tweaker Pad surrounded by the constant commotion and the flow of drug addicts and drugs, I still felt alone. I always had an emptiness or void.

Sometimes when it was bad, I would go to Baldwin, my old school and workplace. I had lifelong friends there, people who cared about me. I'd be able to just visit and to be with normal people, they never let me down, not once. No matter how bad I looked or in what state I was in, I was always welcomed and loved, which made me feel worse. More lonesome and sad that I wasn't like them, a part of their lives, instead, separated from all of the good people in my life, living on my own as a drug addict.

This was a rough time for me. Finally, at one of my lowest points, my dad decided to kick me out of the apartment at his rental property. I came home one day to find all of my things being carried out to the alley, some going into a dumpster and others the garage. My dad, like always, didn't say a word; he just kept working, helping some hired hand carry my belongings downstairs. I was so mad; I started screaming, "What are you doing? Why are you doing this? What's going on? Dad, why would you do this to me? Where am I supposed to go?"

My dad, angry and frustrated started yelling at me and calling me names, screaming that he was sick of me, that I was a "Low-life piece of shit." My own father was calling me names, hating me. Stabbed to the heart, I felt sick as he continued telling me "He never wanted to see me again and that I was ruining his life, I wasn't allowed there. If he saw me or if any of the neighbors saw me they were going to call the police." There was no offer of help, rehab, taking me to a hospital or an intake facility; there was no love or caring. I was a twenty-year-old Heroin and Meth Addict that could die and be gone from his life forever and these would be his parting words. It wasn't about me though, like always with my dad, it was all about him.

This was my father, the man I grew up calling dad, my hero, my guardian and protector, putting me out on the streets, not really concerned or bothered with what might happen to me. I couldn't believe it. I wanted to die, so badly wishing I was already dead so I didn't have to live through this. "I would be better off dead. I deserved it, I deserved to be kicked out, I was worthless," all started flooding my mind as I faced being homeless again. I took Baby and we sat in my car, which like everything else in my life was falling apart and not working. I was sad and angry, not sure what to do. I drove around the block and parked, waiting several hours, I sat in the car with my dog and wrote poems on old napkins to pass the time, poems about death and how worthless I was.

Wanting to be sure my dad was gone before I went back over there; I waited until later in the evening, to return. Leaving my car, I skateboarded over to the now vacant and dark apartment, where I broke in to shower and sleep. Cold and uncomfortable, I slept on the floor with Baby, my pregnant dog, as I started to go through withdrawals and cried myself to sleep.

It was a mission for my dad to keep me out and since I had nowhere to go I wasn't going without a fight. I'd leave in the daytime, trying to sneak in only at night to shower and rest, but somehow, my dad knew. He actually boarded up all of the windows and the door so I couldn't get in. Using a hammer and nails, he put huge pieces of plywood over everything to try and keep me out. The first night I slept in my now broken down car with Baby, cold miserable and alone. I gave my last twenty dollars to a drug addict who promised to bring me drugs if I'd share with him. He never came back.

I had nothing. It was here, this was it, my "Rock Bottom." It was harsh and inhumane, I wanted to die. I took a cab to my mom's, ditching it at a Stop Sign a few blocks from her house. Baby, pregnant and me sick, going through withdrawals, I feigned having to throw up as I opened the door and jumped out, hopping on my skateboard while Baby ran, we made our way through the streets and alleys, losing the cab and making our way to the front of my mom's building. It broke my heart that my dog had to suffer because of me, making her run like that when she was pregnant was criminal. I wasn't good enough for her, I didn't deserve her. I felt so bad. My dad was right, "I was a worthless piece of shit," kept going through my head as we went upstairs to my mom's condo.

My phone, sitting on the table, in the now packed out Coffee Shop is buzzing, so much that it's moving across the tabletop on its own. Coming back to the present, I can't believe how bad I used to be, how I survived. It was, the "Rock Bottom" I had been waiting for. I can remember the feelings, the adrenaline rush of trying to ditch the cab, the heartbreak of dragging my dog along and the tiny ray of hope that started to appear as I skateboarded towards help.

I think of my mom's face when I showed up at her door, her tears of joy, knowing it was time, that I was there to surrender, ready after all of the years of anguish and heartache to go to rehab. My mom never gave up on me, even in that moment, I was loved by her, she took me in and I showered and cleaned up while she made all of the arrangements for me to get the help I so desperately needed. The contrast of how my dad treated me in my addiction is shocking. I think about him, throwing me out on the streets, his own child, not offering a lifeline of any sort, instead, shaming me and making me feel more worthless than ever. Why didn't I remember that? Why didn't I ever see it?

I pick up my phone, on vibrate, it's alive with activity. There are several text messages and a few missed calls. Chase, of course, checking on me, he's always concerned, especially if I'm around my dad or sisters. I quickly text him back, letting him know that everything's fine and that I'll fill him in later. Another is my mom who's watching the kids, most likely ready for me to return; there are a couple of texts from friends and, lastly a call and text from my dad.

My heart sinks; I think to Taylor who was headed over there, she wouldn't, would she? My mind races as I wonder if she rushed over there and shared our conversation. She told me I had until Father's Day though. I try to relax, knowing its days away, but grapple with how she, who supposedly has nothing to do with any of this, is now in control of when I confront my dad. How did that happen? I'm annoyed thinking about it, sad, thinking about my dad and our past.

I sit in the coffee shop literally remembering how awful my dad was and still wrestle with whether he's a loving and caring father or a child molester. It's all so confusing, I have memories of him taking me to the beach, for bike rides, trips to Sea World, The Zoo, taking the little train at Balboa Park a million times, the Merry-go-round, memories of him being a fun laid back parent, but they're intermittent, scattered now. That's not how I think of him anymore. My thoughts of him now are ones that make me sad, or sick, confused. His texts to me too, they're unsettling, putting me on edge, I'm almost afraid of them. I stuff my phone in my bag and head home. Regardless, I'm sad, for whatever reason, I'm not ready to say goodbye to my dad, but I have to.

·Chapter Fourteen·

"I just thought it was a dream I guess." I'm sitting across from Rosie, my therapist, wondering what she thinks. She's pretty remarkable, it's only my second visit, but for some reason I trust her. She's thoughtful, taking what I say into consideration before responding. She doesn't tell me how I should think or feel; she doesn't make suggestions on how I should handle things, or what I should do. Instead, she reasons on everything, teaching me how to draw my own conclusions, which of course, is all new to me.

I had just shared what I thought may have been a dream, only it's a disturbing dream of my dad, one where I think he's molesting me. Rosie writes something in her notebook and then asks me if I can remember any other dreams I've had. I think about her question, "Like recent?" I answer, kind of surprised. I wonder what she's after as she explains, "Any dream, it can be from this morning, last week, a year ago, whatever you can come up with." I take a minute trying to think of something.

Outside of the ones I've been having about my dad, I can't think of a single one. It's quiet. Both of us sit comfortably in her small office, Rosie is patiently waiting while my mind, on a mission, rifles through files, memories, my past, searching for anything that might be considered a dream. "I'm not a big dreamer I guess. I've had a million dreams, but I can't remember any right now." Rosie looks at me and asks, "Not one?" I take a deep breath and sit back, exhaling in defeat, "Nope, not one," I say, a little baffled. Rosie smiles, then helps put me at ease, "Don't worry Kristen, most people don't remember their dreams."

Taking a minute for it to sink in, she's right, even when I've had a dream, I don't remember it, I'll wake up and it's vague at best. Within a matter of minutes, it's usually gone and completely forgotten. "So what does it mean?" I ask her. Rosie and I sit and discuss dreams for a minute and then talk about memories. We're doing the "reasoning" thing. We agree, based on our unscientific discussion that a dream doesn't stay with you for a lifetime usually not even a recurring dream, but a memory does.

I think about it, everything we've discussed, the reality of it, hitting me hard. This meant the memories of my dad were definitely memories, not dreams. It was me that tried to turn them into "dreams." They were so real and scary when I first started having them; it was easier for me if I turned them into dreams. If they were dreams, everything was still okay. Dreams protected my dad, in a way, making it acceptable to keep my relationship with him.

Being pregnant for the first time, I just wanted them to go away, I wanted to enjoy my pregnancy, stay happy and positive. It wasn't easy, at the time, so many things kept surfacing, one right after the other, that I was afraid. I would even try to tell them to, "Stop, get out, leave me alone, and go away." I didn't know what else to do. I couldn't accept that it could be a reality, that my dad could have molested me. Over time, no matter what I tried calling them, memories or dreams, they weren't going away. If anything, over time, they only intensified, filling my head constantly.

Talking about it with Rosie, I share this, then add, "The very first time it came up I wanted to tell someone, I wanted help, but I didn't feel that I could. I didn't tell anyone, because I wasn't sure. I mean, part of me was sure, but I had also spent a lifetime doubting myself, so I guess I just started doubting this too." Sympathetic, she asks, "What parts do you doubt Kristen? Do you doubt a part of it, or do you doubt all of it?" I think about her questions. "I don't doubt that my dad stared at my boobs and..." I stop; it's all I can say.

Three years ago, when I was first pregnant with Jordan, and the thoughts started, I really wasn't sure what was real and what wasn't. That's why I kept pushing them down, not telling anyone, but the more I pushed them down, the more memories came up. The memories I shared with Rosie are from my childhood, they're complex, hard to understand, mostly because the ones I have of my dad aren't all bad. It's the combination of memories, throughout my life, that are confusing. My dad's role in my life, especially as an adult was never clear to me, there was always a disconnect in a way. I always thought it was my fault, because of my being an alcoholic, addict, my fault that he avoided me or treated me like I didn't matter, my lifestyle causing him to avoid me. Now, though I was starting to see it differently, why we were disconnected was starting to make sense to me.

During my addiction, I never remember my dad trying to help me. In my memory, he stayed uninvolved. He seemed to disown me in a sense. After I went to rehab though, for whatever reason, he started showing up for things. I didn't understand it, especially after kicking me out of his apartment. Why now? Was what I would think. I remember his presence making me uncomfortable; he made me anxious, our exchanges were always awkward. I was always torn, trying to be happy for his participation, but questioning it. Was he really there for me? I tried to believe that he was, to feel that way, but something in the back of my mind didn't trust it, didn't trust him. Never understanding why I continued to blame myself, thinking there was something wrong with me.

Once I went to my mom and surrendered to rehab, I think both of my parents had a renewed sense of hope that I was finally going to change. I tried to tell myself that maybe there was a shift for my dad and that's why he was taking an interest. I remember feeling like a fraud. I didn't go to my mom's because I wanted to get sober; I was only there because I was out of options. I did it, just like my first intervention, because I had no other choice. It was all I could do at the time.

I had nothing, I was homeless, out of money, I had a pregnant dog and nowhere to go. My mom, who spent the little spare time she had, becoming an expert in addiction and recovery, had at the ready, a list of Detox Centers, Rehab Facilities and Sober Living Houses. She was dialed in on everything that I needed to get help. My mom was prepared; she had my path to sobriety completely mapped out. The trouble was she was the only one ready to go.

It was during my early twenties that I spent, collectively, over a year in and out of dozens of different types of Addiction and Recovery Centers and Facilities. While all of them, and the people running them were promising to help me attain sobriety, there wasn't a single one that I stayed in where I did not use drugs.

Starting at a Detox Center, in Los Angeles, I didn't even have to find drugs, I think in order to help me through withdrawals, the center pumped me with so much "medication" I could barely function. Wanting the patients to keep a journal, I couldn't even write, could hardly walk and was barely coherent enough to participate in the group counseling. They allowed me to have visits from my dog though. In fact, I remember bartering with my mom, willing to go into rehab, as long as she promised to take care of Baby and her puppies.

I think my mom believed that her refusal to find a home for or take care of Baby would get in the way of my sobriety. I will say, my mom did not like animals at all, I remember begging her to get an animal when I was a kid and she said I could get a fish because they die fast. So when I say my mom wasn't an animal person, she really wasn't, but somehow she understood how important that dog was to me. I think too, she had heard that many times addicts viewed their pets as their "one true friend" and that the animal can be particularly important in their overall progress and recovery. So my mom, completely out of her comfort zone and afraid of PitBulls, came with Baby to the Detox Center to visit me.

My mom thought that keeping me from San Diego was the answer, so from the Detox Center, I went to a beautiful house, in a nicer area of Los Angeles. Rehab places are known to be moneymakers, and this one was no exception. Definitely raking it in, my mom was paying top dollar for me to be there, in one of three bunk beds, in one of four bedrooms, sharing a house with a grand total of eighteen women, and all of us were trying to get sober. The optimal word was "trying." Although the fourth bedroom housed a live-in staff member, the idea of that many women under one roof was insanity, especially women in rehab.

Regardless, while I was making my own adjustments, my mom found a couple that was willing to take care of my dog and the puppies, once they arrived. She agreed to pay two-hundred dollars a week, provide anything they needed and would be able to visit whenever she asked. My mom became a little obsessed with it all; maybe feeling in a way that my dog was somehow an extension of me and that she held the keys to whether I did well or not. Because of this belief, my mom would do absolutely anything to make sure Baby and her puppies were cared for and thriving.

Sadly, at the time I wasn't able to recognize the incredible lengths my mother was going to in her efforts to help me. I just took it all for granted, most of my time spent thinking about how and when I would be able to use drugs and alcohol again while my mom was basically killing herself trying to make everything on the outside work. At one point, after the puppies were born, my mom even brought them all up to Los Angeles to see me. I can't even imagine my mom in the car with one dog, let alone a dog and her eight puppies.

There were so many other incidentals involved, things that were costly, time-consuming and completely out of my mom's arena. Taking them for shots and checkups and over time finding homes for all of the puppies was all-consuming. She also took Baby to get fixed when it was all over, going through the surgery and recovery another trying and difficult task. My mom was willing to take all of this on, while consistently staying involved with me and my rehabilitation and working full-time. Whatever it took, my mom would do, if she thought it would help me.

There were moments that I wanted to get clean, but I didn't think I could do it. It always seemed too hard. I didn't know how to deal with all of the feelings. I couldn't handle my reality. In my mind, I think I had come to terms with the fact that I was a drug addict and would always be a drug addict. I couldn't see myself clean or sober, I couldn't picture myself with a normal life or a job, bills and a house, I couldn't picture me as a regular person. I saw myself as a lifelong drug addict; I even pictured myself dying as a drug addict.

Because I could only see myself this way, I didn't bother to put a lot of effort into the programs or recovery. Not wanting it for myself, it would never happen. It didn't matter what anyone did for me or how much they tried to help me, it would always be up to me. It definitely made me sad, again, I'd reflect on my life and wonder why I turned out like this, I knew there had to be something, there had to be a reason. I was so uncomfortable just existing, always suppressing any type of feelings, constantly being ashamed of myself, covering my body in weird ways, going through life worthless and undeserving, whatever was wrong with me, I didn't think it could get fixed.

Talking about feelings and being surrounded by other addicts and alcoholics only made me want to escape, use again, find relief from having to continually think about myself, my life and my issues. It was only a matter of time before I found a friend, one just as half-hearted as I was about being in rehab and the idea of sobriety. This wasn't a good thing. She was court-ordered, for her, it was a Sober Living House or Jail. Both of us with Junkie Instincts were drawn to each other.

We meshed immediately and started hanging out for meals, in between group sessions and other facility activities. With a stolen credit card number we ordered drugs online, waiting at the door for the packages to arrive and got high on "Soma" Muscle Relaxers and "Special K.", or Cat Tranquilizers, which we had researched ahead and known would be undetectable on our drug tests.

Still passing the tests every time, we eventually graduated to outings. Outings, or short periods of time where we were allowed out of the facility, gave us a taste of freedom. With that freedom, the goal was for the patients to get part-time jobs so we could start earning money, and over time, become self-reliant and responsible members of society. Trying to stay above the fray we went to a Restaurant Supply and bought an Industrial Whipped Cream Dispenser and cartridges, huffing them in an alley and hiding the dispenser in a bush around the corner from where we were patients. The high only lasted a few seconds at best, so becoming dismayed by the tremendous efforts and minimal high, we both decided that passing the drug tests no longer mattered and we bolted for real drugs.

Together, we found a Drug Dealer in the area. Like a Secret Power, a Drug Addict attracting another Drug Addict was innate. He drove us to a seedier part of L.A. where there were crack heads on every corner; most of them afraid to sell to us, thinking we looked like cops. Part of me was afraid; everyone looked much crazier and far worse off than anybody I knew. The girl that I was with, an actual Crack Addict, was looking to buy Crack, while I was open and willing to try anything. I would say, although I loved heroin, my drug of choice under the circumstances was meth. Thankfully for me, the woman we met up with, rough and worn had a caring heart and refused to sell any Crack to me, she refused to get a new person started. Instead, she directed me to a house nearby where I was able to buy and shoot meth.

Required to return to The Sober Living House by the end of our Work Day, we knew they would have been notified that we weren't at our jobs, in addition to never going to work we were both returning under the influence. I was able to maintain, but the Crack had gotten the best of my friend. She went out of her mind and ended up running around naked, acting crazed and disturbing all of the other occupants. Once it was official and I failed the Drug Test, I got kicked out. I'm not sure what happened to her, regardless, I was onto the next place. My mom was broken-hearted but prepared.

I went to a beautiful house, also in L.A., it was just minutes from USC in an average area. With only two beds in each room, there were five rooms housing nine women, one a live-in administrator. I think it was donated by William Shatner's Foundation, and regularly got funding from Stars, I didn't last there either. No matter where I went, I ended up using drugs. I would be sober a few days, and then relapse. I relapsed at every place I stayed in. Maybe Treatment Centers and Rehabilitation Facilities work for some people, but for me, so far, it wasn't the answer.

I eventually ended up in a place where they wanted family to visit. My mom, from day one, had been there one hundred percent, visiting whenever she was allowed, calling, checking on me, and bringing me clothes and toiletries. She even brought Baby, to visit, whenever she could. The puppies had been adopted out, and Baby was now living with her, a woman who never even liked dogs. My mom fought for me in every way possible, her actions proving that her love had no bounds. Regardless of how many times I screwed everything up, she wouldn't stop trying.

My dad came every once in a while, his visits almost always strained were never really welcome. Again, I couldn't explain why I just knew as soon as he was on his way, I would be on edge. I'd be ready for him to go soon after he arrived. Once, on a holiday, I think maybe Easter, he showed up with Marianne and my sisters. For years, all of them had avoided me, refusing to have anything to do with me, and now all of a sudden they were there, sitting in a circle, staring at me.

I didn't want them there. Torn, as always with the obligation I felt towards my dad and his family, I tried to be normal, act like I was happy to see them, glad to be one big happy family, but inside I was an emotional wreck. I reasoned that at least they had made the effort, but all of them sitting there looking at me like I was some sort of lost cause only brought up all of my age-old feelings of worthlessness, just like they always did. Even if they never had a single negative thought about me, my perception of what they thought, was enough to destroy me. I couldn't understand why my dad would want to do that to me. I freaked out, felt sick, started crying, making it all worse. The next day, I found someone with Cocaine and relapsed.

My mom, tireless, wanted me sober and wasn't going to give up; each time I relapsed she'd come up with a new and supposedly better place. I let her believe it was possible, let her keep putting her hope into the thought that one day, at the right place, with the right people, it would happen. It was sad, the entire experience with rehabs, for us at least, was completely discouraging, but no one knew what else to do with me. It was a vicious cycle of disappointment but without other options we would just keep going to new and different places, doing the same things, hoping for a better outcome.

One place I was in, the woman running things even relapsed, pills were found in her desk, she blamed it on one of the patients, but when she failed a drug test, the evidence was in. Most places were normal homes turned into Sober Living Houses, some were more hospital like, all had the same goal, have you work up to having a normal life, routine, time in therapy, and maintaining a part-time job. Random drug tests kept people honest, and hopefully clean. At one point, with undercover drugs, I progressed enough to make outpatient status, able to get my own place.

My mom financed everything, like always, finding a cute apartment for me in Los Angeles, hoping to keep me from my San Diego drug crowd. I had a part-time job, a little money and was inhaling Dust-off Computer Cleaner and the Nitrous Oxide to get high. The high didn't last, but at least I was clearing the drug tests. This was me trying. In my own apartment, drugs from the internet, ones that wouldn't show up on my drug tests were easy to get. For me, because they were fairly mild compared to what I had been using, I thought I was doing well. I didn't want to disappoint my mom, but I knew I couldn't last; something inside me had an insatiable desire for opioids, speed, and pills. I craved alcohol too, I needed it; I physically couldn't go without it. Using all of the small time stuff wasn't cutting it, not for long anyway.

Living in Los Angeles, in a one bedroom apartment, my mom would go to great lengths to visit, bring me new clothes and undergarments, and provide essentials, like paper towels, toilet paper, and cleaning supplies. She'd also bring groceries, help me cook and clean, and take me out to dinner and the movies. She'd stay over, sleeping on the sofa and it was great, I loved it. She'd bring Baby and I would feel so happy, I could almost envision living sober, not quite, but almost.

Then there was my dad, his occasional visits, only reminding me of how uncomfortable he made me. They were completely different. The thought of him visiting alone caused an odd sense of dread. I felt bad; again I was always torn, seeing him as a loving and caring father when he wasn't around and in that same person, a leering and unsafe presence that made me feel uneasy and insecure. As much as I tried to be okay with it, I wasn't, I didn't like it. I was never able to relax if he was around. To make matters worse, he would want to sleep over too. Like my mom, he'd sleep on the sofa, only not like my mom, I had to lock my bedroom door and could barely sleep knowing he was out there.

Pretending to do well, inside I was ready to use, tired of all of the scraps that barely got me high. So, at a routine Doctor's Appointment, left alone in an exam room, I raided all of the cabinets and drawers and helped myself to needles, a wad of alcohol swabs, and a handful of cotton balls. All that was missing was the drugs. I knew at some point, I would get them so I stashed all of the supplies deep into my backpack, hiding them in a pair of socks, my heart soaring at the prospects.

After thirty days I graduated from the Outpatient Program. It was decided that I could move back to San Diego, back to one of my dad's apartments. It had to be a different apartment, the one I had been in before, because of all the drug use, smoking and overall destruction had to be completely gutted and renovated. With everything new and improved he rented it out. My new place was cute, fresh and airy with lots of light and furnished with all of my things from Los Angeles. I even had hopes of being able to take Baby back, reuniting with my precious dog.

I got a part-time job at a Flower Shop in Pacific Beach and my mom helped me get a car. I think for a time, I actually was doing okay, trying to maintain my lifestyle by only using the drugs that were undetectable, ones that I could function with, those and the inhalants. Dust Off, the computer cleaner was one of my staples, I inhaled so much that I started having breathing trouble again and even had a few seizures.

My mom, working full-time still seemed like she was always around, keeping an eye on me whenever she could. We talked several times a day and had routine plans to walk, go for a bike ride, hang out at the beach, or go to the movies and dinner. She would do anything to keep me sober and the entire time I was living a lie. I'd constantly reason that at least I wasn't using heroin yet.

I rarely saw my dad and if I did it was short and sweet. Out of the blue though and right out of rehab, I went on a trip with him, an overnight, just the two of us. I feel squeamish just thinking about it. My dad was going to Lake Havasu to maintain a Vacation Rental and asked me to go. Lake Havasu, a five-hour drive from San Diego, is known for outdoor activities, like boating, camping, and hiking, it's a tourist destination for some. I don't know why I agreed if it was a distraction from using heroin, just something different to do, or what. There may have been a part of me that wanted to be okay with my dad, okay with our relationship, I wished so bad for us to be normal. To this day, it is one of the saddest and strangest memories that I have. It's one of those buried, deep down, forgotten, one of the memories, or "dreams" that came up when I was newly pregnant.

I sit across from my therapist, now describing the trip, wondering again, why? With the apprehension I felt about being around my dad, why would I go? "I think I was in my early twenties, I was back in San Diego, but not completely sober. Rosie listens, writing something down every so often, a question or a thought to talk about later. "I can remember being sad about not feeling comfortable with my own dad, the entire drive, of course, wondering why? Then confused, wondering why I said yes, why was I doing this? My stomach sinks as I continue, "It was a long drive and I think at one point, I was talking myself into just making the best of it. There wasn't anything I could do other than try to make it okay."

Remembering it as I speak, I feel the same internal struggle as I continue, "I just hung out, and my dad did some work, then we went to get something to eat. He had his motorcycle out there and wanted to take it to dinner; I had to be on the back." I feel physically ill as I say it out loud. "I was on the back, behind my dad, having to press my body next to his, hold onto him, it shouldn't have been strange, but it was, for some reason I thought I shouldn't be doing that. I felt like the girlfriend, being on a motorcycle with him, it wasn't comfortable, even though it was my dad."

I stop for a minute, reminded of the mistress thing, I feel disturbed. "In Havasu, most people are couples, and I didn't feel right just me and my dad. It bothered me that people might think I was his girlfriend. It was the same at dinner, just the two of us, away from everyone, isolated and alone, like an affair. I would keep telling myself that I was sick in the head, demented, that there was something wrong with me."

I look at Rosie listening to me and continue, "I always had such turmoil about being with my dad, I was always torn by how I should feel and how I actually felt about him. I didn't want to be there, I wanted to go home. Taking the motorcycle back to the house after I was nervous, it was dark and I didn't want to stay. I was sick to my stomach thinking we'd be alone, under the same roof all night, the entire time telling myself I was crazy. Back at the house, it only got worse. My dad was flipping through the channels and we ended up watching a disturbing movie about incest and sexual abuse." I start to cry, "I don't know why we watched it?"

Rosie asks, "Do you need a minute?" I wipe my tears, grateful for how kind she is, and answer, "I'm okay, it's just so strange, I don't understand it. The movie, Sherrybaby, with Maggie Gyllenhaal, is literally a movie about a Heroin Addict and incest. Why wouldn't my dad turn it off? Why wouldn't I? I just sat there and watched it with him, and I don't know why. I didn't do anything. It was horrible and perverted, and we both just sat there watching it, watching the girl being molested. All of it was disgusting, the entire trip was disgusting." I pause and take a deep breath. "It was me, in the movie; I kept thinking it was just like my life."

It's quiet again. Rosie asks, almost hesitantly, "Did anything else happen?" I think back, remembering that I didn't sleep that night, I couldn't. I stayed awake, my mind racing, trying to get the awful movie out of my head. I was afraid of my dad and not knowing why. "No," I answer. "Well, I guess, I mean, the next day when we were getting ready to leave, I had a seizure. It was from inhaling all the chemicals. I had a seizure and my dad was mad, he was yelling at me, swearing and calling me names. He told me I was lying and kept accusing me of using drugs." Rosie asks if anything else happened but I tell her no. "No, it was just miserable, the ride home was depressing. When I got home I started using heroin again?" Quiet for a minute she looks at me and asks, "Why Kristen?" I feel sad, I don't even answer. Instead, I reason and draw my own conclusions.

·Chapter Fifteen·

I hand over the interest sheet to The Director, as she takes me to the classroom Jordan will be in to show me around. If accepted, she'll start school in the next few weeks, a big "if" and I'm already frantic. Entering the room, anxiety instantly takes over my chest, my entire body seizes up, I feel faint, the smells, the sounds, the fluorescent lights, all of it immediately takes me back. It's been over thirty years and walking through the doors I'm transported, I'm back in school and it's horrific, the fear, the loneliness, the sadness, I'm paralyzed remembering it all. The misery I had for most of my young life, the dread, and unease I constantly felt, all return.

The Director is walking ahead of me, pointing out features of the program, as I drag behind, unsure if I can get through it, or if I'm going to throw-up. I heave lightly, trying to breathe through my mouth to avoid the old, stuffy school smell that's overtaking me. The kids, all so young and innocent, could it really have been that traumatic for me? I start reasoning with myself, thinking of how Rosie and I would discuss the facts, and then draw conclusions. I faintly hear the woman up ahead as she tells me about the schedule, the activities, and naptime.

"Naptime" causes me to cringe. I don't want my girl to have to nap here, I can't imagine, the room darkened, all the children required to lay on cots or mats to rest. Panicking, I think of Jordan being in trouble, unwilling to cooperate, or lie still, never being able to fall asleep. I try to reason on it, but I can't, Jordan would never be able to do it, she's not a napper, my inner dialogue is wild; I can't stay with one train of thought. "Pick her up early, just pick her up," I'm trying not to cry, "She doesn't have to stay, it's only preschool," I try to keep calm.

Jordan, not quite three, should be in preschool, that's all I hear from everyone, and there's a part of me that knows it's true. School nowadays is so important; supposedly if I don't get her into a good preschool now, then she won't get into a good elementary school, high school and so on. It's crazy, the pressure of it all, but it's real and I don't want her to be an underachiever, or unable to socialize or maintain friendships, the things that I'm told could happen if she doesn't start school soon.

I watch all of the children playing, laughing, happy, little beings, all having fun as they buzz around the room. I look at the little coat rack, all of the tiny sweaters and jackets hanging up beside their cubbies, their names taped underneath. The one-foot cubes hold lunchboxes, blankets, dolls, and little cars, treasures from home, things that helped coax them to school or help comfort them while they're here. As I look at the different items, thinking how sweet they are, the woman showing me around says, "No personal belongings are allowed, if they come into the room they have to stay in their cubbies until they go home."

I try to stop the tears from welling up. I can't imagine Jordan getting into trouble for bringing a toy or doll to school, thinking of it having to stay in her little cubbie, untouched until I come for her, isn't that too strict? The woman keeps talking, selling the school, then there's the waiting list, the deposit, it's overwhelming. I picture Jordan's name taped on one of the cubbies with all of the others, I feel sad thinking of her being here without me, I don't want her to go to school. I do the self-talk thing, but it doesn't seem to be working. "Kristen you're fine, Jordan will be fine. She's not you. She's different, her life is totally different. Stop, get a handle on yourself," but I can't, I have to excuse myself and go outside.

I want to run, but I don't. I have to get out of there; I walk to the nearest exit, pushing the door open to a beautiful sunny day, blue skies and fresh air. I let the door shut behind me and lean against the wall trying to breathe. I start bawling my eyes out and I can't stop, within minutes I'm out of control. I go to the car and sit in the driver's seat now hysterical. I know Jordan has to go to school, and I don't want to put all of my issues on her, but I can't stand the thought, I can't even get through the tour.

I dry my eyes and calm down, I call Chase and tell him what happened; I tell him how I fell apart, the smells, the sounds, even the lights making me feel like I did when I was a kid. He reminds me of the same thing I tried to remind myself that Jordan isn't me and she's going to be fine. He tells me he's sorry that happened and how much he loves me, reassuring me that everything will work out. I think of everything going on, all of the stuff with my dad still unresolved, my sister's threat and deadline, therapy. Maybe now wasn't the best time to do this, maybe preschool could wait.

What was wrong with me that I was so worked up about being in a school, about rules or napping? Touring schools shouldn't be this hard. What would happen when I actually found one and dropped her off for the first time? Maybe now was a good time, why should anything from my past affect what I was doing now, especially the stuff with my dad. It shouldn't, not when it came to my family. Jordan is going to love school I tell myself, thinking of all of the positives from the brief tour, it's close to the house, it's clean, and it's only a few hours a day. Feeling better already, I put on my seat belt and start the car, as I do a text comes through. I look at the screen, startled, it's my dad.

I turn off the car and roll down the window. I hadn't seen or talked to my dad in over a week, which for us was unusual. It was devastating to me; I think I was mourning the loss of my father, missing him, or the idea of him anyway. I hadn't confronted him yet, but he was already gone in a way, the memory of us spending time together, now contaminated by thoughts that there was something sinister about him, about our relationship. I couldn't remember the good anymore without thinking of the bad.

He called once, leaving a message, almost like he knew. I didn't return his call, still not prepared to handle us, or our situation, what needed to happen. I was down to the wire, my sister's deadline looming over me, was now just days away. She had text recently too, asking me directly in her message if I had told "Dad" about my memories yet, I didn't answer her. I didn't need her to pressure me; I knew she was right, it was time, I needed to tell him. I look at my dad's text.

POPS

So what's going on?

I start to text back, my heart is racing, and my stomach instantly knots up.

ME

What do u mean

POPS

I don't know, just a sense

ME

I'm having memories of being sexually abused

POPS

By who?

ME

I'm not sure any thoughts????

POPS

Like what?

ME

? I don't know

Several minutes go by, I'm not sure what to expect. I start to feel disappointed, wondering if that's it if that's how my dad is going to leave this.

POPS

Just for the record it wasn't me

The phone stays lit up, the last message sitting there, ominous in a way. I don't even know what to think.

POPS

I never sexually abused you or anyone else and that's that!

I can't believe this is it; this is my dad's reaction. This is MY DAD! Wouldn't a dad pick up the phone and call his daughter if he received a text like the one I sent? Better yet, wouldn't he drop everything and come over? I think I envisioned him coming over; shocked, angry, upset, wanting to know if I was okay, what happened? How could he help, or be supportive? Wouldn't a loving, caring father be incensed, wondering who it was? Wanting to know when and how something like this could happen? Wanting to kill whoever did such a thing to his child, his own daughter?

Not my dad, my dad was worried, like he always was, about himself. There wasn't a single thought about me or how I was feeling, what I was going through. Here I was telling my father, my parent, that I had been victimized as a child, and all he could worry about was how it might affect him. Why would he be professing his innocence when it hadn't even been called into question yet?

I don't know what I pictured, what I thought would happen, I guess I thought my dad would for once, be more concerned about me and my welfare, my mental health, my sobriety. Deep down I wouldn't really want him to come over, I wouldn't want to be around him, not by myself, talking about it, talking about sexual abuse. I guess I just wanted us to be normal, to handle it how a normal father and daughter would handle it, but that's how messed up I am. We're not normal, talking to your dad because you believed he sexually abused you is not normal, nothing about any of this is normal.

I think my dad being concerned about me and caring about how I was doing would have been completely out of character, but it's what I wanted, it's what I've always wanted. It didn't happen that way though, instead, I didn't matter to him. He mattered to him. I break down in tears crushed again, it's too much, the reality of my dad and his reaction is too real, and way too much.

With my kids at my mom's for the morning, my window of opportunity is small to call and talk with Rosie. I dry my eyes, find her in my contacts, and hope she isn't too busy to help me come to terms with my dad's response. It's weird, I'm sad and I'm hurt, but am I really surprised? My therapist picks up and I'm so relieved I completely break down again. I'm not even sure where to start. I'm finally able to tell her about the text messages from my dad. Thinking of his final text, I'm upset, that was how my dad was going to leave things? I never accused him; he just assumed that I thought it was him? Why? I tell myself it's my fault, it's the way I handled it, I shouldn't have done that to him, not by text.

I share what I'm thinking with Rosie as she patiently listens, I want her to weigh in, say something, I want some type of validation. Instead, catching me off guard, she asks, "Do you think he'd be willing to come to therapy with you?" I can't even imagine. Would he come? What would that be like? We'd be in the same room, able to discuss things, face to face, and I wouldn't be alone.

With nothing to lose, I tell Rosie I'll ask. I think about confronting my dad face to face. I'm nervous, knowing now, that I could never have done it alone. I think he'd talk his way out of it, tell me I was sick or there was something wrong with me. More than likely he'd blame me and my addiction for the thoughts or memories, the drugs affecting how I viewed things. I'd doubt myself, doubt all of the memories, the behaviors, everything, believing again, that it was all me, that I was crazy. I wasn't though, I was sure of it. I thought of the "Boob Issue" alone. I lived in a bra, most of my life, never taking it off, not even to shower, especially at my dad's. That definitely wasn't normal behavior, but for someone who had been molested, it was. I matched every single sign in the book about Sexual Abuse, signs that pointed to something happening to me, I matched every one of them.

Was I brave enough to tell him that? Would I be able to tell him that I brought it up to my mom years ago, long before I was steeped in addiction when I was still a teenager? Would I be able to ask him why he never mentioned me when we were together? Why he kept me, and the time he spent with me, a secret from Marianne and my sisters? Would I be able to do it? Could I finally confront my dad in person?

It was interesting, I watched my dad lie about being with me for years, but when I really thought about it, that wasn't all he lied about. Throughout my lifetime, I witnessed my dad being dishonest in dozens of situations; in general, he was never an honest person. I remember him lying in business transactions, financial matters, and even friendships. My dad was generally shady, his actions and how he conducted himself all along revealing his true character, he was a person of little integrity. My dad couldn't be trusted.

I think that's why, when he showed up at rehab, I was apprehensive. Confused, I didn't know what he wanted. I'd think to myself, "What is he doing here?" How was he able to cast me aside for years, never seeming to care whether I was dead or alive, and then show up with a sudden interest in my recovery? There was something about my dad that didn't make sense. There were things I used to overlook, but couldn't anymore. Even financially, my father had never been vested in me, never putting any money towards me or my treatment, any of the things I needed, he was just there. Unaware at the time that my mom had been paying him to let me live in his apartment in North Park, my mom had paid him all along, even before I went to rehab. My mom always paid for everything, my dad never contributing to anything for me, for as long as I could remember.

He had money; he owned homes and boats, fancy motorcycles, vacation rentals, rental properties, why wouldn't he want to help me? The year I spent in and out of all the Treatment Centers, Recovery Places, and Sober Living Houses, it was all on my mom. Even with insurance, my mom spent hundreds of thousands of dollars trying to save me; I think she would have bankrupted herself if she had to, not my dad. Why would my own father hesitate to contribute to anything for me financially? Not just throughout my childhood, but in my recovery? Something that could have saved my life? Why didn't he want to? More importantly, why did I excuse it, or think it was okay? My father wasn't really there for me in any capacity and I never recognized it until now.

I try to remember him as part of my life after returning from rehab, but I can't. From Los Angeles, I moved back into his apartment complex, but I rarely if ever saw him. I didn't think much about it at the time; I didn't want to see him or anyone else for that matter. I was using again, not quite as bad as before I left, but close. Regardless, my dad never reached out to me again, apart from our awkward and disturbing trip to Havasu, we returned to our separate lives. I went immediately back to my heroin addiction and I was okay with it, but why was my dad? Especially since that weekend he had accused me of being on drugs again? My dad thought I was using drugs again and instead of bothering with me, he just disappeared

Cameron, barred from visiting me in Los Angeles, was easy to reconnect with when I returned. Our relationship staying undefined, we were friends with benefits, but in a way, so much more. I used to wonder if the two of us were sober, would we be able to have a normal relationship. We cared about each other, but as addicts, there's a very fine line in caring about and using people. His violent tendencies had subsided and we were compatible, good friends even, but our commonality had always been drug addiction. We had never had a relationship without being under the influence.

There was a part of me that started thinking about the "what if's?" in regards to being sober. How would this person or situation be if I was clean, what would my life look like if I was able to really kick drugs? Most of the time, I couldn't picture it. The idea of Cameron and I together and sober was all in my head. The fact that I could think of myself being sober was new, living sober, at least the idea of it, no longer as foreign or as bad as I thought. I could picture it sometimes. Thinking of being with my mom in the apartment in Los Angeles and only using minor drugs, for me, was as close to sober as I had ever been, and it wasn't that bad. Thinking of myself as a drug addict was easier though, it was already a reality. Shooting up and feeling good, to me continued to be better than all of the "what if's?"

Hooked on heroin within months of my return, it seemed worse than before, I needed it all of the time. Making a promise to myself to use heroin and heroin only, the scary part was that I was able to maintain, it wasn't noticeable to the untrained eye, or the average person, like my mom. To me, I was in love with heroin, the feelings were so good, I felt so happy, and even if it was fleeting, it was better than a lifetime of sobriety, at least in my state of mind. As long as I used every few hours, I would be okay, I did it dozens of times every day without anybody knowing. When I was on meth, and taking pills with alcohol, everybody knew, there was no hiding it. I twitched, I was thin and blown out, I looked like a tweaker. Heroin was different, as long as I had it routinely I was fine, I had a job, my own apartment and for the most part, lived a fairly normal life.

I was back to the people, places, activities, and habits I had before I left; only no one outside of my drug circle knew it. I was functioning so well, I was planning to take Baby my dog on, ready for her to move back in with me, but deep down, I couldn't envision it. I was scared of her and the responsibility she came with, eventually, breaking it to my mom that it would be too much for me. This news, after everything my mom had gone through with her, was another disappointment, but it wouldn't have been fair, that sweet dog deserved someone better than me, someone, normal and sober. I felt horrible about her, but I was living a double life, and it was already taxing, telling a constant stream of lies and covering my tracks became exhausting. I was lying to everyone about everything and I hated it, especially lying to my mom, who continued to love and support me, thinking I was sober.

I had never been worse. I had a bad habit and refused to believe I could ever get out. It was so out of control that if I didn't shoot up, for even an hour, I would start to get sick. It wasn't a joke, it would get extreme, shakes and diarrhea so bad that you don't care what people think, you stand a good chance of messing yourself and it wouldn't matter. Nothing mattered and there was no shame, I was that desperate again. My habit was expensive too; I resorted to hundreds of things that would be considered illicit, illegal and outright cringe-worthy. The prostitution probably the worst, doing things I hated, that made me feel lifeless, had me needing heroin all the more. So I kept the lies going, not one shred of honesty or decency left in me; I tried not to think, about anything, and went about my life.

I kept true to my promise to stay away from other things until I attended a wedding that spring. Old friends, Skinheads, also addicts, were getting married and I was going to be a Bridesmaid. Their Wedding Date was April 20, 2008, or 420, the unofficial cannabis holiday, and honorary time to smoke pot, all of my old ways were about to resurface in my life. The day started off great, shooting up and showering, I drove to The La Valencia Hotel in La Jolla, ready for fun. We met early, in one of the rooms, to start getting ready. I remember feeling so out of place, a bunch of drug addicts, alcoholics, and criminals, in a fancy environment, rubbing shoulders with the rich.

The wedding and everything about it, outside of the location, was cheap starting with our dresses. Flimsy and wrinkled, in need of pressing, they were tacky, even for me. We did our own make-up and hair, used heroin all day, drank bottles of Cheap Champagne, took handfuls of pills and filled the beautiful room with cigarette smoke. I had smoked a couple of packs a day for years and was never without, my cigarette addiction just as bad as the rest of my horrible habits.

The Wedding took place there, that afternoon in an outdoor courtyard. The Bride and Groom saying vows, was meaningless to me, sealing their ceremony with a kiss, it was time for the best part, the reception. All of my friends together partying, and having fun was everything to me, I felt connected, and even if it was short-lived, I loved it. The reception was held about fifteen miles away in an area of Mission Beach, called Marina Village. I parked my car nearby at a friend's and rode with them, all of us looking forward to a party, "Open Bar" and dancing.

Wasted after the first couple of hours, I was ready to leave and decided to walk. Taking my shoes off, I stumbled towards my friend's house to get my car. Walking alone, tired and needing to "Get Well," all I could think about was getting home, when a police car pulled up alongside me, stopping me in my tracks. My heart was racing, "Please don't arrest me, please don't arrest me," was all I could think. "Have you seen a White, Male, about six feet tall, brown hair, with large neck and facial tattoos?" It was my friend, who probably got into a fight or had done something horrible. As a helicopter circled above, I knew it was bad. Answering "No," I started walking away, annoyed that they would scare me like that, just to help them do their own job. Nervous, I willed for them to leave me alone and kept walking, as they drove off continuing their search.

Relieved, I made it to my car in about ten minutes, excited that I'd be home soon. Starting to feel crappy without heroin, I drove faster, stepping on the gas, as I headed to North Park. In anticipation of relief, I wasn't even out of the beach when I hear the siren, "Bleep, bleep," trying not to cry, I look for a place to pull over as a million old feelings wash over me, feelings of shame, sadness, and fear. I'm so nervous again, I feel like I might have diarrhea, I didn't want to go to jail; I was so sick, so sad.

Two police cars are behind me, one cop in each car, I pull out my license, and throw my purse under my feet, as they walk up. They make me get out of my car and I knew I would be going to jail. Forced to walk a straight line, then touch my finger to my nose, I couldn't do either, then the alphabet forward and backward which I couldn't do even if I was sober. On a busy corner, in Pacific Beach, just blocks from my mom's, I thought of her as they read me my rights. They let me get my phone and lock my car, which I couldn't believe, I slid my purse under the seat, hoping to hide it and save myself from a possessions charge on top of a DUI. Cuffed and pushed into the backseat of one of the cars, we went to a nearby sub-station where I blew a .08. "It's your lucky day, you're off to jail," said the cop.

I was so bummed, I had literally promised myself that morning, I was going to kick heroin tomorrow. I really was. I was done, tired, it was too much to keep up the facade. I was starting a new job with a salary and commission, and I was really excited about it, a chance to start fresh, come clean. Dying inside, everyone thought I was sober, including my mom. Crying, I hated my life. Now I was going to have to disappoint her again. The thought of jail, withdrawals, having to go to court, this ruined everything. It was horrible, I was horrible. I pulled myself together, mad at the cop; I didn't want him to have the satisfaction of seeing me falling apart. I was headed to Las Colinas, the Women's Jail in Santee. I hadn't been there in over a year and with anxiety about my future and the start of withdrawals, I felt like I would die. Why? Why did this have to happen?

In the backseat, the cop talks to me, he's surprisingly compassionate, almost fatherly, telling me I should straighten out my life while I still have a chance, adding that I seemed smart and could make something of myself. His unexpected attention and kindness tugging on my heartstrings, I'd wonder how it was possible for a total stranger to care more about me and my substance abuse, than my own father. We talked the entire way, him encouraging me to get clean and me telling him about my plans, my new job. I even shared the fact that I had planned to kick everything tomorrow, only now tomorrow I would be waking up in jail. "There's the bright side,'" he says, "You can still start tomorrow." Only, I don't want to now.

We arrive at the jail a few minutes later, and he wishes me luck, ending by telling me that he really believes in me, and thinks I can do it. I try again not to get emotional, as he leaves, and I wait to be booked. The intake person isn't as friendly, immune to the people; to her, I was just a number. Putting my car keys and phone on a metal tray, the only personal belongings I have besides the clothes on my back, processing starts. Invasively patted down, they check roughly under my bra straps, and along the elastic in my underwear, then go through my hair and check behind my ears, it takes forever and dignity doesn't exist, getting booked isn't for the modest. Processing takes hours, and I'm sicker than a dog, I've lost all track of time. I just want to lay down somewhere, anywhere. Instead, I'm shuffled in for mug shots, and another room where they take my footprints and fingerprints, then finally a holding cell where I'm pushed in, and a huge steel door slammed behind me.

Several women line the walls, the smell of vomit and urine, with icky body odors, waft through the air. Most of the women are loud and obnoxious, talking non-stop, jailed for everything from shoplifting to prostitution, maybe even worse. We all wait together. Starting withdrawals, I laid on a bench, cold and clammy, chills and tremors; with waves of nausea and heaving keep me awake and suffering through most of the night. The next day, after processing goes through, I can sign all of the paperwork and am free to go until my court date.

Still having the shakes and random bouts of diarrhea, I have the option of taking the trolley or calling my mom. As hard as it will be to let my mom know what happened, I make the call. I can tell she feels blindsided, she's in disbelief telling me how hurt and angry she is. I cry, so sad to be in this situation again. I sit out front waiting for her, and as awful as everything is, and as terrible as I feel, all I can think about is heroin and "Getting Well."

My mom pulls up twenty minutes later, I get in the car and she won't even look at me. I sit next to her wishing with all of my heart that I was sober and that things were different. I hated myself, why did I keep living this way? How could I keep putting my mom through this? All of these months, she thought I was clean, and the entire time I was lying. She's had no idea, and now she thinks it was just alcohol, blaming the "Open Bar" at the reception. "I'm disgusted by this Kristen, I don't get it, I don't get your choices!" Apart from that, the ride to my car was silent, me never mentioning that my license was confiscated and temporarily suspended, I let my mom drop me at the corner across from my car. I get out and she doesn't say a word. "Bye mom, thank you. I'm sorry, I'm really, really sorry." Still nothing, okay then. I slammed the door shut, and she drives off.

I think of what she said about "choices" and wonder if all of this was choice. I guess so, but why? I didn't understand my "choices" either. I get into my car, pulling out my purse from under the seat. I stop along the Bay at a Public Restroom, it's empty and I go into a stall, having everything I need to "Get Well," with me. Within minutes I'm feeling better. Finally able to go home, I make a quick call and then stop at my dealer to buy a baggie of heroin. Set for the evening, once I get home, I shower, and shoot up again. Feeling elated, for the time being, I'm no longer concerned about my "choices," my new job, my plan, or even my poor mom.

·Chapter Sixteen·

I decide I'm going to use until my hearing and then I'll kick heroin for good. Giving myself a new deadline makes me feel in control, like I'm in charge of my heroin addiction, instead of it being in charge of me. With that settled, I was able to salvage my job with Pro Flowers and started working there full-time the following day. Straight away I had to start lying again. Forced to lie, for the time being, one lie wasn't enough to cover my addiction. There had to be a million lies, big lies, little lies, my entire life became predicated on how good of a liar I could become. Sadly, I was a master liar, and no one seemed to ever question me, not even my mom. Why would she? With my new job, recent arrest, jail stint, and upcoming court date, to her there was no possibility that I would be using.

My mom through the years had become somewhat of an addiction and recovery specialist. Because of how bad my problems were, she used her spare time to educate herself, learning as much as she could about the disease and recovery. In an effort to be proactive, she joined groups, attended seminars and went to a weekly program with others like her, who had a loved one struggling with addiction. She donated to charities, supported fundraisers, raised money, ran marathons, and tried her best to keep informed on every topic relatable to helping me.

With all of her insight and knowledge, I was leery about being around her and the possibility of her detecting my drug use. My mom and I were fairly connected and would spend time together regularly, so I blamed my new job, learning about flowers and flower arrangements, along with being tired, to try and avoid her. Lies, lies and more lies.

During this time my mom purchased a table at a huge Fundraising Event in San Diego, a big celebration to raise money for a Local Non-Profit called Second Chance. It was a Re-entry Program that helped people who were getting out of prison, become successful, employable, and self-sufficient. My mom loved to be involved and I think felt good about contributing what she could, in hopes that eventually I too would be a success story. She invited several friends, some work colleagues and me. I think she expected me to go, but the last thing I was interested in was going to a fancy gala for Sober People. That type of event wasn't my thing; it never had been, especially at the time. Putting on a front while using heroin, I wanted nothing to do with any of the things she was involved in. With no intention of going, I told her I wasn't sure, blaming it on my job and whether or not I'd have to work.

As the date of the big event approached, I decided it was the least I could do in exchange for all of the things my mom had done and continued to do for me. Feeling guilty for a million reasons, and under the guise of sobriety, I attended. My addiction at this point was so severe; I timed everything so that I would never be without drugs in my system for too long. Shooting up before I went and giving myself an hour max before I stepped out to "Get Well," I put myself together focusing on making sure my bruised and spotted neck was camouflaged with concealer and powder and my blood-dotted arms were covered with a sweater.

Arriving ready to leave, I showed up feeling superior almost, like I knew a secret. These people may have stopped using drugs, but I didn't have to, look at me, I could shoot up all day and no one could tell. I didn't want to be sober, not really. To me it was all a big joke, I even looked down on them. I remember thinking they were weak at first, "Look at me I have a year, or a month or even a day." Initially, it was all a bunch of crap to me.

Having been in and out of voluntary programs, involuntary programs, sober living houses, shelters, and hospitals, the idea of doing any of it again, wasn't for me. Sobriety wasn't for me. Counting the minutes, I sat next to my mom at her $10,000 table with all of her friends and work associates, feeling bored and out of place. The event highlighted testimonies from different people who battled drug and alcohol addictions most of their lives, some far worse than mine, involving deaths, prison sentences, loss, and complete and devastating hardships. Some were more walk in the park stories to me, people who thought just being an alcoholic was bad.

I listened, unsympathetically, wishing that alcohol was my only issue. Because the program had helped them all, they shared their success stories, crediting Second Chance for helping them become sober heroes, and becoming accomplished and responsible members of society. I won't lie, some of them were total tearjerkers and I was moved, not enough to change, but moved.

Once they finished, there was a brief intermission that was going to be followed by a Special Presentation and an Award Ceremony. I checked my phone and stepped outside for a smoke. On the countdown to leaving, I was getting antsy, knowing I'd have to take care of myself soon. I finished my cigarette and went back inside just in time to see a hot ex-addict getting started on his bad boy tale. He was a sure success story for this type of gathering. Growing up in a broken home, molested by a babysitter, and abandoned by his parents, as a teenager; he had met with all the wrong people and all of the wrong circumstances, getting iced up and becoming a drug addict, drug dealer, and rough and violent criminal, that had been in and out of prison.

He shared his personal experiences very tenderly; raw with so much emotion it was hard to watch. When he finished, he read a beautiful poem about sobriety and the gratitude he felt being in recovery. He, with the help of the Re-entry Program, had changed his lifestyle one hundred percent, becoming clean and sober, getting a full-time job and becoming a responsible and caring individual.

I was definitely intrigued, hanging on every word, I sat back and tried to relax as a ten-minute video of him and his life played out on a huge screen in front of me. Daydreaming of him and my prospects, I watched his documentary with a renewed interest in him and his story. He was so sexy to me, not too straight-laced or uptight, he was my type for sure, a bad boy gone good. For the first time, that I could ever remember, I wished I was sober, so serious about it, I felt sick that I wasn't. Completely taken with him and his story, I would have done anything to be sober at that moment.

When the video was over, and during a Standing Ovation, he accepted an award as two women stood nearby, waiting to congratulate him. One was his mother, who had appeared in the video, the other woman, I assumed was his girlfriend. They were both crying, most likely total tears of joy for the turnaround he made. They hugged him and were posing for photos, as I watched from my seat. At my table, I freely shared how hot I thought he was and not mincing words, that I was interested in him. The table, of mostly women, thought it was great, everyone encouraging me to go and meet him, to let him know how much I loved his speech and video. "Look, he has a girlfriend," I pointed out.

The star of the event, he was walking around in my estimation, like a peacock, enjoying his fans, the compliments, and adoration. I remember thinking the girl with him was cute, but maybe they weren't that serious, they weren't close, or holding hands they weren't acting like a couple, maybe she was his sister, maybe I had a chance.

One of my mom's more confident friends, excited at the idea that we could be a match, grabbed my hand and started dragging me out of my chair to meet him. "Come on," she said, "I'm going to introduce you." Making our way through the crowd, she stepped in front of him and stuck out her hand introducing herself. The "Mayor of Cougar Town," she was my mom's age and had no hesitation coming right out and asking him if he was single. He stepped back, grinning, a rush of red covering his cheeks, I think not knowing if he should be nervous or flattered, he was momentarily speechless. I stepped forward, telling him, "Your speech was very inspiring." Hesitant about how he was going to respond, I thought he seemed preoccupied, too busy to bother with me, but surprisingly, he came back with, "Are you in recovery? Want to go to a meeting?"

We exchanged numbers and he text me a couple of hours later. It was late and he offered to bring over Jack in the Box, addict food in case you're unaware. The bummer was I really wanted him to come over, but Cameron was with me and we were using heroin. I felt heartsick, I really liked him, Chase Campbell definitely had more going on for him then Cameron. It wasn't right though, I had started out by lying to him, telling him I was in recovery. For the second time in as many hours, I shot heroin into my veins, as I wished again, that I could be sober.

Chase called again the next day, wanting to make a plan for the weekend. I was so excited, I could hardly contain myself. He invited me to a meeting, then a bonfire at Crown Point, a Bay Front area near my mom's house. I went for a wax, picked out my outfit and tried not to think too much about the fact that he was sober and I wasn't. It definitely kept running through my head, knowing it would ruin any chance for us. I didn't want him to know and hoped with all my heart he wouldn't find out. The voice in my head telling me, "You better do something, you better get sober."

I didn't listen at all during the meeting and only talked with Chase at the bonfire, we talked about our pasts, our lives, and how he got sober. He kissed me, several times. I really felt like there was chemistry between us. I was already falling in love. On our way home we stopped for Mexican Food and hung out for as long as possible, to me his journey and struggles with addiction weren't that different than mine.

There was a spark of hope that if I really wanted to I could do the same thing, I could change my life. We made plans for a second date and spent hours texting and talking on the phone, he was beautiful to me, so funny; I loved his sense of humor, and the silly voices he made when he was joking around. Something about him and being with him made me happy, I felt like we belonged together, feeling lighthearted and excited, I wanted to spend more and more time with him. I even wanted to be sober, I just didn't know how to do it, and so far wishing hadn't made it so.

We were both super busy, so making a relationship happen wasn't easy. Chase worked full-time at the Second Chance Program as one of their trainers, went to meetings all of the time, and lived twenty miles away in a Sober Living House in Imperial Beach, which meant he couldn't stay over. That helped me hide my addiction. I was working too, had started attending my mandatory DUI Program, which began with group counseling every week and was spending what was left of my time organizing my heroin use.

Yes, it was that bad that I had to plan it or risk getting sick and being found out. I knew too, that at some point, I was going to have to choose between Cameron and Chase. I started limiting my time with Cameron in hopes that our parting ways would be easier. I didn't think I had those types of feelings for Cameron until he wasn't around as much. He and I had shared such a history, over eight years on and off, of good times, crazy times, scary situations, trying circumstances and thousands of hours in full-blown addiction, part of being with him a habit and part must have been some form of love.

On our second date, Chase and I went to the beach, we both loved the ocean, which was a huge plus for me. He was sexy, strong and muscular, with the best tattoos, and build. I couldn't stop thinking about how good looking he was, I didn't think I was good enough for him. I was attracted to everything about him, his style, his mannerisms, his strength, and especially his sobriety. He was everything I wanted in a man, and he was reliable and responsible, which I wasn't used to. When he took an interest in me, wanting to get to know me and find out more about me, I was touched. Chase was kind and caring and made me feel safe, in a world that had never been safe to me. Our shared love of the beach and swimming in the ocean, along with everything else, made us perfect for each other.

After the beach, we went back to my apartment where we showered, cleaned up and then I made dinner for him. I think he knew that something wasn't right. I wore a swim shirt to cover my arms and thought it would be a dead giveaway, but he didn't say anything. On top of that, I couldn't stay awake and kept nodding off, he confronted me but I lied, just like I always did, hurting myself and all of the people that cared about me. Here was the perfect person for me, but I wasn't sober, and I didn't think I could get sober. I knew if I wanted to be with him, long term, I had to do something, I wouldn't be able to hide it for much longer, he was onto me.

Showing up unannounced at my apartment one afternoon when I thought he'd be at work, Cameron and I were together just hanging out and smoking weed. When I heard someone coming up the stairs, I panicked and made Cameron sneak out the back door. I rushed around, gathering everything up in a trash bag, thinking I could get it to the dumpster without anyone knowing. Tapping on the door, my heart sank when I saw him. I tried to keep him at the door not wanting him to smell the weed or see everything disheveled, but I knew it was too late. I was scared. He asked if I was hiding someone, then he asked me point blank if I was using drugs. I couldn't lie. I told him I was just smoking weed.

Letting him in, I made a scene about how bad the trash smelled, grabbed the bag and headed down the stairs to toss it. I saw Cameron driving away as I threw the dumpster lid open, and pitched my evidence in. Letting the lid slam shut, I turned around to Chase standing there, the reformed bad boy looking so sad and disappointed, I thought he might cry. He threw the lid open and jumped in, digging around for my trash, which he found, ripping the bag apart to find needles, cotton balls, burnt spoons and even a small baggie of heroin. He started calling me names like "Liar and Junkie," making a huge scene, using the intimidation tactics from his program, he wouldn't let-up.

Going on and on, he started telling me he had to worry about Aids now and that because I deceived him, I owed him money for all of our dates, dinners and the movie we went to. I stood there in tears for a while, telling him how sorry I was, how much I liked him and wished I was different. I left to walk back upstairs and he followed me, asking if he could wash his hands before he left. I cried even harder, he was so clean, possibly OCD, just like me when I wasn't using.

Instead of giving up on me, Chase was relentless, obsessed even, constantly calling me, harassing me and badgering me to get clean. He'd text and leave messages telling me I needed to stop using and get help. I thought it was because he was so mad and he felt betrayed, but I think it was his way of caring, showing me by trying to get me to do something about my addiction, that I was important to him. I kept telling him that I was sorry, but he wouldn't let up.

It was so bad I remember changing my number, wanting him to leave me alone. It was a difficult situation, I knew I needed to quit drugs, but I also knew I couldn't do it. The string of Treatment Centers hadn't even able to help me and they were experts. I really believed I was a lost cause, but Chase didn't. Chase refused to believe that about me and he refused to give up on me, at one point even telling me to use weed for now, as long as I stopped using heroin. Then he told me about a drug that was supposed to help kick heroin, so I went to my doctor for Suboxone. Not covered by my insurance, I was so hopeful I spent my entire paycheck on it.

Chase came over, showing up because he couldn't call me, he made me flush everything I had down the toilet, all of the hidden heroin, the pills, alcohol, the pot, every bit of it gone. Then he told me, "Please, you need to get clean, you know I love you, right?" I loved him too. Even though he was mad at me and lost all trust and respect for me, he stuck by me the whole time. We spent the evening together and talked about the future and plans, what could be. I remember him being so excited, telling me that November 18, 2008, would always be special, it would be my Sobriety Date. In the back of my mind, I remember thinking, that it was too soon and that it was a lot to live up to, but I also knew if I didn't get sober now, I would lose him forever.

The next night at the DUI Program I was super sick from not using heroin; I had barely made it through my first full day without it. I felt so horrible, I wanted to die. I took the Suboxone to help, but it wasn't the easy way off of heroin that I thought it would be. Sitting in the program, it was the last place I wanted to be, but my attendance was mandatory and I couldn't miss. Giving up, I sat in class texting the dope man, making plans to "Get Well," as soon as it was over.

Sitting in the group counseling session, the DUI Counselor called on me, asking me if I was still using. I told her and the people circled around me, what was going on. Raw and honest, I shared that I was trying to stay sober and that I was only one day without drugs and I couldn't do it, it was too hard for me. Getting emotional, I started crying and kept saying, "Screw it, I just can't do it." Some of the people looking on started tearing up too, "I am just going to be a drug addict, that's what I am; I have to just come to terms with it. I am a junkie and I'm going to die a junkie."

Once we finished, the DUI Instructor came up to me and, with most of the group already gone told me, "Just don't use for tonight. Go home take a bath, drink some hot tea. It's one night, you can use tomorrow if you want, but just for tonight, don't use." I left the program thinking that I could do that. I believed that I could go home and not use for one night. I went home and did it. I got through that night and I never used again. Just that one night, knowing that I could make it through gave me momentum and with Chase, I was motivated, I finally wanted to get sober, and I finally believed it was possible. November 18, 2008, really was my Sobriety Date.

Over an hour had passed; I was still sitting in the car, in the parking lot at what could be Jordan's new school. I'm amazed and so grateful to be sober. I think back to meeting Chase, remembering almost every detail perfectly. Chase came into my life at the right time and showed me that someone could care about me, that I was worthwhile and could be loved. I had a reason to try, when so many times, trying for myself was never enough. Chase made me think that I could do better, have a better life, he showed me that it was possible, that he would be there to help me. Meeting him made me believe in myself and that I could, if I really wanted to, get sober.

I remember the DUI instructor too, so brilliant setting such a small and attainable goal, her words forever etched in my mind, "Just get through this one night." My mom too, from the time I was little, always, always there for me, no matter the cost or what she had to go through. She made sacrifice after sacrifice to try to save me, never giving up on me, even while most were advising her to cut me off and let me figure it out for myself. I believe without Chase coming into my life, I would likely be dead. Without my mom there for me through the years, sticking by me no matter what, I would have died too. The DUI Instructor, basically a stranger, played a huge role and sadly, I don't even know her name.

I can't say the same about my dad. I can't say that he was ever there or that he helped me through any part of my addiction. I don't remember him, in all of the years I struggled, I can't picture him trying to help me I think about the texts from my dad, they make me sad. The strangest part is I feel sorry for him, I'm worried about him, how he's feeling, wondering if he's okay. I scroll through our texts and reread them. This can't be it; this can't be the way this ends. I text my dad and wait.

ME

Would you be willing to meet with me in Therapy?

·Chapter Seventeen·

My dad agreed to meet me at the therapist's. I'm early, our appointment isn't for another twenty minutes, but I wanted to arrive ahead of time, before him, ready and waiting. I was afraid of having to walk in together, afraid to be alone with him. At the same time, I was sad, feeling sorry for him, wishing, like I always did, that things were different. I sit in the car thinking about the past, my dad, Marianne, and their whole sordid family. Looking back it all made sense, why I was the way I was. Why I had the need to get obliterated and try to void out feelings.

I flash to me with blood dripping down my arms, not caring, excited about registering, loving everything about needles and drugs, hollow inside, living to shoot up. I picture myself with a needle in my arm, or in my neck, it still excites me sometimes, something about it, knowing I could be free of feelings. I think back to my first few months of sobriety, I kept a needle hidden away. Bringing it out when I was alone, shooting water, just to feel it again, to register, to see the hole in my skin, and the blood. Something about it so comforting, representing relief, in my head, a single needle able to rescue me from all of the things that troubled me.

I didn't want to be sober, not at first. I'd go back and forth thinking of sobriety than thinking of being high, the thoughts of being high always winning out. If Chase wasn't holding vigil over me the first few days, I definitely would have relapsed. Chase and I were dating even though it was frowned on for anyone new in recovery. The guideline was a year before getting into a romantic relationship, but we were in deep. Chase had been sober for nearly two years, and I only had a few days when we decided we were going to go against the odds and stay together.

I stopped heroin cold turkey and it was rough, most addicts, try to taper off, but for me, it was too late. I had my sobriety date, according to Chase and a single day under my belt. I almost relapsed so many times. I was so sick; I can't even describe how sick I was. It was worse than the most horrendous bought of the flu, with fever and chills, cramping, diarrhea, and vomiting. My body ached like it was going to shrivel up and disintegrate, I couldn't move, the pain so severe I would black out and then wake up having hallucinations, I could hardly take it.

To make matters worse, I kept trying to pick a fight with Chase, hoping he'd leave me or want to break up with me so that I would be worthless and alone again. I would be able to use. Chase was unbelievable, he was so aware, he knew what I was doing and he refused to give up on me. He stood by me through it all, he helped me get sober. When it finally dawned on me that he wasn't going anywhere, that he was committed to me and my sobriety, I knew he must have really loved me. Something finally clicked. I knew that I loved him too and that I never wanted to go back to feeling so worthless and alone again. I finally felt ready to stop, I was finished with being sick and feeling bad, I was ready to be sober and believed with all of my heart that it was possible.

It wasn't easy. Getting Sober will most likely be the most difficult accomplishment I have ever achieved. It took everything I had, and then some. Once I was through the worst of it, I had to change everything about my life. I changed my phone number, my email, even moving and changing my address. I stopped all contact with anyone from the past that was a part of my previous way of life. I basically started over, living life in a sense as if I was part of some sort of Witness Protection Program with a new identity

I also dedicated myself to keeping busy, working, exercising, and attending meetings. Chase, at the time, was almost militant about attending meetings so we both went as often as possible. When I was first sober, one of the hardest things for me was that I wasn't used to thinking and feeling so much. I was flooded with thoughts and feelings all of the time and, I didn't know how to handle it. The worst was that I started obsessing about what could have happened to me. It seemed that Chase, as well as many of the people I was meeting in recovery, had a background that involved some sort of trauma. Now sober, I would question what happened in my own life, wondering more than ever why I was the way I was.

As the months passed, even though I was in recovery and doing well, shooting up never left my mind. I would constantly envision myself with needles and drugs, picturing a tie off on my arm and being ready to go. Using drugs was my default setting and I had to figure out how to change it.

Sobriety came with a huge learning curve; I had to reeducate myself on living normally, how to have a quiet and calm life free from anything remotely like my life in addiction. I had to develop self-control and coping skills. I lived in years of shame, never feeling good about myself and now I was trying to build self-esteem and develop character. Being inclined to lie and steal, or take the easy way out of situations, behaviors that were a part of my everyday life, all had to go. It took effort and I had to work to become a new and improved version of myself and, it wasn't happening overnight.

I guess I thought it would be easier, a part of me believing that once I was able to get sober, I would magically morph into a good person, with good qualities and better habits. I was finding out that it was going to take determination on my part and I was going to need help. Attending The Twelve Step Program was one of the things that anchored me in my recovery, that and getting a sponsor, working the steps, and reading the "Big Book." Also, a good friend told me about a Positive Thinking Book called You Can Heal Your Life, by Louise L. Hay that really motivated me to work on myself, it helped me clean up a lot of old ways of thinking.

One of the fun parts about my personal recovery was that I connected with a lot of my longtime friends, people I had known from a young age, all of us former drug addicts and alcoholics, now Chasing Sober together. We had been in some of the same circles; our lives are interwoven through years of addiction, jail time, rehab, and sobriety programs. Seeing them weekly at meetings, working their own program, we were able to support and encourage each other which was super encouraging to me.

Chase and I were in a good place too, we were in love and we were planning to go the distance, but our relationship wasn't without challenges. We met in September of 2008 and I started my recovery in November of the same year. We moved in together a few months later, finding out that living together wasn't the easiest, even though we really cared about each other.

Our shared background, unrealistic expectations, shortcomings and all of the things we needed to juggle to stay in recovery was a lot to get used to. Then there was work and finances. Chase was still working at Second Chance and actually was part of a television series on Sundance called "Get to Work," which highlighted him in action. He was good at what he did and I loved watching it each week. His fame was short-lived and after the series ended, he started looking for a new job. We moved into a Rental Property of my moms, a cute little house, and we loved it.

For the most part, we got along well and had a good time, but long-term addiction creates some pretty selfish tendencies, tendencies we both had to work on. Whatever was going on we both were willing to keep trying, we were determined to stay together and make things work. I think because we both spent so much time in unsafe surroundings and unhappy environments, we did our best to create a safe, happy and fun life for ourselves.

Chase proposed in the spring of 2010. Before he did, being the traditional type, he wanted to go to my dad and ask for my hand in marriage, which under ordinary circumstances would have been fine, but my family was anything but ordinary and the circumstances were strained. I rarely saw my dad, Marianne or my sisters and I knew when I introduced Chase to everyone, things would be awkward. I was actually nervous for Chase to meet them, embarrassed about how they treated me. The strangest part was that Chase and my dad got along fine, but he was on to Marianne and my sisters from the start.

Waiting several months after their first meeting, Chase wanting to surprise me, made a plan with my dad to meet privately, telling him he was in love with me and asking if he could marry me. My dad, of course, said yes, and agreed to keep Chase's Surprise Proposal a secret from my stepmother and my two sisters, and more importantly me. My dad broke his promise within a few days, telling me all about it. Not only did he tell me, but he also told Marianne and my sisters, ruining everything about it. Just like that, Chase was a witness to my family, and how uncaring and selfish they all were.

In a crowded restaurant in Pacific Beach, my dad, who openly admitted to me that he had sworn to secrecy, sat and told me that Chase was planning to propose to me and that he had accidentally told everyone. My feelings were all over the place, a part of me thrilled to think that Chase wanted to marry me and was planning a surprise proposal, and another part of me crushed that my dad, man of zero integrity, told people ahead of the event, including me. He ruined my surprise. To make matters worse he started sharing the reactions of my awful stepmother, and sisters, telling me none of them were even happy for me. He literally sat there, stammering through a tale about how angry they were that I was engaged ahead of my half-sister Taylor, who had been living with her boyfriend for over five years.

"Can you believe it?" he laughed, "They're livid, they're all so pissed and now they're afraid you're going to get married first." I sat there brokenhearted, this was my dad, ruining everything Chase had planned, not caring about him or appreciating that he was respectful enough to even involve my dad. My dad was exactly the same, all these years later, happy to ruin anything that went well for me, he hadn't changed a bit. He sabotaged my proposal, betrayed Chase's trust and now wanted to sit here, with me in complete shock and trying to recover, while he continued to laugh and gossip about it.

Like always, our time together left me questioning myself, feeling bad about things and confused. Why would my dad want to cause a division now, before I was even engaged, all of the things he shared sure to mar how I felt about inviting my sisters to my engagement party, my shower and even my wedding. I had even planned to include Marianne in the things she wouldn't be included in with my dad, to do the right thing, put my best foot forward.

I was so sad, I wanted my sisters to be excited for me, I loved them, I was hoping for a fresh start, I wanted them to be my friends and now it was all ruined. Thinking about why my dad would be so cruel, I don't get it. Instead of being proud of me, thrilled that I was off drugs and that my life was going well, that someone decent loved me enough to want to spend his life with me, he shit all over everything. What should have been a happy, celebratory time in my life, instead, like anything that involved my dad, ended up being hurtful and confusing. He was a grown man, why? Why did he always want to ruin everything for me? Worse, why did my dad want to ruin me?

Getting together with my dad was new since I had become sober, and it didn't happen very often, especially with all the buttons I knew he could push. I guess in a way, I was wary of him, unsure of how our relationship would be. Unclear of how he, Marianne and my sisters were going to fit back into my life. Working the steps and reading the "Big Book" helped, meetings too, forgiveness was a big topic, but it didn't come easy.

This time period was years before I had any of the memories of Sexual Abuse, but I had a lot of other so-called "resentments" towards my dad for so many things. I think not being there for me, never protecting me from Marianne and her form of abuse and, mostly for the years of causing divisions between me and my sisters. The odd thing about people is no matter how bad their bad side is, you can almost always find good. There was and always would be a part of me that loved my dad and, would try to see the good in him. I just had to find a way to allow him and his family to be a part of my life on new terms, my terms.

Chase proposed in the spring of 2010 and of course, I said yes. Even though my dad had thrown a wrench in Chase's big surprise, Chase still caught me off guard, taking me for a quiet dinner at one of our favorite restaurants, followed by a casual walk on the beach. He got down on one knee and with tears in his eyes, said the most beautiful things I think I've ever heard. He really loved me, more than I had ever been loved in my life. Putting the engagement ring on my finger, I'm not sure which of us cried more. It was one of the most exciting times in my life. I couldn't wait to be Mrs. Chase Campbell. I promised myself I would appreciate the entire experience, from the planning to the parties, to the wedding itself, I was going to enjoy everything. I was on a natural high, happier than I had ever been.

My mom, crazy about Chase, was thrilled, but much more practical she insisted that she and I get started planning right away. Just being engaged and wearing my beautiful ring had my heart singing. My life was like a modern-day fairytale for addicts. Less than two years ago, I was a complete junkie, on a sure path to death from a Heroin Overdose, and now I was in love, had been sober for an entire year and was soon to be a Married Woman. My Wedding now would be a far cry from the farce Prison Wedding years ago. I think I was so happy I thought my heart would burst open.

It wasn't all confetti and rainbows though, we both decided to quit smoking cigarettes before we got married, we wanted our wedding to be not only drug and alcohol-free, but smoke-free too. Ready to move forward without our bad habits, it was rough. We were edgy, grumpy and outright mean. Then to make matters worse, Chase broke his hand, and it was seriously intense. Being former Drug Addicts, he couldn't take any narcotics and was stuck toughing it out with over the counters like Advil and Tylenol. His arm was in a cast for weeks and he couldn't do anything about the pain, which made him pretty unbearable.

We were so stressed, on top of quitting smoking and Chase's Broken hand, our finances were shaky and we couldn't afford to do much, like go out and have fun, even dinner or a movie was a stretch. Everything was too expensive after paying our monthly expenses and putting money towards our wedding. So there we were, stuck together under very tense circumstances, with no distractions. It was super challenging. Sometimes in order to keep the peace, Chase would go in the other room and play video games, while I zoned out on Keeping up with the Kardashians. I remember thinking if we could make it through that time period, we could make it through anything.

Still reminiscing as I head inside, Rosie greets me with a warm hug and reminds me that I'm in a safe environment, and this is my opportunity, to be honest and open, about everything. We sit and wait making small talk until my dad arrives. I can hear his car pull up out front, him getting out and shutting the door, his footsteps, and then the doorbell. Rosie goes to answer the door and I sit by myself and wait.

Alone, I think back to my wedding day. Chase and I were married on September 25, 2010, forever one of the best days of my life. I had never felt so beautiful or so loved. We were married in Point Loma, in a beautiful setting with an amazing view, surrounded by all of the people in our lives that meant the most to us. I loved everything about it and tried my best not to let my dad, Marianne or my sisters ruin it. From the time I was engaged until my wedding was over, I experienced a million emotions, that I wasn't used to dealing with, most positive and very exciting, but some extremely stressful and even scary. Chase, again, very big on being at the meetings and working the program, insisted I do the same. I think staying in that routine really helped.

My mom was honestly a saint, helping at every turn, as well as covering every expense, from the Engagement Party to the Rehearsal Dinner, to the venue and everything to do with the actual wedding. My dad, true to character never contributed one penny, but had a list of personal family and friends that he wanted to be included, at one hundred dollars a plate. I was so delusional about it all at the time, I think subconsciously I questioned it, but like always I overlooked it. Throughout the entire process, my dad didn't lift a finger, contribute anything financially, or put forth any effort in any way to help. Disassociating it, I continued to think he was the most loving and caring father.

Although, my dad, his wife, and my sisters, were welcome and included every step of the way, nothing they were involved in was ever easy, or without some form of conflict. My goal, with Chase's help, was to stay positive; regardless of what any of them were saying or doing, or how they were acting. With my mom helping, everything was planned to perfection, I had both of my sisters and Chase's Sister, the one from the gala, in my wedding, my dad walked me down the aisle and gave me away and, apart from all of the undercurrents from him and his family, everything was amazing. It was one of the best days of my life.

I was so grateful and overflowing with joy and appreciation the entire day, I was thrilled with everything about my wedding and looked forward to being able to have fun with all of the guests at my reception. Of course, it started off fabulous and once we arrived with the Wedding Party and did the customary introductions, the music played, dinner was served and the party was started. It was after this that Chase and I took a few minutes to show our love and heartfelt gratitude to the ones who supported us the most.

Through a poem that I read, I thanked my mom for her years of self-sacrifice, love, and commitment to me, touching on my battle with addiction and her refusal to give up on me, ultimately saving my life. I also thanked her for all of her financial contributions to everything throughout my life, but more importantly her example of character, appreciating her strength and stability and how she handled life with so much integrity. It was because of those qualities that I was even alive, never once did she let me down, even in our most challenging times. Emotional and heartfelt there were a few other things but when I finished, there wasn't a dry eye in the entire room. It was very moving, honest and sincere. It was truly how I felt, it honored and credited the one person in my life who had been a constant, never giving up on me and making everything throughout my life and my entire wedding experience possible.

As I finished, I noticed both of my sisters in angry tears, making a scene and storming out, with their mother in tow. It was Cinderella come to life at my very own wedding. My dad, the divider, instead of letting it go rushed over to me moments later to share that they were angry that my mom got all of the credit and I didn't mention any of them, going as far as including that they felt they had been through hell too and deserved acknowledgment. It was unbelievable, I had simply written and read a poem for my mom, who did everything, paid for everything, and is everything to me and, they were finding fault with it.

I can't say I was surprised, but I was sad, feeling like the three of them, even on a very special occasion, could not be happy for me. As much as I tried to extend nothing but love and welcome them into one of the most beautiful days of my life, I never felt that they were at my wedding to celebrate or to enjoy the day and be a part of all of the excitement. I'd see them throughout the event, clumped together like always, better than everyone, too good to socialize with my friends or Chase's Family, judging everyone and everything. For me even now, sober and on my Wedding Day, they were able to make me feel like I didn't measure up.

My mom sent us to Hawaii for our Honeymoon, her Wedding Gift to us was ten days in Maui. It was definitely the way to wind down and relax after months of being constantly busy, planning, preparing and working towards our wedding. I know there were things that weren't perfect, didn't go as well as I hoped and could have gotten the best of me, but I really set the goal to make the most of all of that time and enjoy it and I did. For me, regardless of what anyone else thought, it was the perfect ending to a really wonderful time of life. It was surreal really to think that I could be the focus of so much positive energy, love, and support, I can't be certain but I think Chase felt the same way. It was truly a great experience.

Getting back to reality wasn't as easy. Chase ready to pave his way to a more lucrative and rewarding career took an entry-level job in Human Resources at a Fortune 500 Company. Having to learn from the ground up, he spent the first few months working long hours and even bringing work home. He was a hard worker and very disciplined, he dedicated himself to do well and do his best to make a good life for us. Even though he would be stressed and short-fused from time to time, I couldn't have been more proud.

At this same time, I had my own amount of stress going on. My mom with a renewed interest in me being a College Graduate had offered to pay all expenses and help us out financially if I went to school. Putting all of my anxieties and phobias about school aside, I started college just before our wedding and was getting all of my pre-requisites out of the way, in order to get into one of the local Universities. I wanted to do something where I could help people and according to my mom, the way to do it was with a degree behind your name, my end game was to get a Degree in Psychology. Never being much of a student, I wasn't doing that well initially and was fairly discouraged. With all of this added to a new marriage, wedded bliss wasn't exactly what we were experiencing.

Daily life for both Chase and I was very busy. With so much going on, and responsibilities in other areas, neither of us stayed on track with meetings or working our recovery programs. I wasn't as worried about what might happen or the possibility of relapse as I used to be. I didn't want to get too self-confident, but I was actually too busy and too tired to even think about alcohol and drugs. Although we were fairly exempt from our old lifestyles, there were still times when that way of life or things about it would creep in, at least for me. Fear of police, being pulled over and being arrested were fears that I had and I didn't know if they would ever leave.

One of the first times I was pulled over as a sober person, was just as scary as when it happened to me in addiction. Having been pulled over and arrested many times, my last was only a few months before I kicked heroin, which had been over three years ago. I honestly hadn't heard a siren, been pulled over, or had anything to do with the police since my final arrest in 2008.

I was sober and law-abiding, but was still completely unsettled by anything to do with the police. So when I got pulled over with a friend, after going to breakfast, just hearing, "Bleep, Bleep..." the sound alone seared through my nervous system and made me a nervous wreck. I thought I was going to mess myself and throw-up at the same time. Panicked, I felt like I had the wind knocked out of me and I struggled to breathe normally. All of this and my friend, the driver had no reaction at all, she was completely unfazed. I sat, dying for both of us, as two cops approached her car, one on each side.

I looked rugged, wearing one of Chase's Oversized Raider's Sweatshirts and Jeans, I had showered and pulled my hair into a ponytail and wasn't wearing make-up. The cop on my side popped his head in my window and asked for my I.D. Startled, I rummaged through my wallet and handed it over, wondering why. I felt judged like he was only running my I.D. because of my appearance, mostly my sweatshirt and tattoos, I was scared. My friend, behind the wheel, was going through it with her own cop, only he seemed more relaxed, and friendly. I heard her ask why we were being pulled over and his answer was, that her brake lights were out.

Questioning why they'd need my I.D. for that, I go to every worst-case scenario I could think of, ultimately thinking it was something from my past that wasn't cleared up and I was going to jail again. I wasn't at all confident, even knowing I hadn't done anything. I think I was so used to going to jail, I couldn't calm down. Something inside reminding me this scenario, at least for me had never really ended well. I sit quietly listening as my friend tells her cop that she didn't have her license. My heart sank.

With my policeman back at his car running my I.D., I use the opportunity to text Chase. My hands are shaking so bad, I fumble with the letters, misspelling everything. I tell him we're getting pulled over and they took my I.D., asking him, "What if I go to jail?" Then texting in all caps, "I DON'T WANT TO GO TO JAIL," followed by, "I'll let you know."

In my head, I've almost always gone to jail. I was so used to it not working out for me and going to jail, that's all I could think about. Old memories flood my mind, none of them good. I was under the influence and when I'd go to jail, I'd go through withdrawals in there almost every time. I always thought I would mess myself, the fear of police, jail, and consequences, causing such a strong reaction in my body. I'm still having all of those feelings now, only I'm a law-abiding citizen and I still think if I don't get to a restroom soon, I'm going to have a problem. I'm so uncomfortable I want to cry.

The officer on my side comes back and hands me my I.D. asking me "How come you have a record?" I just look at him, not knowing what to say. "You mean my past?" I ask, unclear. I want to ask if I can have a minute to head over behind the bushes and go to the bathroom, that's how bad it is, but instead, I sit silent afraid of him. He's rough and unfriendly, mean even, I think to myself, maybe he's a Charger's Fan.

I want to lighten things up, I haven't done anything, but I'm afraid to make small talk, he looks mad like he wants to take me down a rung. I keep my mouth shut remembering some advice from an attorney in my past, "Don't ask, don't tell," in other words "Keep your mouth shut, only speak when you're spoken to, and one-word answers, no details." Remembering my schooling I keep quiet.

He looks at me and asks again, "How come you have a record?" I look at him blankly, trying to think of a one-word answer for that. My friend over on the other side of the car has fared better, with a written warning to repair her brake lights and not having her license, her policeman is gone, already back at their car. She leans over and looks at my cop, "Bad Choices," she says, "But she's been sober for over three years. Isn't that great?" He smiles and congratulates me, returning my I.D. "Have a nice day ladies," he says then walks away.

Confused, I wondered if it was all me, in my head, all of the reactions and responses based on my history, instead of what was reality and what was actually happening. My thoughts of him changed from mean and scary, to nice, just like that. Why? Because I didn't get arrested? Would I ever be like my friend, who didn't react? Calm throughout, getting pulled over and being okay with it? Of course, she had never been arrested nor had a bad experience with the police. She had never been to jail, didn't have a record or a history of addiction. My life had changed, I had changed, in a million ways and all for the better, but no matter how much progress I made, my past was still there, underneath it all, ready to take me back. I knew in time, I would learn how to get a handle on my reactions, a part of self-control, it was a part of the sober living learning curve. My friend starts the car and we make a beeline for a Starbucks with a restroom, hoping I can make it.

As the years went by, life definitely became brighter, I rarely if ever even thought about my old life. There were reminders all around but over time, that wasn't who I was anymore. I worked hard to change, I loved Chasing Sober, I was finally loved and felt happy. Chase and I were Best Friends and were both proud of how far we had come. It wasn't perfect, but it was so good. For me, my sobriety made me feel so accomplished, and for someone who had never really accomplished much of anything, it was the best feeling in the world. I had been sober for almost five years and married three when I found out Chase and I were going to have a baby. We were both thrilled. Having a child of our own was a dream and we couldn't wait to be parents. We were committed from the start to do our best to be good parents and have a happy family life.

It was after my first doctor's appointment, the one that confirmed the plus sign on my pregnancy test that something popped into my head, something horrible. It wouldn't go away. The first few times, of course, I thought I was crazy, willing my thoughts to stop, but they wouldn't. The more I tried to stop them, the worse they would get. I didn't want anything like that in my head, I was so happy and excited to be pregnant, it was like a dark cloud of dreary memories came and settled in. I was still thrilled about having a child, still enjoying that experience, but the memories stayed. I kept it to myself, begging them to stop, go away, and let me live my happy little life, but they were here to stay.

Thinking back to when I first started having the memories of my dad, I feel sick. I'm still waiting in my therapist's office, I can hear Rosie and my dad talking, it's been a while. He's probably grilling her on her qualifications, wanting to see her degree. I know he won't like that she works out of her house, she won't be good enough for him, he'll think she's a sham.

My dad comes in and sits down, slouching in his chair, "Hey Kris," he says and I already want to cry. How can I still love him so much? Why do I feel sad for him? He's casual in jeans, a polo shirt, and tennis shoes. I watch him, trying to figure him out, his body language, how he's acting, but I can't. I'm going to cry. Rosie starts as I try to keep composed. "Kristen has been having some thoughts about the past that won't go away, so we're here to discuss them, together, to find out more about them." My dad looks at me and asks, "Like what kind of thoughts?" I brace myself and say "I feel like you've always stared at my boobs." I take a deep breath and add, "Actually, I think you may have done more."

My dad scratches his head and looks at Rosie and then to me, "So this is about boobs?" he looks at me, explaining, "Well, um, geez, half of the world's population goes around topless. I mean, boobs are everywhere, are we just talking about boobs?" Speechless, I look at Rosie, waiting for her to say something, anything. I can't believe this is my dad's response. It literally makes me sick. Rosie as if she's reading my mind, tells my dad, "We're not just talking about "boobs," but if we were, we are talking about your daughter's "breasts," and if you touched them at any time in her life it's not only considered Sexual Abuse, but it is against the law. My dad laughs nervously, and looks at me, "Boobs? Really? So you think I touched your boobs? Well, I mean, geez, they're just boobs. This is what all of this is about? So I looked at them or I touched them? Or what? Uh, well, I mean if I did, I don't remember."

I think even the therapist is surprised by him. It's shocking really, a grown man, a father, acting like his daughter's breasts are unimportant, trivial, something "half of the world's population has, and is exploiting, or as he so eloquently stated, "are running around topless with." I feel invisible, I don't matter. To him, me and my body are insignificant, my memories too, my feelings, all of it falls to the wayside with him. Everything I believe my dad has done to me, sexual abuse included, all of it is now casually excused by him saying, "If I did, I don't remember."

My dad not remembering means I am worthless to him. In my dad's assessment of me, I am so worthless; I don't even merit him remembering? I try not to cry, not to overthink, stay focused, present for the rest of our conversation. We talk about other things, it's big and scary, our discussion unearthing things from long ago, so many things that aren't right, inappropriate.

My dad finds blame with me being messed up first, then it's because of the drugs, then maybe it was my friend's father, my mom's boyfriend, ready to pass the blame the list goes on. He doesn't stop, in a shocking confession, he admits to having and reading all of my "Smut Letters." Openly stating that he saved them and he has them in his storage. I might be sick as he goes on, letters to me from several convicts and letters I may have written to them, and never sent. As he speaks, I remember wondering what happened to them and the box that was under my bed. I picture the box, from years ago as the memory of it flashes through my head. I feel dirty even thinking of them. My dad explains he found them when he moved me out, I correct him. "Threw me out you mean." He continues, "Well anyway I read those letters and there was one where you describe someone, on you, you were passed out and, I don't know, you couldn't breathe, well anyhow, maybe it was one of those guys from the letters?"

I look at him in disbelief, "You're sick dad. There's something wrong with you those letters were private, you didn't have any business taking them or reading them. You kept them? I mean, why would you want to? It's all so repulsive, it's something someone perverted would do and for the record, it isn't any of the people that you mentioned. My memories are of you dad.

My dad stands up, "Is that it? Are we done here?" Looking down at me he seems mad. I can't believe he's mad at me. It's outrageous. "Really, is that it Kristen?" I look at him, not sure what to do or say, "I guess if you're done? I mean there are other things, there are a lot of things, but you don't seem like you want to talk about them." My dad looks flustered, and glares at me, "You're sick," he says, then walks out without looking back.

I sit in my chair and start sobbing, looking to Rosie to help me make sense of everything. Sadly there's no making sense of any of this. We discuss, my dad's body language, agreeing that emotionally he was immature and on the defense coming in. We discuss how he minimized the topic, minimized me and, my body. My dad acted like even if he had done it, it wouldn't have been an issue, at least not to him. We discuss the fact that my dad never denied doing anything to me. That was it, there wasn't anything else to talk about, except how I was going to handle this and the feelings I had about it. What was I going to do now?

I'm stunned that my dad didn't deny any of it. How could he not remember? Was that even an excuse? I'm shocked that he didn't fight for his innocence; my dad wouldn't even put up a fight for me. Not once did he say he would never do anything like that, or that he loved me. He never really questioned any of it, instead, like always, he blamed other people, putting the focus on someone else. I feel sick and betrayed, bringing up the letters? Why would any father ever read, let alone keep all of those sickening letters? It was surreal. This was it; this was going to be our end, our goodbye.

More than anything, I was scared. My mom took a week off to stay with me and the kids during the day while Chase was at work. We had all of the locks changed and had cameras installed. We read that some people who are confronted about the abuse become suicidal and want to kill themselves. Sometimes they're so upset that they've been exposed, they'll go after the accuser. I honestly didn't know what to think, I was afraid for myself and my kids, but I was also sad and worried about my dad.

My mom was all business about the entire thing. Practical, she was ready to put it all behind us and move on. She didn't believe in dwelling on the past or even talking about it, especially when it came to me. I think she tried to stay neutral about her opinions of my dad, only briefly even commenting on everything. It was an odd thing to discuss. Maybe it was all too hard for her, my past too painful. I think she just wanted to enjoy where we were now, relish in the fact that she had me back and that I was doing so well, especially in light of what I had been dealing with.

My dad never reached out to me, months went by and I would wonder about him, wonder how he was, questioning whether he thought of us at all, did he even miss me? Did he miss his Grandchildren? Was he okay? That day at Rosie's he just disappeared, I never talked to him again, never talked to Marianne or my sisters. Marianne left a scathing personal message on my Facebook Page, telling me I was sick and needed help, that I was horrible my entire life, always causing problems for them. There on social media, for the world to see, so I blocked them all, from everything. My Phone, Facebook, Instagram, life.

I didn't block my dad from my phone, I think I hoped he would call, reconsider, at some point and take accountability, but it never happened. My dad dropped off the face of the earth after that, at least to me. I didn't see him for years, in my mind; I pictured him so alone, so sad, despondent, maybe even suicidal, then one day I see him. He's fine, he's happy, just out riding his bike with a friend, enjoying the day, not a care in the world. I tear up, a rush of adrenaline washes through me. I keep driving, in a way relieved that he's okay but, in another way, I find myself crushed that life just went on for him, he's unscathed, like always, I didn't matter.

·Chapter Eighteen·

Time, the great healer of heartache and loss eventually took over and softened the blow of my dad and his reaction to what I believed happened to me. My dad walked out of the therapist's office that day and out of my life. It was the last time I would see or hear from him and I don't know why but I was devastated. I think at first, it was almost like he had died, it was that painful. There were days that I would miss him so much that I would just cry; grieving him and feeling his absence in my life.

To confront him was by far one of the most difficult things I had faced since becoming sober. Losing him to the circumstances, regardless of how dysfunctional our relationship had been was heartbreaking. I honestly didn't expect it to be so hard. Gratefully, having a husband and family to take care of, and a busy life, I wasn't able to stay down for long, I had to pick up the pieces and move forward. I was also concerned about my sobriety, aware that these were the types of situations that would cause people to relapse.

As hard as it was and as sad as I felt, once I decided to put it all behind me and focus forward, within a few weeks I noticed that all of the sordid memories and thoughts of the past had stopped. They were gone, along with my dad, they had disappeared and left in their place was a sense of peace, something I had never experienced before.

I knew all along that confronting my dad would end our relationship, more than likely it was the reason I continued to put it off for so long. I just didn't know that I would take it so hard. In the end, even with the memories gone and being freed from dwelling on my past, in a way I didn't feel like it was over, for some reason I didn't feel like I had closure. In place of what used to trouble me and occupy my thoughts was a need for validation.

There was a part of me that wanted my dad to admit to what he had done and not just the sexual abuse. I felt a need for him to acknowledge that he allowed my stepmother to treat me abusively too. I think of all the years that he wouldn't get involved when I needed him to, when I needed him to step in and protect me. Then there was the constant divide he caused, between me and my sisters, alienating us from each other, ultimately destroying any chance for us to have a relationship. It wasn't realistic for me to even think about. In my head, I could picture it, but it would never happen. I don't think my father was capable of telling the truth, or accepting any of the blame or responsibility when it came to me.

In the therapist's office, the last time we were together, I asked him why he always lied to Marianne and my sisters about being with me. His answer was that "It was just easier." Did that even qualify as an answer? There were hundreds of things that I questioned or wondered about, things I had to let go, move past, but there were other things that I wanted my dad to acknowledge, to admit to. I guess I wanted him to take some accountability for what went wrong in my life. In my mind, it was the answer, if that happened, then I would have closure; I would be able to move on.

In time, all of it subsided, my thoughts and feelings about my dad and his accountability eased up. In the back of my mind though, the desire I had for him to provide some sort of closure for me was always there. I tried to move on and I did, but from time to time something would come up, something that reminded me of him and how much I missed him. Then the whole closure issue would reappear.

Randomly, I gave Jordan a handful of Tic Tacs one day not thinking too much about it. Staring at them in her hand, she looked at me and asked, "Hey Mom, remember before, there was that man that gave me these?" Amazed that she could remember, it was my dad. My dad always had Tic Tacs, they were his thing. I think he gave her a couple but she wasn't even two, it was close to the end of our relationship. It had been well over a year and Jordan was three now. I looked at her and smiled, "Hmmm, I'm not sure." Not giving up she tries to remind me, "Remember that guy, you know him mom, he's called Pops." Trying not to react, I tell her I don't remember and go in the other room and break down.

There were other things that would come up, reminders of my dad. Holidays, Birthdays, certain places, beaches, a bike ride. It was interesting that now, it seemed like I could only see him in a good light. In his absence, I would mostly recall all of the fun times and happy memories. I knew it wasn't accurate though, it happened with my addiction too, sometimes exaggerating all of the fun and excitement, while playing down the hardships, years of desperation and, heartache. Trying to stay positive, I wanted to focus on and remember all of the good, the past was over and it was time to let it go. Or was it?

I continued in therapy, trying to sort out all of my feelings about everything that happened. Initially, it was challenging, but along with therapy, I attended my Twelve Step Program regularly. Choosing to go to an all women's group, they were the best and all of them were extremely supportive. On one harrowing afternoon, where Rosie and I talked about some pretty unsettling things, I went to the meeting that evening and afterward, told a few close friends about what I had been going through over the past year.

These were girls my age that had been in and out of alcoholism and addiction with me for years. Friends, from my past, doing their best to work the program, they were there every week Chasing Sober with me. When I shared that I had memories of my dad molesting me and that I had confronted him and was in therapy, one of them looked at me and without hesitating said, "You told me and my sister that your dad molested you years ago." Continuing she adds, "In fact, we always thought it was strange that you still hung out with him, especially after what he did to you." I didn't remember at first. I couldn't believe that I told anyone. Letting it sink in, I started to tear up and asked, "Really?"

I didn't remember a lot of things at first, but over time, as more and more things like that started happening and, more and more people shared their stories and insight, I did remember. I was able to start putting all of the pieces together so that no matter how much I would doubt myself, there were clear signs that my dad was guilty.

I did my best to put it all behind me and focus forward, in the beginning, even avoiding all of the places that I thought I might run into my dad. Over time though, I just started living my life, trying not to think about any of it. I'd take my kids to our favorite beaches, we'd go on bike rides, and I'd jog on the boardwalk. Outside of the one sighting, I didn't run into my dad, Marianne or my sisters at all, and it was fine, perfect even.

I was more and more comfortable with the fact that my dad was no longer a part of my life. The loss I originally felt was definitely diminishing. The only thoughts that lingered were of my dad not admitting to it. Apart from his text messages, he never verbally denied any of it, but he never admitted to it either. I continued to have a burning desire for him to just confess, to apologize to be remorseful, somehow I wanted him to care enough about me to at least give me that, to at least let me have closure.

Instead, I never heard a word from the man that is, until one random day over two years later, when a letter from him showed up in my mailbox. With my heart racing, I was so excited; I could hardly contain myself wondering what he wrote. In a Business Envelope, I ripped it open and within seconds was instantly deflated. It was typed, a form letter, buttoned up, boxy, like it was written by an attorney. The letter said, "He missed me, because of what I believed happened and that he never thought it would mean he wouldn't see me or hear from me for this long." It goes on to say, "He went for professional help and wants to try to repair our relationship." I'm confused, why is my dad sending a letter? I don't understand, why is it typed? Why wouldn't he just call me? Why did he let it go for two years? Once again, like always, my dad avoids any accountability.

The letter states that, "He knows the deep hurt and confusion my recollections have created for me and that he can appreciate how upsetting that would be." I read over parts of it again, it doesn't even sound like my dad. I keep reading and it says, "He understands that abuse has long-lasting effects on the victim and he's truly sorry that I may have experienced anything of this nature." May have? He follows up, "However, with that being said, I did not ever do anything remotely like that, as I said before, I miss you, Jordan, Ryder, and Chase very much."

It's the worst letter I've ever read, it's disappointing and I don't get it. Like ripping a Band-Aid off of a wound that I thought was healed, all of the thoughts, feelings and hurt, start to reemerge. I'm so sad, why on earth would my dad send me a Business Letter? Why typed? Is it even from him? Or is it from a lawyer? He ends it by saying "I hope you'll contact me to see if we can get back to some sort of reconciliation." In typed writing, it finishes with "Love always," and in handwriting, it's printed, "Your DAD."

I read the letter several times, trying to make sense of it. I can't though, so I decide to text him.

ME

I miss you. I'm so confused by everything.

My dad didn't respond to my text for over a week. I think at first I was sad, I wanted him to call, I wanted to reconnect and, I thought it was all going to work out for the best. I wanted to be optimistic about us and the future. I knew realistically though, it was never going to happen. My dad was emotionally immature, narcissistic even, he wasn't capable of making things right or doing his part to make things work between us.

I mean really, he sends me a form letter wanting to reconcile, seems to blame me for not being in touch and doesn't acknowledge his role in any of the damage he did in my life, then he has the nerve to wait over a week to respond to my text? They were games I no longer wanted to play. By that point, I knew I couldn't do it. I had been in such a great place without him in my life, without any of them. I wasn't prepared, nor did I want to face my dad and all of the baggage that came with him.

Before I received my dad's letter, I was happier and more relaxed than I had ever been. I was on cloud nine, Chase and I had recently found out that we were expecting our third child and we were thrilled. It was possible that it would even be my first pregnancy without memories of sexual abuse or flashbacks to my past. I was looking forward to having a good pregnancy, a happy and carefree pregnancy. I was in such a great place in life, that just the thought of having to try and fit my dad and his family back into our lives started causing all of the old feelings of doubt and worthlessness to resurface. I also started feeling apprehensive and anxious for the first time since my dad's departure.

I went to see my therapist, even though I had already decided on my own not to entertain any thoughts of seeing my dad or reconciling. I think him not texting me back or calling was in a way, a telltale sign that he hadn't changed at all. It was still all about him, he was above it all. He was waiting all that time for me to make the first move, all of the responsibility for our relationship fell on me. It was up to me, like always, to make things right with my dad, to be the one to reach out. I wouldn't do it, not anymore. I was strong enough to recognize that his one-sided relationship was no longer worth it. I went on with my life and my life couldn't have been better.

Still obsessed with having some type of closure, I don't believe it's a coincidence when my dad and I have a chance encounter down at the beach. I hadn't seen or spoken to him in over two years and it had been over a month since I had received his odd letter. That day, in a strange twist, my dad just happened to show up at the same beach, on the same day and at the same time as me.

It was gorgeous out, a beautiful summer day and I was sitting with a friend feeling so grateful for a beach day when everything changed. Chase was with us and had gone up to get our cooler out of the car. He called me from the top of the ramp to give me a head's up, "Bub, your dad's here, he's on his way down there?" I froze. I was instantly anxious and could feel my stomach knot up.

Chase had the day off work and we originally planned to take the kids out of preschool and spend the day as a family. In a strange twist, we took the kids to school, deciding it would be nice to just relax for a few hours at the beach with friends. Relieved now that my children weren't with us, I watched as my dad walked by, not noticing me or my friend.

He set up his chair and his umbrella less than thirty feet away. I tell her about Chase's call and point out that my dad was there. She's known him for years and knows everything about our situation. We hadn't been there long, both of us were still in our cover-ups with our bags still packed, and she asks if I want to leave. "No, I'm going over there," I tell her. Watching as my dad sits down and pulls out his sunscreen, my friend, afraid for me, begs me not to go. "At least wait until Chase gets back," she pleads. "I can't wait, not anymore," I say as I stand and leave.

I walked over; feeling like it was meant to be. I just have to get to the bottom of it; I need him to come clean. I need closure. It's all that's left, the only thing remaining from my past that troubles me. Catching him off guard, he's putting on sunscreen and he doesn't stop or even look at me. "Hey Dad, can we talk for a minute?"

He doesn't look at me, even as I crouch down to his level. "Uh, yea, I guess, sure," he continues sitting in his beach chair rubbing in his lotion. Before I can say anything, he angrily stammers, "We haven't talked in two and a half years, it's all your fault." So he's the victim? That's how he wants to start this off, "Dad, you haven't even tried to reach out." Still putting on his lotion, he sputters, "I tried calling, you never called me back, I was blindsided, cut-off. "Dad, you know that's not true, I took you to therapy, you're messed up." Rubbing lotion all over his face now, he fires back, "It's been the worst two years. The worst thing that could ever happen, you did it to me."

I'm stunned, "Dad, how do you think I feel? I had the experiences, I have the memories." The lotion is making me crazy. Now he's putting it on his arms and chest, at the same time, he says, "You're accusing me of something I didn't do. You're the one that's messed up. Marianne and I, we have a good sex life, we always have." Ignoring his sex life comment I continue, "Dad, I dressed like a boy, I was depressed, anxious, even suicidal. I told my mom, I said something to my friends when I was younger. Do you think I want this to be true?"

Squirting a huge blob of sunscreen into his hand, I want him to stop and just focus, have a reasonable conversation, but he won't, he rubs his hands together and starts on his legs, never once looking at me, "No, that's why you must be messed up. My other daughter's stand behind me." I look at him annoyed, "So it's all about you Dad?" Without stopping, he answers, "Yes, you ruined my life."

I'm hurt, I can't believe after all of this time my dad is still making it all about him. "You should have called me dad, even the day I text you that I thought I had been molested! A parent that cares and is loving would pick up the phone and call, come over, ask how they can help, ask who did such a thing, say they're going to kill them, I got NOTHING! You text back that just for the record it wasn't me! Really, you don't think you're guilty? No one thinks that way dad. No one who's innocent thinks of himself."

I start crying, even though I'm mad and I don't want to. My dad is still putting on sunscreen, so much it's just ridiculous now. He's not even looking at me and doesn't seem interested in anything I'm saying, but I have to get it out. "You should have thought of me, what I was going through, how hurt I was, you could have shown some concern. You weren't even worried that I could get pushed into using again, back to addiction. No dad, you were only concerned about yourself, just like my entire life."

He finally takes a break from the sunscreen overload and stammers, "Uh, well, I mean, when you sent that text, I was trying to think back, I thought maybe it was one of your friend's dads or one of your mom's boyfriends." Wiping away tears, I don't believe him, "If you didn't do it, dad, why didn't you fight for me, plead your cause, profess your innocence. If someone thought I did something to them and I was innocent, I'd fight for them, I would do everything I could to prove that they were wrong. You just walked away, walked out of my life. I wasn't even worth fighting for, not to you. Why didn't you fight for me dad? Why? "

Unaffected by anything I've said, my dad replies, "I tried to call." Hurt that he's not being honest, I tell him, "You didn't dad, cell phones don't lie, there's nothing from you, there's not a text, missed call, voicemail, there's nothing. You're not being truthful dad, why? You waited for two years! Then you sent me a form letter, the saddest strangest letter, you really think after all that time, after everything that happened, that's how you should contact your own daughter? You honestly sent a typed letter, a business letter? Do you really think you understand what I've been through? You don't dad, you have no idea or you would have shown you cared, you would have asked about me, been concerned about me, you wouldn't have made it all about you!"

Again, not acknowledging me or anything I've said he responds, "Well, uh, I tried to go to a therapist myself, a real one with an office, not a bogus one at some obscure woman's house, in the business because she has an ax of her own to grind. The therapist I went to said to write a letter and see if gets anywhere. Oh, and by the way, my therapist said your therapist can't be any good if she's working out of her house like that. She probably put all those weird ideas in your head."

I can't do this anymore; he's only focused on himself, on how he feels. He's not even being honest and now he's blaming my therapist, "Dad, why don't you just admit it, I'm not even mad about it, I won't tell anyone. Please admit it so I can move on. I'm begging you dad, I just need closure." Crossing his arms as he sits sprawled out in his beach chair; I continue to kneel next to him waiting for him to free me. Instead, defiantly he says, "I'm not admitting to something I didn't do, I have a pretty good memory and I don't remember doing that."

I watch him, saddened. He can't honestly be back to that, back to whether he remembers or not. "Dad, you didn't do it or you don't remember doing it? There's a big difference?" My dad is all of a sudden silent. He's done. He's not going to answer. I stand up, my legs feel weak from kneeling all that time, I turn and leave; disappointed that I don't have the closure I so desperately want. Or do I?

I walk back over to where we're sitting and Chase stands up to hug me. I immediately fall apart. Overwhelmed with emotions, I can't stop sobbing. My dad meanwhile, goes for a dip in the ocean, packs his belongings and leaves. That was the last time I ever talked to him. I haven't seen or heard from him since and I don't believe I ever will.

·Chapter Nineteen·

My Obstetrician and I are going over my exam, finishing up my appointment, I'm huge and my baby is due in two-weeks. "He's ready Kristen, he's going to be big," she tells me as we sit at her desk and go over my chart. It's quiet, nervous, I make small talk, sharing, "This has been my best pregnancy out of the three, I've never felt better." It's true, it's been amazing. "I've enjoyed it so much that I'm going to miss being pregnant."

I'm honest, I have been so happy; I've loved being pregnant this time. I'm not sure if it's because I haven't had to contend with memories of my past or if it's the fact that I've been able to move on, putting all of the issues with my dad and his family behind me. No longer a part of my life, I rarely, if ever, think about any of them or what happened.

My doctor is all business, friendly but distracted, I wonder if she was even listening. She writes something in my file then looks up, "Great, so we have your C-Section scheduled for March 19, at 10 a.m., over at Scripps La Jolla. I have on record that you prefer Toradol for pain is that still your preference?"

My heart stops, I've been planning for this moment for days, practicing even. "Well, actually no," I answer, "This time I'd like to just go with the normal painkillers." I am matter of fact. I do my best to stay calm but inside the alarms sound. Inside I'm panicking. I'm anything but calm. Just saying the word painkillers, I feel my body come to life. The idea that I'll be able to take them and have those feelings again is exciting. "Too exciting," says the voice in my head. It's acceptable I tell myself, I am having major surgery, after all. People in recovery do it all of the time and they're fine. I make a promise to myself that I'm only going to use them for the first few days, the days I'm in the hospital and that's it, I won't take any home. It's already starting, I know it, I'm already deluding myself.

My doctor doesn't look up or say anything, she's unfazed. I wonder again if she's listening. Maybe she's suspicious, looking through her notes she'll be reminded that I'm in recovery, she'll shoot me down, tell me no. Instead, she writes it down and says, "Okay, we're all set, I'll need to see you once more between now and then, but everything seems good. Do you have any questions for me?"

Wow, she's not mentioning anything about the drugs. Does that mean I'm going to get them? It was that easy? No questions asked? Trying my best to sound normal, I answer, "No, no questions, I guess I'll see you next week. Thank you. Thanks again." I'm in shock. I can't believe it was that easy for me, a former addict to get drugs. I am getting opiates, just like that. I think back to my last two pregnancies, both of them Cesareans, I can remember the pain being so excruciating and I was so uncomfortable afterward, I could hardly enjoy my new babies. Jordan is going to be five in a few weeks and Ryder will turn four in two months, I was so different then, I was in such a proud phase of my sobriety. With only a few years sober, I refused to touch anything. Now though, I feel stronger, I think I can handle it. I have over ten years of sobriety, and I don't want to endure that pain if I don't have to. I'm in such a great place I don't have to go that route this time.

Convincing myself that it's not a big deal I walk out to my car obsessed. I can't stop thinking about having drugs this time around or how great it will be to feel good, to be able to relax and enjoy my new baby. I won't be suffering or in agony and, I won't be fighting off all of the doctors and nurses constantly pushing me to take narcotics. I'll already be taking them, so they can just keep loading me up. "Do you hear yourself, Kristen? Your focus is on getting high," the voice in my head starts in. Hushing it, I justify things, telling myself that I deserve it, I'm entitled and, I will be okay. Besides, I know tons of people in recovery who have done it, considering it a "Freebie" to take pain meds for a medical procedure, surgery, even dental work. It's not thought of as a relapse; you don't lose anything. In fact, you're still considered "sober," and get to keep your Sobriety Date.

Driving home, I'm on a high, it's a beautiful day, I'm in perfect health and, my new baby will be here soon. I can't wait I hum to myself, feeling exhilarated. "Don't kid yourself, you're on a high because you're thinking about getting drugs," the voice in my head, reminds me, with a ring of truth. Ignoring it, I know I'll be fine, taking painkiller's for surgery is completely normal and allowable. "No, not really, not for you," warring words start to fill my head. "If it's completely normal and allowable then why are you being so secretive?" I wonder. Am I being secretive? Rationalizing, I decide it's not a secret; I just haven't had a chance to tell anyone yet. Pulling into my driveway, I turn off my car and close my eyes, trying to get a handle on all the thoughts racing through my mind. It's right, the voice in my head is right. I am being secretive and for someone in recovery, with a past like mine, being secretive is never a good sign.

That night, Chase and I are in bed, he's half asleep and I'm reading from my "Big Book," hoping to get some kind of insight on my decision to accept opiates for pain. Making it sound professional now, that alone tells me I can't be trusted on this topic. I am an alcoholic and a drug addict, wanting and using is in my blood, of course taking painkillers sounds amazing, of course, I'm going to opt for them, but is it the right thing for me to do? Is it the right thing for my family? Will it jeopardize my sobriety? I want to talk to Chase about it, see what he thinks and, ask him how he feels. I look over but he's already dozing off.

Perfect timing I think, he won't want to talk; groggy, he'll agree with me and say it's fine, then give me the green light so he can go back to sleep. "You're scheming, just like a drug addict," warns the voice in my head. "Quiet you," I warn it back. "Chase," I nudge him awake. "Chase, I need to ask you something." I watch him, wondering if I should wait. "Chase, I think I am going to take the painkillers this time. When I go in to have the baby, I'm..." Chase leans over and stares at me, "What?" He sits up, looking puzzled, "You're kidding right?" Shaking his head, "No way, there's no way Kristen, you're not taking drugs, are you out of your mind?" Reaching over to turn on his light, he runs his hand through his hair and gets out of bed. I know him, he has to stand up, it helps him stay calm, gather his thoughts. He stands, walking to the end of the bed and faces me, "I don't know where this is coming from but you can't be serious. I can't believe you're even thinking about using? Do you really think you can take drugs like that and just be fine?"

He paces back and forth, most likely overthinking it all; he's getting worked up as he waits for me to answer. Watching his reaction, I feel annoyed that he doesn't think I can handle it. "I am serious Chase, I do think I can take painkillers now; I mean, I've been sober for over ten years and, I'm in a really good place. With my dad out of my life and the past behind me, I'm stronger than ever and I've never felt more confident. So, yes, I think I can and, I think I will."

Chase comes over and sits on my side of the bed. He looks at me, pained, "There's no way, I won't let you. Babe, you're our rock, if you go down, we all go down, and I can't let that happen. We need you, we all need you. I won't let you do that to yourself, to us, or to our family." I listen, a part of me knowing he could be right, but there's another part of me that wants to try it. I want to do it anyway. "Look, I get it," I tell him. "I understand how you feel, but I think it will be okay, I'll be okay, I mean it's what, two, three days tops, that's it. Then it's over, I come home with the baby and life goes back to normal, just like now. We're good, I mean look at us, we've never been better and the kids are perfect. I honestly think it will all be fine.

Chase without skipping a beat and with tears in his eyes looks at me, "Yeah but what happens when we don't go back to normal? When you're not fine? You're lying to yourself; you know that right? You can't open up all of those Opioid Receptors and then just snap back to normal. Surgery is known to take people from recovery. Drugs are drugs, they will take you down, wipe you out, wipe us all out. Is that what you want?"

Chase stands up and walks to the doorway. Standing there in his boxers and a wife beater, I smile thinking of the first time we met and how sexy I thought he was. Here we were all of these years later and I still feel the same way about him. Now we're married, about to have our third child and, with over a decade of sobriety for both of us it's just like it was in the beginning, drugs are still an issue. Feeling like I'm losing the battle, I tell him, "It's not going to be like that, I promise, plenty of people at my women's meeting have done it and they're all fine."

"So that's where you came up with this crazy idea, at a meeting? Did they tell you about all of the people that aren't fine? The ones that lose twenty or thirty years for a normal knee or hip surgery, or some other medical procedure, people that have lost everything over taking one lousy painkiller. Did they tell you about the people who've lost their lives, the ones who have died? Look you got through it before without them and you'll get through it again without them, you have to do it that way, it's better. Please, don't take a chance; don't risk everything we have, everything you have, not for a few painkillers.

I think about what he says feeling disappointed, I know he's right. In the big picture, was it worth it to take a chance? Not ready to give in so easily, I try to buy a little time, "I am going to think about it and we can talk again in a few days." He looks at me and smiles, "No, sorry, case closed Mrs. Campbell, it's a definite no from me. I'll be there, standing guard, watching over you, I won't let you take any painkillers. Goofing around now and pretending he's playing football, he acts like he's blocking, "I'm going to be your Defensive End, running interference, no drugs for you." Running in place and grunting like he's knocking player's out of the way, "I won't let it happen, not now, not ever." Laughing, and lightening the situation, he finishes his performance and starts to walk out of our room.

Hey, where are you going? I ask. Still walking down the hall and imitating a Sports Commentator's Voice, he answers, "We're done here, Chase Campbell, comes through for the team, pass intercepted on the opioids in the final play. It's game over and the crowd goes wild." Finishing with fake cheering, and before he's out of earshot, he calls out, I'm getting a bowl of cereal, you've stressed me out, Bub."

The next morning, I wake-up to Jordan holding Chase's phone out to me, it's my mom, on speakerphone. "Mama, it's G, she wants to talk to you. Daddy called her to tell her you can't take any meds at the hospital." Great, I think, wondering what else my five-year-old heard. "Are you there? Is anyone there? Hello?" My mom's voice calls out from the phone as I take it from Jordan, "Mom, hang on." I sit up and send Jordan back out so I can talk. "Okay Mom, I'm here, what's going on?" Taking her off speaker, I hear her say, "You tell me Kristen?" as I put the phone up to my ear. My mom is outraged, incensed that I would even be thinking such a thing.

Once she lets off a little steam, we have a very frank discussion about the whole painkiller issue. We go back and forth a bit, basically, a similar conversation to the one Chase and I had before we went to bed last night, minus the football plays. My mom, as practical as ever, tells me she's going to do some research and call me back. I get up and get a cup of coffee, giving Chase a hard time for calling her, but actually grateful that they both care so much. As grateful as I am for their concern, I feel like it's too late, I really want the "pain meds."

"Why though?" I never would even consider it before. I think back to my other two kids, I mean it was definitely painful; the first couple of days the hardest, but it wasn't unbearable. There wasn't any part of me that was willing to take drugs, even with all of the hospital staff offering them up at every turn. I think about the people working in the hospital, they don't care about recovery; they just want you better so they can discharge you. I remember both times they were pushing pain meds, around the clock, some trying to talk me into them so I could get up and walk, start moving around a little easier. I mean, I told them all of the time, every one of them, "I'm in recovery, I'm a recovering Drug Addict, I don't want any narcotics." I felt like I needed a guard 24 hours a day, it was so non-stop. Still, I held my ground not taking anything other than the Toradol or Regular Tylenol and, I was fine.

Why did I stay so strong then, shouldn't I still be that way, refusing opioids at all costs? What got into me that I'm even contemplating "using drugs" now? I should be more proud of my sobriety than ever, especially after navigating through the past few years. I know it's not about the pain, I just want to be high and not in a relapse. My heart sinks, it's true, it really has nothing to do with the pain. I think of my innocent, unborn child coming into the world while I'm high. Not having drugs in over ten years I'm sure I would be looped, I feel sickened thinking of my baby being welcomed by me as a drug addict, that's what it would be. His mom would be high and unlike ordinary woman with pain killers for a few days, his mom could or could not, end up being addicted again. What was I thinking, there is no way I would ever want any of my kids to see me high, on anything, not with my background. There was no way I was taking anything. "Really, are you sure about that Kristen?" asks the voice in my head.

Over the next few days, my mom and I have had several opportunities to talk about "Opening the Opioid Receptors," and how it could trigger a former addict to start using again. In deep, she shares a story of a friend's situation where a routine operation with "normal pain medication" for her daughter, who was in recovery, reactivated the addictive tendencies and it led to her eventual overdose and death. Working every angle, my mom as expected knows her stuff. She's actually done a ton of research and has even started a "file." Throughout my life whenever my mom was working on a project, planning an event, a vacation, or dealing with something important, she would always start a file. I know this matter has become a top priority of hers when she tells me she started a "file."

Exactly one week later, sitting in my Obstetricians Office again, I'm a week out from my delivery date and it's my last Prenatal Appointment. Looking at all of the stuff on her desk, I notice a Coffee Mug that says, "Don't mistake your Google Search with my Medical Degree." I don't remember seeing it before and I have to laugh as I pan over to my Mom, sitting next to me with her "file."

On a mission, she wanted to come to ensure that I wouldn't be given anything narcotic. I'm glad she and my doctor know each other, their discussion may be awkward when my mom shares her research proving that pain meds can, and in most circumstances do, open the Opioid Receptors back up. I told my mom it wasn't necessary, she didn't have to worry, I promised both her and Chase that I would tough it out deciding for myself not to touch the pain meds and opting to have my third child exactly as I had my others, completely sober.

My doctor comes in and we go through pretty much the same thing we went through last time, only this time, I have to ask her to change my preference for pain medication back to Toradol. It's funny, just like last time she has no reaction, she jots it down, once again unfazed. I think back to last week, the excitement flowing through my veins, ecstatic at the thought that I could have a "freebie" or be able to have drugs without a relapse. Again, it wasn't really about the pain for me, it wasn't physical, it was all mental. My brain right away honed in on the opportunity to get high and tried disguising it as something that would be "okay." I'm not judging anyone else, but based on my reaction alone and where it took me in that short period of time; it will never be okay for me.

Within a few minutes, there's a fairly tense conversation about the topic of drugs and recovery, Opioid Receptors and the huge responsibility that comes with the dispensing of narcotics. My mom is pretty direct and the doctor isn't really agreeing with her, or her information, at one point referring to my mom's email, stating that she can appreciate her stand but that to date, there hasn't been enough research. I look over at my Mom, "You emailed her?" I ask. Although I am involved in the discussion, I mostly listen. I understand both of their viewpoints, but for me as a person in recovery, my sobriety isn't anyone else's responsibility; it's mine and mine alone. I can't hold anyone else accountable for me or the decisions I make.

I think of all of the times I was offered pain meds by doctors and nurses. If recovery isn't their field and if they've never had any experience with a recovering drug addict, what would they know? My own doctor, well aware of my background and my recovery still felt it was okay to allow me to have narcotics, believing it would not affect me. They're just trying to do their job, take care of their patients; following normal protocol. I've had some of the most extraordinary doctors and nurses and I can't fault any of them for doing their job. Again, my sobriety is up to me.

The following week my beautiful baby boy arrives. Maximus Christian Campbell is born and to me he is perfection. As predicted he's big, weighing in at ten pounds, he's beautiful and healthy and, I couldn't be happier. I made it through the surgery with only non-narcotic medication and felt fine. I was completely alert and aware of every moment, able to welcome my newborn son in a complete sense of clarity and with a heart overflowing with love.

The recovery wasn't as easy. The severe pain started within a few hours and the medication they gave me caused me to itch, which they calmed with Benadryl. I ended up not high, but still out of it, barely able to keep my eyes open for hours. As promised, Chase was with me through it all, only with poor cell phone reception in my hospital room, he was often in and out fielding all of the calls from family and friends. Max seemed to come into the room with me and, was allowed to stay from the start which I loved. My nurse was beyond warm and friendly. Coming in she introduced herself, asking me right away, "Kristen, how's the pain? On a scale of one to ten, what do you think? I look at her and feeling foggy answer, "I'm not sure, maybe a seven." Noting it on my chart she says, "If you want something other than Toradol, let me know, I have an arsenal of drugs."

Immediately, I'm in my head again, I'm interested. From the start I know it's not about the pain. My ears perk up, I think about an arsenal and I can't swallow. In my Benadryl Haze, I can feel myself liven up, my heart starts racing, there's an old sense of excitement. "An arsenal, huh?" I look at the nurse, not bothering to explain, "No thanks, I'm good, I'm *Chasing Sober.*"

For photos please feel free to see our Instagram Page
@chasingsoberthebook

·Epilogue·

Sharing a story that included Sexual Abuse was never my intent. When we started writing *Chasing Sober* several years ago, it was a simple rough draft of my personal journey from addiction to sobriety. My desire has always been to try and help others by showing that no matter how bad things were, sobriety was not only possible but achievable. In the midst of writing this book, when I discovered I was pregnant, I started having the memories of my dad. The book unfolded along with what I was currently experiencing in my life and although it was sad and uncomfortable, by including everything and staying truthful and honest, I believed I could bring the most benefit and inspiration to those that decided to read my story.

When I first got sober, it was the only thing I had ever accomplished. Now, I feel I have accomplished so much more. I really am grateful and constantly count my many blessings, especially when it comes to my family, my continued sobriety and the love and support I find in my relationships with others.

For many people who share a personal account of their life there's a big ending, one that promotes the idea that in order to really be happy in life, you have to have a successful career, acquire some measure of material wealth or achieve some level of social status, if not all of the above. In my life, after everything I've experienced, I thought all I needed to be happy was to feel good about myself and to love and be loved. To be genuinely happy though, at least for me, I think there's a need to give back or to help others. I believe my purpose is to share my story and as the cliché goes, if I can help just one person, for me then I can really say I am genuinely happy.

Thank you for purchasing and reading my book. If you need to get started in your own personal recovery, please find an Alcoholics Anonymous or Narcotics Anonymous Meeting near you. To start may be the most courageous step you'll ever take, to continue, the best thing you'll ever do.

·From the Author·

Knowing each other for over three decades, Kristen and I have been close friends for years. I was one of the ladies that worked at Baldwin Academy who was always a steady and welcoming presence to Kristen, loving her and trying to help her regardless of her circumstances. Never really aware of how bad Kristen's life was, writing the book was a revelation that addiction had come close to taking the life of one of my closest and dearest friends. To be a part of her life has been exceptional and the changes she has made more than remarkable, she is one of the funniest and most genuine people I know and I just love her.

Living in San Diego and sharing many common interests, we remain close and I am honored to spend time with her and her growing family. We both look forward to pursuing other ventures with this book, hoping to use the opportunity to bring an awareness of what drug use can lead to for younger people and inspire or motivate those that are already in addiction or struggling with sobriety. Kristen's message of Recovery and Chasing Sober is one of possibility for all of those that are suffering, and although what works for one person may not work for another, there is always, always help and a solution.

In order to have a better understanding of what Kristen believed helped her and continues to help her the most, I attended dozens of Alcoholics Anonymous Meetings, and am an enormous believer in this incredible resource as a must for any person wanting to get and stay sober. Attending Open and Women Only Meetings that allow those who are not alcoholics, I was constantly amazed and humbled by the experiences. The rooms are full of warm, welcoming and open people with huge hearts, ready to help and encourage others. I want to thank all of the ladies that I've met, they are truly outstanding individuals and I am honored to have witnessed their love in action.

This book is dedicated to those *Chasing Sober* everywhere, may they find peace and solace in a life well-lived, full of love and happiness, and may they always stay addiction free.

There's never an end when you're *Chasing Sober*

Made in the USA
Middletown, DE
17 July 2019